Contested Imaginaries of Future Technologies

Sören Becker • Benno Fladvad
Editors

Contested Imaginaries of Future Technologies

Geographical Perspectives

palgrave
macmillan

Editors
Sören Becker
Marburg University
Marburg, Germany

Benno Fladvad
University of Hamburg
Hamburg, Germany

ISBN 978-3-032-11496-9 ISBN 978-3-032-11497-6 (eBook)
https://doi.org/10.1007/978-3-032-11497-6

This book is an open access publication.

Open access funding provided by the Open Access Publishing Fund of Marburg University and the Open Access Fund of University of Hamburg.

This Palgrave Macmillan imprint is published by the registered company Springer Nature Switzerland AG.
The registered company address is: Gewerbestrasse 11, 6330 Cham, Switzerland

Preface

In what ways do technologies shape future visons, and how do these visions influence our understanding of space? In times of catastrophic future scenarios and ever-accelerating conjunctures of technological solutions to climate change and ecological crises, human geography is an essential discipline for examining the role of technologies in shaping our future visions. This book therefore sheds light on an ongoing debate: the role of technologies in addressing future crises, and their underlying social expectations, spatial links, and contestations.

Even though *the future* is one of the main themes of this book, it obviously has a past. It is the outcome of several thematic sessions held at the Royal Geographical Society Conference in London and the German Congress for Geography in Frankfurt am Main in late summer 2023, in which almost all contributors of this book participated. These sessions emerged from our observation that many geographers and social scientists, especially those specializing in cultural and political geography, are currently engaging with the contested nature of various future technologies, including climate engineering, artificial intelligence, augmented realities, renewable energy, and low-carbon technologies, which are often considered as key solutions to the multiple socioecological crises and to achieving sustainable planetary futures. Yet, despite this vibrant debate, characterized by criticism and scepticism, but also by analytical acuity and theoretical depth, the research landscape appeared fragmented and dispersed. Given the variety of technologies and the thematic areas they are associated with, this is no surprise. However, our impression was that these debates had great potential for synergy and mutual learning, particularly since many of them emphasize the relevance of social, or rather sociotechnical, imaginaries, which are embedded in, and often legitimize, the spatial and material implementation of future technologies.

Against this backdrop, this book brings together scholars who explore the co-production of imaginaries and technologies, emphasizing the many ways in which they intersect with the production and contestation of space. The eight chapters offer different geographical and space-sensitive perspectives on technologies within the thematic areas of energy transitions, digitalization, and planetary governance. While this book is intended primarily for an academic audience, we hope that it will also be valuable to readers with a more applied focus, as most of its contributions are not only theory-driven but also empirical in nature.

We would like to express our sincere gratitude to the participants of the sessions at the conferences in London and Frankfurt, and particularly to the contributors of this book, who have accompanied us over the last two years, broadening our horizons with their thought-provoking and innovative contributions. Moreover, we would like to thank Jean-Baptiste Goeh-Akue for his tireless editorial support, his feedback and valuable suggestions, as well as his meticulous attention to detail regarding references and literature. We would also like to thank Helia Seif for her valuable assistance in compiling the list of abbreviations and conducting literature research. Finally, we are very grateful to our publisher, Palgrave Macmillan, especially to Rachael Ballard for her support and patience, as well as to the University of Marburg and the University of Hamburg, for their financial support, without which this book would not have been published open-access.

Marburg, Germany Sören Becker

Hamburg, Germany Benno Fladvad

September 2025

Contents

Part II Digital Promises

Part III Engineering the Planetary

List of Figures

List of Tables

Notes on Contributors

Sören Becker is Assistant Professor of Human Geographies of Sustainable Transformation at Marburg University. His research focuses on infrastructure transformations, digital platforms, and regional development strategies.

Tabea Bork-Hüffer is Professor of Human Geography at Heidelberg University. She is a digital, social, and cultural geographer with a particular interest in how the entanglement of digital technologies in everyday lives affects social inclusion and exclusion, social sustainability, and well-being.

Zoé Chateau is a Research Fellow in Geography at the National Research Institute for Agriculture, Food and Environment in France. Her research explores the socio-spatial dimensions of sociotechnical change and controversies, with a focus on energy and forest transitions.

Patrick Devine-Wright is Professor of Human Geography at the University of Exeter. His research focuses on social and spatial dimensions of low-carbon energy transitions, specifically understanding controversies over the setting of large-scale infrastructures for electricity generation and transmission.

Benno Fladvad is Assistant Professor of Natural Science Peace Research with a focus on Climate and Security at the University of Hamburg. His research focuses on environmental justice and environmental security, nuclear justice, energy transitions, sociotechnical imaginaries, as well as democracy in the Anthropocene.

Iris Hilbrich is a Researcher and EU Framework Coordinator at the Center for Innovation Systems & Policy at the Austrian Institute of Technology. Her research focuses on emerging technologies, climate policy, responsible research and innovation, as well as energy justice and just transition.

Craig Henry Jones is a Lecturer in Management and Society in the Department of Organisation, Work and Technology at Lancaster University. His research focuses on the NewSpace Economy and the different ways in which extraterrestrial resources and territories are (re)imagined by different actors. Broadly, this research draws upon intersections between Science and Technology Studies, geosocial imaginaries, and extractivism.

Jacqueline Kowalski is a PhD Candidate and Research Assistant in the Department of Geography, University of Innsbruck. Her work focuses on social geographies, (in)equalities, digital geographies, and alternative futures, with a particular interest in desired futures of young people with disabilities.

Les Levidow is a Senior Research Fellow with the Radical Anthropology Group, The Open University. His research covers controversial technologies in the agriculture and energy sectors. He is also editor of the journal *Science as Culture*.

Matthias Naumann is Professor of Human Geography at the Institute of Geography and Geology, University of Würzburg. His research focuses on urban and rural development, infrastructure transformations, and the political geography of conflicts and populism.

Delf Rothe is a Senior Researcher at the Institute for Peace Research and Security Policy at the University of Hamburg. He has published widely on issues including the securitization of climate change, climate-induced migration, security technologies, risk, and resilience.

David Philipp Rudolph is a Senior Researcher in the Department of Wind and Energy Systems at the Technical University of Denmark. His research is concerned with socio-spatial implications of the energy transition and contestations over the planning and deployment of renewable energy infrastructures, with a particular focus on social justice, community participation, and people–place relations.

Christina Walter is a PhD Candidate at the Institute of Geography, University of Augsburg. Her research explores the relationships between water, society, and the digital. Theoretically, her work is situated at the intersection of political ecology, Science and Technology Studies, and digital geographies. Her doctoral project investigates how emerging digital infrastructures reconfigure the water sector in the East of England.

List of Abbreviations

2D	Two-dimensional
3D	Three-dimensional
ACMI	Africa Carbon Markets Initiative
AfD	Alternative for Germany
AI	Artificial Intelligence
AMC	Asteroid Mining Company
ANT	Actor-Network Theory
AR	Augmented Reality
BECCS	Bioenergy with Carbon Capture and Storage
CCS	Carbon Capture and Storage
CCU	Carbon Capture and Utilization
CCUS	Carbon Capture, Use and Storage
CDR	Carbon Dioxide Removal Technologies
CEO	Chief Executive Officer
CEUD	Centre for Excellence in Universal Design
CFSP	Common Foreign and Security Policy
CO_2	Carbon Dioxide
CSGP	Common Security and Defence Policy
CSO	Civil Society Organisation
DAC	Direct Air Capture
DERM	Digital Earth Reference Model
DestinE	Destination Earth
DF	Danish People's Party
DG DEFIS	Directorate General "Defence Industry and Space" (EU)
DG R&I	Directorate General "Research and Innovation" (EU)
DSI	Deep Space Industries
DTE	Digital Twin Earth

DTE4Security	Digital Twin Earth for Security Project
EC	European Commission
ECHA	European Clean Hydrogen Alliance
ECMWF	European Centre for Medium-Range Weather Forecasts
EDF	European Disability Forum
EO	Earth Observation
ESA	European Space Agency
EU	European Union
EUMETSAT	European Organisation for the Exploitation of Meteorological Satellites
EUSPA	EU Agency for the Space Program
FoE	Friends of the Earth
GEO	Group on Earth Observations
GEO-DAMP	Geospatial Data Management Platform
GHG	Green-House Gas
GNDE	Green New Deal for Europe
H	Hydrogen
HCI	Human-Computer Interaction
ICT	Information and Communication Technology
ICMS	Industrial Carbon Management Strategy
IPCC	Intergovernmental Panel on Climate Change
IOGP	International Organisation of Oil and Gas Producers
ISDE	International Society for Digital Earth
ISRU	In-Situ Resource Utilisation
IT	Information Technology
LNG	Liquefied Natural Gas
NASA	National Aeronautics and Space Administration
NSE	NewSpace Economy
NEOs	Near Earth Objects
NGO	Non-Governmental Organization
PCI	Project of Common Interest
PtX	Power to X
SAI	Stratospheric Aerosol Injection
SatCen	Satellite Center
SCOT	Social Construction of Technology
SPA	Strategic Pipeline Alliance
SRM	Solar Radiation Management
SRMGI	SRM Governance Initiative
STI / STIs	Sociotechnical Imaginary / Imaginaries
STS	Science and Technology Studies
UD	Universal Design
UK	United Kingdom

UNEP	United Nations Environment Programme
USA	United States of America
VR	Virtual Reality
XR	Extended Reality

CHAPTER 1

Introduction: Towards Geographies of Sociotechnical Imaginaries

Benno Fladvad and Sören Becker

1 Introduction

Technologies are everywhere. They are an integral part of our everyday lives, surrounding us, helping us, making us mobile, feeling proud and happy. If they don't work, however, they let us despair; they thwart our plans and make us feel helpless. In short, technologies greatly influence what it means to be a human and a social being, contributing to our sense of self, health, wellbeing, security and societal positioning—albeit, of course, not all humans and societies have equal access to and ability to use technologies. In contrast to everyday devices that we use at work and at home, technological infrastructures such as roads, energy grids, water and sewage systems, digital infrastructures and supply infrastructures are rather invisible and often taken for granted (Bowker, 1994). Working at macro-scale, they are generally understood as things, or as a distributed networks

B. Fladvad (✉)
University of Hamburg, Hamburg, Germany
e-mail: benno.fladvad@uni-hamburg.de

S. Becker
Marburg University, Marburg, Germany
e-mail: soeren.becker@geo.uni-marburg.de

S. Becker, B. Fladvad (eds.), *Contested Imaginaries of Future Technologies*, https://doi.org/10.1007/978-3-032-11497-6_1

of things, “that enable the movement of other matter […] as objects that create the grounds on which other objects operate” (Larkin, 2013, p. 329). They function as the hidden backbone of our societies, allowing them to operate efficiently and seamlessly.

It should be noted here that, especially when it comes to border infrastructures, their basic feature is obviously not only to enable flows, movement and mobility, but also to impede them, hence producing immobility, violence and injustice (Kathiravelu, 2021). Yet, technological objects (including everyday devices, production technologies and large-scale infrastructures) cannot be considered merely as artefacts or physical entities, but as interconnected socio-material assemblages: as complex systems of relations between humans and non-human matter that are imbued with and reproduce asymmetric power relations, socio-ecological grievances, diverse social meanings and contested imaginaries of the future (Harvey et al., 2017; Anand et al., 2018; Hornborg, 2019).

The contested, political nature of technologies becomes most apparent when new or emerging technologies are introduced and discussed. Consider, for example, new infrastructure projects such as wind energy. While some see them as a promise, carrying expectations and visions of progress, sustainability and modernity, others perceive them as a threat that contributes to profound and often negative socio-economic changes and reveals violent processes of displacement and dispossession (Appel et al., 2018), sometimes resulting in instrumentalization by right-wing populists (Naumann, 2021). Historically, the introduction of the railway or the steam technology, as well as the weaving loom, is a striking example of this ambiguity between promise and threat—not only imaginatively but also materially. On the one hand, these technologies enabled the Industrial Revolution, sparking further technological, scientific and societal progress. On the other hand, they gave rise to and legitimized mass slavery, ongoing colonization and the rise of European imperialism (Hornborg, 2019; Headrick, 1981).

Today, this dialectic has not fundamentally changed: especially the combined grand challenges of environmental deterioration, including climate change, and digitalization (Lenz, 2021), are the main drivers bringing forward a wide range of contested future technologies. Propelled by the aspiration to mitigate or control climate change, and to preserve the prevailing market-driven order, speculative and emerging technologies such as solar geoengineering or large-scale green hydrogen are currently being discussed at the forefront of climate policies (Sapinski et al., 2021;

IEA, 2024). Proponents of solar geoengineering argue that the apparent inefficiency of conventional climate policies generates a moral obligation to promote respective technologies that aim to control climate change and thereby alleviate its direct impacts on the global poor (Svoboda et al., 2018). By contrast, others argue that this logic risks normalizing a potentially hazardous, incalculable and inherently undemocratic technology undermining and further delaying effective decarbonization policies (Biermann et al., 2022). A similar polarization can be observed in the case of green hydrogen. Whereas some have already declared the "hydrogen age" (Dincer, 2023; Dincer, 2020), celebrating its versatility and its potential to contribute to a rapid and effective decarbonization, others emphasize that the hype surrounding hydrogen conceals its inefficiency compared to traditional green energy production and generates new forms of "green colonialism", as well as multiple environmental injustices at the water–energy–food nexus (Müller et al., 2022; Kalt & Tunn, 2022; Nature Editorial, 2022).

Alongside the discussions around climate and environmental governance, processes of digitalization and datafication (i.e. converting aspects of social life into data) are bringing forward several future technologies such as artificial intelligence, extended reality and digital twins. These approaches are likewise contested. Political ecology-inspired analyses, for instance, have demonstrated the extent to which climate artificial intelligence (i.e. diverse digital applications intended to ameliorate environmental and climate threats), driven forward by tech companies such as Palantir and Microsoft, is, despite its ambitions to contribute to climate justice, deeply embedded in global racial capitalism, thus reproducing injustices and problems it paradoxically intends to solve (Nost & Colven, 2022). Similarly, feminist-intersectional critiques have highlighted how city digital twins, which are increasingly being used for urban management and planning, are embedded in and perpetuate gendered and racialized hierarchies privileging white masculinity (Rose, 2024). However, discussions are also taking place around the appropriateness of digital technologies in a degrowth context (Meyers, 2023) and new forms of digital socialism (Morozov, 2019), thus pointing to the potential of digital technologies to transgress and go beyond growth-driven paradigms. Against the background, and the various, often concealed, socio-ecological implications and drawbacks of digital technologies, scholars are therefore increasingly debating whether digitalization is "a problem solver or a fire accelerator" (Lenz, 2021, p. 188).

These ambiguities and the necessarily contested nature of future technologies are the starting points of this book. However, our ambition is not to engage in normative assessments on whether and under which conditions certain future technologies are or may be helpful, sustainable, just and democratic. Nor is our aim to spread technophobia and expand the comprehensive critical literature on the drawbacks and necropolitics of technological fixes and data-driven climate policies (Nightingale et al., 2020; Dunlap & Laratte, 2022). Rather, with this introduction and the following chapters, our intention is to imbed the controversies around future technologies in a critical analysis regarding the co-production of technologies and spatialized future visions from the regional to the planetary scale. Following the hypothesis that neither technological progress and polices, including the imaginaries surrounding and guiding them, nor the production and contestation of space evolve independently from each other, with this book we intend to address the question of how distinctive socio-spatial visions are built around and gain power through technological policies and advances. Targeting the intersection of cultural and political geography, and inspired by Science and Technology Studies, we seek to understand how these "sociotechnical imaginaries" (STIs)—a term prominently coined by Shaila Jasanoff and Sang-Hyun Kim (2009, 2015) and one of the guiding concepts of the book—intersect with and are contingent on the production and contestation of space. In short, our main intention is to bring distinctively geographical perspectives into this strand of research. We believe that this undertaking is not only a fruitful social-theoretical endeavour, but also sheds lights on the ways in which technological policies and advances influence the (re)organization of space in the Anthropocene.

In the following three sections, we will elaborate on this argument on the geographies of sociotechnical imaginaries in greater depth. In section 2, we contend that spatiality is an inherent dimension of sociotechnical imaginaries, i.e. sociotechnical imaginaries and imaginaries of spatial order and development are mutually intertwined. To substantiate this argument, we will draw both on the literature on sociotechnical imaginaries and on work from human geography focusing on spatial and geographical imaginaries. In section 3, we will discuss how future technologies and pathways for sociotechnical development are socially shaped, yet not to be considered deterministic. To this end, we will engage with long-standing debates in Science and Technology Studies (STS) and their uptake in human geography. This demonstrates that future technologies provide a fertile research field to understand not only the extent to which technologies are power-laden and inherently normative, but also sites of conflict where antagonisms as well as contradictions between different sociotechnical trajectories become apparent. Section 4 will provide an overview of the individual chapters and develop the cross-cutting themes of this book into a research agenda. Considering the co-constitution of sociotechnical and place imaginaries, the representational spaces of future technologies and their performativity in terms of spatial transformation will enable us to move beyond a mere critique of technological fixes and allow us to understand the latter as products of specific socio-spatial visions of the future.

2 Sociotechnical and Geographic Imaginaries

One of this book's main arguments is that technological progress and materialities, as well as the imaginaries attached to them, are constitutively and inextricably linked to production and contestation of space. Conversely, we argue that spatial (or geographic) imaginaries, including imagined spatial orders, influence and prefigure the planning, design and application of technologies and material infrastructures. The way we imagine specific spaces and places—politically, legally, performatively and culturally (e.g. as unused and full of untapped resources, as religious sites or Indigenous territory) —has direct implications for their technological and infrastructural furnishing, for example, when it comes to questions of energy production or agriculture. Furthermore, how we imagine and experience space is a matter of technological mediation and enactment (White & Wilbert, 2009). Our conceptions of the world are largely influenced by how it is being scientifically and technologically surveyed, monitored and represented (e.g. by digital maps), and culturally interpreted and normatively evaluated (e.g. by media technologies). For instance, the application of remote sensing technologies and associated imaginaries of risk, vulnerability and possibility can reproduce past imaginaries of the Arctic as a resource frontier and result in visions of Arctic spaces threatened by multiple dangers, requiring political intervention and control (Johnson, 2024). At the same time, technologies and scientific knowledges cannot be separated from the societal and spatial context which has brought them into being. Certain types of energy production, for instance, fossil, nuclear or renewable, are not only sociotechnical assemblages, but also at once products and mirror images of broader normative and (geo)political orders and acts of future-making. In short, space and technologies (including their scientific underbelly) are being co-produced and mutually intertwined, both imaginatively and performatively, as well as materially (Chateau et al., 2021).

In the social sciences this idea of coproduction has been prominently discussed by Actor Network Theory (ANT) and Science and Technology Studies (Latour, 1994; Jasanoff, 2004). In particular, Sheila Jasanoff and Sang-Hyun Kim's notion of "sociotechnical imaginaries" (Jasanoff & Kim 2009, 2015) has been highly influential in capturing the simultaneous production of technologies and social order. Understood as "collectively held, institutionally stabilized, and publicly performed visions of desirable futures, animated by shared understandings of forms of social life and social order attainable through, and supportive of, advances in science and technology" (Jasanoff, 2015, p. 4), STIs not only provide insights into how societal norms, values, etc. are reflected and embedded in technologies, but also into how desirable societal futures are technologically mediated and stabilized. The concept therefore "pulls together the normativity of the imagination with the materiality of networks" (Jasanoff, 2015, p. 19) and is intended to "occupy the blank space between [...] the construction of imaginaries in political and cultural theory and of sociotechnical systems in STS" (Jasanoff, 2015, p. 5). To this end, it not only allows insights into the material and technological dimension of the often implicit and taken for granted shared understandings, visions, expectations and practices of societies, on which their existence, their self-understanding and coherence rests—commonly understood as "social imaginaries" (Castoriadis, 1987; Appadurai, 1996; Taylor, 2004). It also foregrounds the ways in which specific future visions, e.g. of capitalism and growth (Beckert, 2016), sustainability (Adloff & Neckel, 2019), climate change (Levy & Spicer, 2013) or energy production (Marquardt & Delina, 2019), are materially stabilized and gain power.

Yet, this focus on the stabilization of dominant imaginaries—the focus of Jasanoff and Kim's earlier writings, in which they focused on national STIs of South Korea and the United States (Jasanoff & Kim, 2009)—does not mean that the concept of sociotechnical imaginaries is blind to pluralism and contestation. In arguing that "[m]ultiple imaginaries can coexist within a society in tension or in a productive dialectical relationship", Jasanoff (2015, p. 4) has more recently refined and expanded the understanding of STIs towards an inclusion of alternative, counterhegemonic and more distributed imaginaries that are being formulated by diverse actors—social movements, expert groups, communities or transnational corporations—on various scales. This multi-scalar understanding of STIs and the attentiveness to more marginalized imaginaries has been welcomed by critical social scientists and taken up particularly in the field of energy social science research, partly in response to the sociotechnical transitions approach, which has often been subject to criticism regarding its limited attention to power and cultural meanings (Geels, 2019). These studies, ranging from empirical case studies (Smith & Tidwell, 2016; Delina, 2018; Marquardt & Delina, 2019; Benediktsson, 2021) to literature reviews (Rudek, 2021; Kuchler & Stigson, 2024) and analytical propositions (Longhurst & Chilvers, 2019), place special emphasis on the multiplicity of energy futures, on power, antagonism and the fact that the invocation of "desirable futures" is always dialectically accompanied by its opposite, i.e. by the undesirability of an imagined future trajectory (Jasanoff, 2015, p. 5). The potential changes and promises inherent in a sociotechnical imaginary, e.g. of infrastructure projects or artificial intelligence, are rarely evaluated as equally positive by all those affected, and may invoke dystopian feelings of fear, leading to populism and anti-democratic tendencies (Naumann, 2021; van Veelen et al., 2021). The questions of what constitutes a desirable future, how it is implemented and for whom it will be beneficial are therefore not only questions of power and competing hegemonies but also go to the heart of democracy and justice (Fladvad, 2023, p. 498).

Despite this emphasis on the contested nature of STIs and its implications for spatial politics, it is remarkable that with few exceptions (Chateau et al., 2021) geographers have hitherto paid only limited attention to the framework and its potential for a distinctively geographical perspective. The neglect of this gap is particularly striking given Jasanoff's (2015, p. 20) emphasis on the importance of space as an analytical category (among others) through which sociotechnical imaginaries can be operationalized and unfold their explanatory power. As she puts it:

> Sociotechnical imaginaries tackle head-on, and more symmetrically, the complex topographies of power and morality as they intersect with the forces of science and technology. As the term itself suggests, the concept allows for spatial imaginations to preexist and channel the spread of science and technology. (Jasanoff, 2015, p. 23)

Space, therefore, is not only the context or container within which sociotechnical imaginaries unfold (e.g. national visions of green hydrogen production); instead, spatiality, and in particular the concept of scale—though controversially discussed in human geography (Marston et al., 2005)—is in itself a central and defining feature of STIs, as it helps to normatively legitimize the formulation and stabilization of specific imaginaries:

> From an imaginaries perspective, moreover, space and scale are linked in a normative coupling [...] For imaginaries not only help to reconfigure actors' sense of the possible spaces of action but also their sense of the rightness of action, at scales ranging from locality to nation [...] to continent [...] and to the planet itself. (Jasanoff, 2015, p. 23)

It is precisely here where this book aims to contribute. Bearing in mind human geography's extensive engagement with geographical and spatial imaginations, developed since the so-called spatial turn in the social sciences (Soja, 1989; Gregory, 1994; Massey, 2005), it aspires to bring decidedly geographical (or spatial) perspectives into research on contested future technologies and to combine these with the lens of STIs. To this end, we follow Chateau et al. (2021), who, in focusing thematically on energy transitions, argue for a deeper and systematic integration of STIs and spatial imaginaries, defined by Watkins (2015, p. 509) as "socially held stories, ways of representing and talking about places and spaces". Socio-spatial imaginaries, they argue, are deeply intertwined with the way we imagine and carry out technological progress: "[S]pace, as lived, imagined and practiced, influences the construction, circulation, framing and uptake of STIs. [...] A two-way relationship therefore appears to exist by which space influences STIs, and STIs influence space" (Chateau et al., 2021, p. 3). In drawing on Watkins' (2015, p. 521) threefold typology of spatial imaginaries, they argue that STIs and spatial imaginaries feed into and reinforce each other. Hence, a distinction can be made between (1) "place imaginaries", i.e. collectively shared understandings and visons of how technological progress or developments shape the characteristics of specific places such as cities; (2) "idealized space imaginaries", which refer to normative spatial attributions through which spaces are characterized, differentiated and valued in the context of technological changes and transformations, i.e. a rural idyll, a high-tech-cluster or an ungoverned and unused territory; and (3) "spatial transformation imaginaries", understood as generalizable ideas and visions, such as globalization, localism, or sustainability, which prefigure technological progress and are reproduced by it. Therefore, while spatial imaginaries and STIs should not be confused or unified, their joint consideration sheds light on the manifold ways by which technological visions are co-designed and co-constituted by society's shared, yet often contested, visons and understandings of space and spatial transformation.

To delve deeper into human geography's engagement with imaginaries and imagination, it is necessary to explore some more theoretical explanations of what in fact is meant by geographical and/or spatial imaginaries (these will be used interchangeably hereafter). This will also enable us to demonstrate how geographical/spatial imaginaries and STIs tie in with each other on a conceptual level.

First, it is important to distinguish the term geographical imaginaries from the notion of geographical imaginations, which denotes "the role of the imagination in shaping geographic thought, perception, and models of the world" (Yusoff & Gabrys, 2011, p. 530). The term thus refers to human geography's theoretical gaze, emphasizing a specific imaginative sensitivity towards place, space, nature and landscape (Gregory et al., 2009, p. 282; Howie & Lewis, 2014). Moreover, using the plural form highlights the existence of multiple forms of geographical knowledge production, originating from diverse social-theoretical and philosophical traditions (Gregory, 1994). The term geographical imaginaries, by contrast, is understood as more or less conscious and taken-for-granted constructions of the world and its spatial orderings, expressed in ideas, narratives and bodily and material performances (Gregory et al., 2009, p. 282; Chateau et al., 2021). Being largely influenced by the theoretical tradition of social imaginaries (Castoriadis, 1987; Taylor, 2004) and Edward Said's (1978) influential post-structuralist theorization of "imaginative geographies", it is commonly understood as collectively shared and normative visions of (other) places, which stabilize the collective self-understanding of communities or societies, and which guide their courses of action. Geographical imaginaries are therefore particularly attentive not only to spatial visions, ideas, fantasies and desires, which construct and give meaning to our lived "reality", but also to manifold processes of othering, i.e. to spatialized practices and discourses through which societies identify themselves as distinctively different. Geographical imaginaries are therefore always characterized (to some degree) by normative and power-laden processes of ordering the world into categories of them and us, self and other, good and bad, familiar and alien, near and far, and superior and inferior (Gregory et al., 2009, pp. 282, 369; Gregory, 2004).

Second, these distinctions are obviously not merely ideational or semiotic constructs, and hence objects of ideas, fantasies, desires and meanings, but are similarly embedded in socio-material practices of worlding: of ordering space through material borders, political institutions, financial mechanisms, infrastructural projects, etc. Following Watkins (2015), it therefore seems best to conceive geographical imaginaries ontologically as performances, as socio-material and bodily practices through which geographical imaginaries materialize. Such a conceptualization draws attention to the ways geographical imaginaries legitimize and organize social practices, as well as to the manifold practical enactments through which geographical imaginaries themselves are being developed, disseminated and reproduced. This perspective sheds light on the more implicit, embodied and often unconscious performances, bodily expressions and socio-material practices of e.g. infrastructuring, bordering, policy-making, producing, planning, etc., through which geographical imaginaries become lived reality. This ontological priority of social practices, as claimed by the protagonists of the so-called practice turn (Knorr Cetina et al., 2000), means to develop a sensitivity towards the ***actual doing*** of imaginaries: how they are being lived, enacted, communicated, challenged and contested in both quotidian and exceptional moments of social life.

Third, it is essential to think of geographical imaginaries as constructs, which are always expressions of social contestations, and competing hegemonies. Drawing on recent attempts to delineate a "post-foundational geography" (Landau-Donnelly & Pohl, 2023), we conceptualize geographical imaginaries, even—or especially—when they appear as quasi-natural entities such as the nation (Anderson, 2016 [1983]), as being characterized by radical negativity, contingency and antagonism. Negativity refers to the fact that spatial orderings necessarily require a certain degree of othering (see above), meaning that spatializing practices always depend on a constitutive outside, which may be invisible, but is never erasable and ever-present in the form of a "flickering by-product of every production of space" (Landau-Donnelly & Pohl, 2023, p. 487). Relatedly, contingency highlights that any given spatial order is just one out of many often concealed and marginalized possibilities, (i.e. spaces could always be otherwise). Finally, antagonism, understood as an ontological and inerasable condition hegemonic conflict (Mouffe, 2005), refers to the characterization of space as a site and historical product of contestation and social struggle. Moreover, it also emphasizes the importance of power relations in the production of space. How spaces are being used, valued, imagined, governed and technologically furnished are therefore always questions of who has the power to control and exercise authority over others.

In sum, geographical or spatial imaginaries can therefore be understood as more or less conscious and taken-for-granted constructions of the world and its spatial orderings, expressed by and embedded in social practices. They must be distinguished from geographical imaginations, which rather refer to human geography's ways of knowledge production, and are characterized by normative and power-laden processes of othering, i.e. of ordering the world into spatialized categories. Finally, following post-foundationalist insights, they are characterized by radical negativity, by contingency and by antagonisms. It is precisely these attributions which render geographical imaginaries a very suitable complementary concept for investigating the spatial dimensions of STIs. They are intended to conceptualize and to highlight the inherent spatial dimensions of STIs and to bring more theoretical depth into respective research, especially in view of the characterization of STIs as normative, powerful and highly contested drivers of space-making processes. The next section will sketch out the research field of future technologies to substantiate this argument further.

3 Imaginaries of Futures and Future Technologies

As explained, this book sets out to analyse the development and contestation of imaginaries around future technologies from the vantage point of human geography. Recently, questions concerning the future have increasingly cropped up as a topic of interest in different branches of human geography (Bunnell & Yeo, 2025; Gong, 2024). Set next to work on climate scenarios, many authors identify a paradox here: although we are increasingly aware of how natural systems will likely change, social and cultural scientists are, for good reasons, more reluctant with probabilistic predictions of future developments. Müller-Mahn et al. (2025, p. 177) take a critical stance on the dangers of "reducing the future to trends and probabilities", inviting the risk of "falling into the traps of deterministic thinking". This also implies not resorting to crises as the only way of thinking futures. To solve this, Chakkalakal and Ren (2022) propose focusing on future epistemologies and future practices (even unfolding today), and the role of social positions and struggles in negotiating and contesting them. This links to notions of prefigurative politics that, as Jeffrey and Dyson (2021) underline, involve both spontaneous and stratregic agency even beyond formalized plans and linear conceptions of the future.

Meanwhile, practices of futuring, and thus the creation of future visions, are set in the present constellation, opening up a temporal politics as described by Oomen et al. (2022, 252): "images of the future shaping the possibility space for action, thus enacting relationships between past, present and future."

Building on this, we contend that the normative and contested character of sociotechnical imaginaries becomes most apparent during times of ongoing technological change, when competing technologies and underlying future visions emerge (Kim, 2015; Storey, 2015). It is in such situations of technological promise and contingency that the concomitant visions of technological and societal futures become easily detectable and comparable. However, the link between emergent technologies and potential futures is not straightforward, either. With a plurality of technological futures competing, it remains unclear which of these will prevail in the future (Rotolo et al., 2015). Recent work in innovation studies questions the straightforward connection between technologies and futures, as even newly developed technologies may fail to anticipate future social or political developments (van der Duin et al., 2024). This also complicates the assumption that technologies will solve social issues—both present and future—a claim that has been challenged by critical work on technological solutionism (Morozov, 2013). In related work, authors criticized the shortcoming of technologies that are, at best, designed to solve specific problems, often coming back to Maslow's (1966) classical observations regarding the functionality of an automated car wash: a machine fine-tuned for this one purpose, but treating every object put on its line as if it were a car. An observation condensed in the famous quote "I suppose it is tempting, if the only tool you have is a hammer, to treat everything as if it were a nail" (ibid., pp. 15–16). So the question remains, who designs tomorrow's hammers and how can this be detected today?

In fact, discussions about how technologies are shaped by social groups or historical circumstances have a long history. Particularly throughout the 1980s and 1990s Science and Technology Studies made significant contributions to the discussion of how social processes define and coproduce technological development. Winner (1980) famously captured this issue in his statement that "artefacts have politics", which are inscribed in the design and functional requirements of different technologies. From a constructivist viewpoint, the School on the Social Construction of Technology (SCOT) (Pinch & Bijker, 1984) differentiated the initial phases of open, flexible technological development, from later processes of closure regarding functions and design when a technology was entering a process of stabilization. In contrast, Hughes (1987) highlighted the role of system builders and standardization processes ensuring the alignment of elements in what he termed "large technical systems", such as electricity infrastructures. However, developments are obviously not always straightforward, and especially Actor Network Theory (ANT) reminds us of the contingency, unexpected effects or even defects of sociotechnical networks (Callon, 1990; Latour, 1994). Both the SCOT and ANT accounts were, in turn, criticized by more structuralist perspectives (e.g. Russell, 1986; Winner, 1993), who argued that both schools ignored the underlying social relations and emerging alternative technological options that may be foreclosed in the play of social powers. Criticizing both Winner's oversimplification and SCOT's perceived naivety regarding power relations, Jasanoff (2020) has positioned her approach of sociotechnical imaginaries as mediating between these poles. As explained in the preceding pages, in this book we therefore uphold the idea that imaginaries help us to link technologies and their genealogy to the underlying social expectations and spatial imaginations that shaped them.

Since these early debates of SCOT vs. ANT, there has been a fruitful interchange between Science and Technology Studies and human geography regarding the role of technology in defining and constructing space (Warf, 2017). Appadurai (1990) conceptualized the "technoscape" as a sphere of globalization in which largely mobile technologies facilitate the circulation of materials and information. Hinchliffe (1996) warned against adopting a one-sided, managerialist approach to technology as suggested by dominant modernist accounts. Since then, geographic work has encompassed diverse contributions, such as "technonatures" in cultural geographies (White & Wilbert, 2009), engagements with "technological fixes" in critical geography and political ecology (Ekers & Prudham, 2017), as well as work on the uneven access to technology in urban geography (Graham & Marvin, 2001). Though these approaches differ in their conceptual and epistemological positioning, they all caution against simplified or deterministic readings of the relations between space and technologies. Mann (2009), for example, discusses the various applications of cell phones in rural areas such as telemedicine, thereby questioning simplistic dichotomies of urban and rural, respectively modernity and backwardness. More recent contributions shed light on technologies emerging in the Global South, thus highlighting developments beyond Silicon Valley and other centres of the global technology industry (Quet et al., 2025).

Obviously, technologies and space co-constitute each other in ways more complex than often anticipated. Perceiving this relation through the lens of sociotechnical imaginaries opens further pathways to illuminate aspirations about social orders and possible futures.

4 Towards Geographies of Sociotechnical Futures

This anthology exemplifies future technologies in three areas that are prominent in scientific inquiry and public debate. The first part, "Mobilizing and Contesting Low-Carbon Futures", is dedicated to low-carbon energy technologies, particularly renewable energies as a major field of technological visions for mitigating the ongoing climate crisis (Sovacool, 2019; Urban & Nordensvärd, 2023). Three chapter contributions highlight the contested nature of different energy transition pathways, each of which is legitimized by sociotechnical imaginaries. Chateau and Devine-Wright distinguish four competing sociotechnical imaginaries linked to divergent place-specific notions of national identity in France, ranging from conservative and eco-modernist positions to advocates of decentralized energy systems and anti-capitalist critiques. Naumann and Rudolph discuss how shortcomings in infrastructure provision are integral to representations of rural spaces in Denmark and Germany. They demonstrate how this issue has become a focal point in recent right-wing populist mobilization, while at the same time carrying potential for alternative, utopian visions of rural autonomy and self-management. Levidow maps industry and European Commission documents, as well as the positions of critical civil society actors, on hydrogen and carbon capture, exploring opposing views on the primacy of renewable energy and the role of natural gas in the European energy transition.

The second part of this book, "Digital Promises", focuses on debates surrounding initiatives for "smart cities" and artificial intelligence as a second significant field for both technological development and negotiation of related futures (Marvin et al., 2015; Bunnell & Yeo, 2025). Adopting an infrastructural perspective, Walter analyses the introduction of a digitally monitored water transportation system from water-rich to more water-scarce regions across England, questioning emerging technological and infrastructure fixes. Subsequently, Kowalski and Bork-Hüffer offer a critical examination of the current extended reality (XR) boom, employing feminist, postcolonial and crip theory to develop a perspective on the inclusive co-creation of XR for producing more desirable futures.

The third and final part of the book, "Engineering the Planetary", broadens the debate to include technologies that target the planetary scale and beyond. Rothe reconstructs discourses and practices of infrastructuring to produce a digital twin of planet Earth in response to planetary and European security threats. Hilbrich opens a North–South perspective, tracing how carbon-dioxide removal and solar radiation management technologies are discussed in Germany and South Africa. Lastly, Jones questions the promises and representations developed by the New Space Industry to promote asteroid mining in outer space, while omitting issues of responsibility for space debris and justice on Earth.

As an outlook, the contributions in this book speak to a possible future research agenda for a joint analysis of sociotechnical and spatial imaginaries. To this end, we build on the three-dimensional typology developed by Watkins (2015) and Chateau and Devine-Wright (2021) that was introduced above. It distinguishes between (1) "place imaginaries", (2) "idealized space imaginaries", and (3) "spatial transformation imaginaries". These concepts cut across the contributions in this book, opening new perspectives on the embeddedness, representations and performativity of sociotechnical imaginaries.

First, various contributions in this book highlight the contestation arising at the intersection of sociotechnical and place imaginaries. While Chateau and Devine-Wright underline that place imaginaries are contested in themselves, Naumann and Rudolph stress the role of poor infrastructure provision for both imagining and creating peripheries. Levidow, further, discusses how a lighthouse project for a hydrogen pipeline in Malta becomes enmeshed in conflicts around corruption in national energy policies. Hilbrich points out that the location of researchers impacts on their evaluation of geoengineering imaginaries. Obviously, place and identities should neither be considered fixed nor isolated (Massey, 2005). Capturing the relation between sociotechnical and place imaginaries therefore implies going beyond both given notions of "energy regions" and "car cities", or place imaginaries mobilized in opposition to new infrastructure (Devine-Wright, 2013). Instead, it requires opening a multi-scalar perspective on how circulating future technologies potentially constitute and reframe sociotechnical relations and identities concerning place. Importantly, this approach features different positionalities and transcends binary distinctions such as rural peripheries versus urban centres and the Global North versus the Global South.

Second, representations of technological futures generate idealized spaces that link with development strategies for businesses, regions and economies. Levidow and Jones both underline this point in their analyses of European Union hydrogen policy documents and the space industry's public relations material, respectively. Such documents produce idealized representational spaces, both reflecting businesses' interest for attracting private or public funding and generating blueprints for future spaces. Generally speaking, such representations are an important cornerstone in future-making, communicating and delineating what is thinkable and feasible when constructing futures (Chakkalakal & Ren, 2022; Oomen & Hajer, 2024). Sociotechnical imaginaries here serve as a key to contextualize technological visualizations in strategies of economic policies and accumulation, as well as the power relations inscribed into these representations. To analyse these, the focus should be the negotiations, conflicts and omissions defining the development of technological visions and strategies, and how these feature in the production and contestation of representational spaces.

Third, sociotechnical imaginaries of future technologies are performative as they pertain to prospects for actual spatial transformation. As Rothe and Walter emphasize in their contributions, imaginaries of future technologies not only regard representational spaces, but produce material infrastructures already today. The SRA water pipeline discussed by Walter is a case in point for new technical infrastructures re-routing material circulations to address future environmental issues or scarcities. Future spatial transformations can be considered a boundary object (Gong, 2024) engaging different stakeholders in political processes and material projects today. Resulting from the contested character of technological visions discussed in this book, this does not necessarily follow hegemonic imaginaries as in Levidow's discussion of hydrogen policies. Instead, there is scope for alternative imaginaries and approaches to thinking technological transformation differently—in the format of decentralized energy initiatives, projects for rural autonomy or participatory technology development. Kowalski and Bork-Hüffer, finally, make a strong point about addressing the needs and desires of disadvantaged people for creating more inclusive digital technologies. Thus, sociotechnical imaginaries are not a carefully defined prescription for future spatial transformations; rather their contestation invites researchers to challenge ready-made assumptions about technologically driven spatial transformation.

References

Adloff, F., & Neckel, S. (2019). Futures of sustainability as modernization, transformation, and control: A conceptual framework. *Sustainability Science, 14*(4), 1015–1025. https://doi.org/10.1007/s11625-019-00671-2

Anand, N., Gupta, A., & Appel, H. (Eds.). (2018). *The promise of infrastructure*. Duke University Press.

Anderson, B. R. O'G. (2016). Imagined communities: Reflections on the origin and spread of nationalism (Revised ed.). Verso. (Original work published 1983).

Appadurai, A. (1990). Disjuncture and difference in the global cultural economy. *Theory, Culture & Society, 7*(2–3), 295–310. https://doi.org/10.1177/026327690007002017

Appadurai, A. (1996). *Modernity at large: Cultural dimensions of globalization*. University of Minnesota Press.

Appel, H., Anand, N., & Gupta, A. (2018). Temporality, politics, and the promise of infrastructure. In N. Anand, A. Gupta, & H. Appel (Eds.), *The promise of infrastructure* (pp. 1–38). Duke University Press.

Beckert, J. (2016). *Imagined futures: Fictional expectations and capitalist dynamics*. Harvard University Press.

Benediktsson, K. (2021). Conflicting imaginaries in the energy transition? Nature and renewable energy in Iceland. *Moravian Geographical Reports, 29*(2), 88–100. https://doi.org/10.2478/mgr-2021-0008

Biermann, F., Oomen, J., Gupta, A., Ali, S. H., Conca, K., Hajer, M. A., Kashwan, P., Kotzé, L. J., Leach, M., Messner, D., Okereke, C., Persson, Å., Potočnik, J., Schlosberg, D., Scobie, M., & VanDeveer, S. D. (2022). Solar geoengineering: The case for an international non-use agreement. *Wiley Interdisciplinary Reviews: Climate Change, 13*(3), e754. https://doi.org/10.1002/wcc.754

Bowker, G. C. (1994). *Science on the run: Information management and industrial geophysics at Schlumberger, 1920–1940*. MIT Press.

Bunnell, T., & Yeo, S. J. I. (2025). Futures. In A. I. Ashutosh & J. Winders (Eds.), *The Wiley Blackwell companion to cultural and social geography*. Wiley-Blackwell. https://doi.org/10.1002/9781119634294.ch24

Callon, M. (1990). Techno-economic networks and irreversibility. *The Sociological Review, 38*(S1), 132–161. https://doi.org/10.1111/j.1467-954X.1990.tb03351.x

Castoriadis, C. (1987). *The imaginary institution of society*. Polity Press.

Chakkalakal, S., & Ren, J. (2022). Un/doing future, unsettling temporalization. *International Journal of Urban and Regional Research, 46*(4), 845–850. https://doi.org/10.1111/1468-2427.13101

Chateau, Z., Devine-Wright, P., & Wills, J. (2021). Integrating sociotechnical and spatial imaginaries in researching energy futures. *Energy Research & Social Science, 80*, 102207. https://doi.org/10.1016/j.erss.2021.102207

Delina, L. L. (2018). Whose and what futures? Navigating the contested coproduction of Thailand's energy sociotechnical imaginaries. *Energy Research & Social Science, 35*, 48–56. https://doi.org/10.1016/j.erss.2017.10.045

Devine-Wright, P. (2013). Think global act local? The relevance of place attachments and place identities in a climate changed world. *Global Environmental Change, 23*(1), 61–69. https://doi.org/10.1016/j.gloenvcha.2012.08.003

Dincer, I. (2020). Covid-19 coronavirus: Closing carbon age, but opening hydrogen age. *International Journal of Energy Research, 44*(8), 6093–6097. https://doi.org/10.1002/er.5569

Dincer, I. (2023). Hydrogen 1.0: A new age. *International Journal of Hydrogen Energy, 48*(43), 16143–16147. https://doi.org/10.1016/j.ijhydene.2023.01.124

Dunlap, A., & Laratte, L. (2022). European green Deal necropolitics: Exploring 'green' energy transition, degrowth & infrastructural colonization. *Political Geography, 97*, 102640. https://doi.org/10.1016/j.polgeo.2022.102640

Ekers, M., & Prudham, S. (2017). The metabolism of socioecological fixes: Capital switching, spatial fixes, and the production of nature. *Annals of the American Association of Geographers, 107*(6), 1370–1388. https://doi.org/10.1080/24694452.2017.1309962

Fladvad, B. (2023). Infrastructuring environmental (in)justice: Green hydrogen, indigenous sovereignty and the political geographies of energy technologies. *Geographica Helvetica, 78*(4), 493–505. https://doi.org/10.5194/gh-78-493-2023

Geels, F. W. (2019). Socio-technical transitions to sustainability: A review of criticisms and elaborations of the multi-level perspective. *Current Opinion in Environmental Sustainability, 39*, 187–201. https://doi.org/10.1016/j.cosust.2019.06.009

Gong, H. (2024). Futures should matter (more): Toward a forward-looking perspective in economic geography. *Progress in Human Geography, 48*(3), 292–315. https://doi.org/10.1177/03091325231224434

Graham, S., & Marvin, S. (2001). *Networked infrastructures, Technological Mobilities and the urban Condition*. Routledge.

Gregory, D. (1994). *Geographical imaginations*. Blackwell.

Gregory, D. (2004). *The colonial present: Afghanistan, Palestine, Iraq*. Blackwell.

Gregory, D., Johnston, R., Pratt, G., Watts, M. J., & Whatmore, S. (2009). *The dictionary of human geography* (5th ed.). Blackwell.

Harvey, P., Jensen, C. B., & Morita, A. (2017). *Infrastructures and social complexity: A companion*. Routledge.

Headrick, D. R. (1981). *The tools of empire: Technology and European imperialism in the nineteenth century*. Oxford University Press.

Hinchliffe, S. (1996). Technology, power, and space—The means and ends of geographies of technology. *Environment and Planning D: Society and Space, 14*(6), 659–682. https://doi.org/10.1068/d140659

Hornborg, A. (2019). *Nature, society, and justice in the Anthropocene: Unraveling the money-energy-technology complex*. Cambridge University Press.

Howie, B., & Lewis, N. (2014). Geographical imaginaries: Articulating the values of geography. *New Zealand Geographer, 70*(2), 131–139. https://doi.org/10.1111/nzg.12051

Hughes, T. (1987). The evolution of large technical systems. In W.E. Bijker, T.P. Hughes & Pinch, T.J. (Eds.): *The Social Construction of Technological Systems: New Directions in the Sociology and History of Technology* (pp. 51–82). MIT Press.

International Energy Agency (IEA). (2024). *Global hydrogen review 2024*. IEA. https://www.iea.org/reports/global-hydrogen-review-2024

Jasanoff, S. (2004). *States of knowledge*. Routledge.

Jasanoff, S. (2015). Future imperfect: Science, technology, and the imaginations of modernity. In S. Jasanoff & S.-H. Kim (Eds.), *Dreamscapes of modernity: Sociotechnical imaginaries and the fabrication of power* (pp. 1–32). University of Chicago Press.

Jasanoff, S. (2020). Imagined worlds: The politics of future-making in the twenty-first century. In J.-P. Voß & R. Meyer (Eds.), *The politics and science of prevision* (pp. 18–34). Routledge. https://doi.org/10.4324/9781003022428-2

Jasanoff, S., & Kim, S.-H. (2009). Containing the atom: Sociotechnical imaginaries and nuclear power in the United States and South Korea. *Minerva, 47*(2), 119–146. https://doi.org/10.1007/s11024-009-9124-4

Jasanoff, S., & Kim, S.-H. (Eds.). (2015). Dreamscapes of modernity: Sociotechnical imaginaries and the fabrication of power. University of Chicago Press.

Jeffrey, C. & Dyson, J. (2021). *Geographies of the future: Prefigurative politics. Progress in Human Geography, 45*(4), 641–658. https://doi.org/10.1177/0309132520926569

Johnson, B. T. (2024). This world of tomorrow: Sociotechnical imaginaries of security in the Canadian Arctic. *Critical Studies on Security, 12*(2), 187–208. https://doi.org/10.1080/21624887.2024.2304413

Kalt, T., & Tunn, J. (2022). Shipping the sunshine? A critical research agenda on the global hydrogen transition. *GAIA—Ecological Perspectives for Science and Society, 31*(2), 72–76. https://doi.org/10.14512/gaia.31.2.2

Kathiravelu, L. (2021). Introduction to special section 'infrastructures of injustice: Migration and border mobilities'. *Mobilities, 16*(5), 645–655. https://doi.org/10.1080/17450101.2021.1981546

Kim, S.-H. (2015). Social movements and contested sociotechnical imaginaries in South Korea. In S. Jasanoff & S.-H. Kim (Eds.), *Dreamscapes of modernity: Sociotechnical imaginaries and the fabrication of power* (pp. 152–173). University of Chicago Press. https://doi.org/10.7208/chicago/9780226276663.001.0001

Knorr Cetina, K., Schatzki, T. R., & von Savigny, E. (2000). *The practice turn in contemporary theory*. Routledge.

Kuchler, M., & Stigson, G. M. (2024). Unravelling the 'collective' in sociotechnical imaginaries: A literature review. *Energy Research & Social Science, 110*(2), 103422. https://doi.org/10.1016/j.erss.2024.103422

Landau-Donnelly, F., & Pohl, L. (2023). Towards a post-foundational geography: Spaces of negativity, contingency, and antagonism. *Progress in Human Geography, 47*(4), 481–499. https://doi.org/10.1177/03091325231156928

Larkin, B. (2013). The politics and poetics of infrastructure. *Annual Review of Anthropology, 42*(1), 327–343. https://doi.org/10.1146/annurev-anthro-092412-155522

Latour, B. (1994). *We have never been modern* (3rd ed.). Harvard University Press.

Lenz, S. (2021). Is digitalization a problem solver or a fire accelerator? Situating digital technologies in sustainability discourses. *Social Science Information, 60*(2), 188–208. https://doi.org/10.1177/05390184211012179

Levy, D. L., & Spicer, A. (2013). Contested imaginaries and the cultural political economy of climate change. *Organization, 20*(5), 659–678. https://doi.org/10.1177/1350508413489816

Longhurst, N., & Chilvers, J. (2019). Mapping diverse visions of energy transitions: Co-producing sociotechnical imaginaries. *Sustainability Science, 14*(4), 973–990. https://doi.org/10.1007/s11625-019-00702-y

Mann, M. (2009). The cell-phone-in-the-countryside: On some of the ironic spatialities of technonatures. In D. F. White & C. Wilbert (Eds.), *Technonatures: Environments, technologies, spaces, and places in the twenty-first century* (pp. 85–104). Wilfrid Laurier University Press.

Marquardt, J., & Delina, L. L. (2019). Reimagining energy futures: Contributions from community sustainable energy transitions in Thailand and The Philippines. *Energy Research & Social Science, 49*, 91–102. https://doi.org/10.1016/j.erss.2018.10.028

Marston, S. A., Jones, J. P., & Woodward, K. (2005). Human geography without scale. *Transactions of the Institute of British Geographers, 30*(4), 416–432. https://doi.org/10.1111/j.1475-5661.2005.00180.x

Marvin, S., Luque-Ayala, A., & McFarlane, C. (2015). *Smart Urbanism. Utopian Vision or False Dawn*. Routledge.

Maslow, A. H. (1966). *The psychology of science: A reconnaissance*. Harper & Row.

Massey, D. B. (2005). *For space*. Sage.

Meyers, M. (2023). Artificial intelligence in a degrowth context: A conviviality perspective on machine learning. *GAIA—Ecological Perspectives for Science and Society, 33*(1), 186–192. https://doi.org/10.14512/gaia.33.1.13

Morozov, E. (2013). T*o Save Everything, Click Here. The Folly of Technological Solutionism*. Public Affairs.

Morozov, E. (2019). Digital socialism? The calculation debate in the age of big data. *New Left Review, 116*(117), 33–67.

Mouffe, C. (2005). *On the political.* Routledge.

Müller, F., Tunn, J., & Kalt, T. (2022). Hydrogen justice. *Environmental Research Letters, 17*(11), 115006. https://doi.org/10.1088/1748-9326/ac991a

Müller-Mahn, D., Runkel, S., Schlottmann, A., & Stephan, C. (2025). Geographies of the future. *Geographica Helvetica, 80*(2), 177–185. https://doi.org/10.5194/gh-80-177-2025

Nature Editorial. (2022). Overhyping hydrogen as a fuel risks endangering net-zero goals. *Nature, 611*(7936), 426. https://doi.org/10.1038/d41586-022-03693-6

Naumann, M. (2021). Infrastruktureller Populismus. *Geographische Zeitschrift, 109*(4), 208–226. https://doi.org/10.25162/gz-2021-0004

Nightingale, A. J., Eriksen, S., Taylor, M., Forsyth, T., Pelling, M., Newsham, A., Boyd, E., Brown, K., Harvey, B., Jones, L., Bezner Kerr, R., Mehta, L., Naess, L. O., Ockwell, D., Scoones, I., Tanner, T., & Whitfield, S. (2020). Beyond technical fixes: Climate solutions and the great derangement. *Climate and Development, 12*(4), 343–352. https://doi.org/10.1080/17565529.2019.1624495

Nost, E., & Colven, E. (2022). Earth for AI: A political ecology of data-driven climate initiatives. *Geoforum, 130*(5), 23–34. https://doi.org/10.1016/j.geoforum.2022.01.016

Oomen, J., Hoffman, J. & Hajer, M.A. (2022) Techniques of futuring: On how imagined futures become socially performative. *European Journal of Social Theory, 25*(2), 252–270. https://doi.org/10.1177/1368431020988826

Oomen, J., & Hajer, M. (2024). Futuring. In C. Overdevest (Ed.), *Elgar Encyclopaedia of environmental sociology* (pp. 319–326). Edward Elgar. https://doi.org/10.4337/9781803921044

Pinch, T. J., & Bijker, W. E. (1984). The social construction of facts and artefacts: Or how the sociology of science and the sociology of technology might benefit each other. *Social Studies of Science, 14*(3), 399–441. https://doi.org/10.1177/030631284014003004

Quet, M., Kameda, K., Pourraz, J., & Rault-Chodankar (Eds.). (2025). Technoscientfic globalisation from below. Mattering Press.

Rose, G. (2024). Visualising human life in volumetric cities: City digital twins and other disasters. *Dialogues in Urban Research, 81*(7), 77. https://doi.org/10.1177/27541258241288812

Rotolo, D., Hicks, D., & Martin, B. R. (2015). What is an emerging technology? *Research Policy, 44*(10), 1827–1843. https://doi.org/10.1016/j.respol.2015.06.006

Rudek, T. J. (2021). Capturing the invisible: Sociotechnical imaginaries of energy—A critical overview. *Science and Public Policy.* https://doi.org/10.1093/scipol/scab076

Russell, S. (1986). The social construction of artefacts: A response to Pinch and Bijker. *Social Studies of Science, 16*(2), 331–346. http://www.jstor.org/stable/285210

Said, E. (1978). *Orientalism*. Pantheon.

Sapinski, J. P., Buck, H. J., & Malm, A. (2021). *Has it come to this? The promises and perils of geoengineering on the brink*. Rutgers University Press.

Smith, J. M., & Tidwell, A. S. (2016). The everyday lives of energy transitions: Contested sociotechnical imaginaries in the American west. *Social Studies of Science, 46*(3), 327–350. https://doi.org/10.1177/0306312716644534

Soja, E. W. (1989). *Postmodern geographies: The reassertion of space in critical social theory*. Verso.

Sovacool, B. (2019). *Visions of energy futures. Imagining and Innovating Low-Carbon Transitions*. Routledge.

Storey, W. K. (2015). Cecil Rhodes and the making of a sociotechnical imaginary for South Africa. In S. Jasanoff & S.-H. Kim (Eds.), *Dreamscapes of modernity: Sociotechnical imaginaries and the fabrication of power* (pp. 34–55). University of Chicago Press. https://doi.org/10.7208/chicago/9780226276663.001.0001

Svoboda, T., Irvine, P. J., Callies, D., & Sugiyama, M. (2018). The potential for climate engineering with stratospheric sulfate aerosol injections to reduce climate injustice. *Journal of Global Ethics, 14*(3), 353–368. https://doi.org/10.1080/17449626.2018.1552180

Taylor, C. (2004). *Modern social imaginaries*. Duke University Press.

Urban, F., & Nordensvärd, J. (Eds.). (2023). *Handbook on climate change and technology*. Edward Elgar.

van der Duin, P., Trott, P., & Ortt, R. (2024). Failed technology management: Introducing 'future technology myopia' and how to address it. *Technological Forecasting and Social Change, 198*, 122927. https://doi.org/10.1016/j.techfore.2023.122927

van Veelen, B., Rella, L., Taylor Aiken, G., Judson, E., Gambino, E., Jenss, A., Parashar, A., & Pinker, A. (2021). Interventions on democratizing infrastructure. *Political Geography, 87*, 102378. https://doi.org/10.1016/j.polgeo.2021.102378

Warf, B. (2017). *Handbook on geographies of technologies*. Edward Elgar.

Watkins, J. (2015). Spatial imaginaries research in geography: Synergies, tensions, and new directions. *Geography Compass, 9*(9), 508–522. https://doi.org/10.1111/gec3.12228

White, D. F., & Wilbert, C. (2009). Introduction: Inhabiting technonatural time/spaces. In D. F. White & C. Wilbert (Eds.), *Technonatures: Environments, technologies, spaces, and places in the twenty-first century* (pp. 1–30). Wilfrid Laurier University Press.

Winner, L. (1980). Do artifacts have politics? *Daedalus, 109*(1), 121–136. http://www.jstor.org/stable/20024652

Winner, L. (1993). Upon opening the black box and finding it empty: Social constructivism and the philosophy of technology. *Science, Technology, & Human Values, 18*(3), 362–378. https://doi.org/10.1177/016224399301800306

Yusoff, K., & Gabrys, J. (2011). Climate change and the imagination. *WIREs Climate Change, 2*(4), 516–534. https://doi.org/10.1002/wcc.117

PART I

Mobilizing and Contesting Low-Carbon Futures

CHAPTER 2

Competing Sociotechnical and Spatial Imaginaries: The Controversy Over Wind Energy Deployment in France

Zoé Chateau and Patrick Devine-Wright

1 Introduction

Driven by different imperatives such as responding to climate change, diversifying away from nuclear energy and meeting EU renewable energy targets, successive policies have aimed to accelerate the deployment of wind energy in France. They have generated increasing controversy at the national level and prompted a variety of actors to articulate contrasting visions of (un)desirable energy futures to support their perspectives on deployment, crystallizing in different sociotechnical imaginaries (STIs). These antagonistic perspectives are fuelled not only by different visions of the stakes and means of France's energy system transformation—or

Z. Chateau (✉)
French National Research Institute for Agriculture, Food and Environment (INRAE), Cestas, France
e-mail: z.chateau@exeter.ac.uk

P. Devine-Wright
University of Exeter, Geography, Exeter, UK
e-mail: p.g.devine-wright@exeter.ac.uk

S. Becker, B. Fladvad (eds.), *Contested Imaginaries of Future Technologies*, https://doi.org/10.1007/978-3-032-11497-6_2

whether such a transformation is even necessary—but also by powerful spatial imaginaries relating to the development of rural spaces and territories. The chapter focuses on this intersection and explores the different visions of sociotechnical and spatial order that become manifest in the controversy over the deployment of wind energy from 2015 to 2022. It examines how different sociotechnical imaginaries compete at the national level, and analyzes their interrelations and co-construction with spatial imaginaries, arguing that space is crucial to how different (wind) energy futures are imagined. This section sets the conceptual background for the chapter by bringing together different strands of literature on sociotechnical imaginaries, the geographies of energy system change and spatial imaginaries, and then provides more context for the case of France. The second section outlines the methods used to conduct the research. The fourth section elaborates its results, presenting four national-level sociotechnical imaginaries and elaborating their co-construction with different spatial imaginaries. The final section discusses their implications.

1.1 Conceptual Background

Sociotechnical imaginaries capture how visions for energy system transformation advance imagined social, political and economic orders. Read as normative commitments, they extend beyond energy systems and have implications for the (re)production of power relations between actors and groups (Jasanoff & Kim, 2009, 2015; Jasanoff & Simmet, 2021). They are invaluable for exploring how controversies over sociotechnical pathways and artefacts are shaped by competing imaginations that go beyond the future of energy, involving social values and collective visions of the good society (Jasanoff & Kim, 2015) that may clash with one another. The geographical dimensions of STIs have appeared as a theme in the literature, touching on various aspects. Recent work has shown how STIs can *emerge* from collectives working at different scales and highlighted how more "local" STIs are *shaped* by place-specific histories and relationships with energy production (e.g., Marquardt & Delina, 2019; Molden & Meehan, 2018; Smith & Tidwell, 2016). Some have explored the processes by which STIs *move* across scales and contexts and *circulate* between groups, either bottom-up or top-down, for example analysing how national STIs interact with more local imaginaries (e.g., Burnham et al., 2017; Eaton et al., 2014; Lambert, 2022; Levenda et al., 2019; Schelhas et al., 2018; Trencher & van der Heijden, 2019). Others have examined the *geographical futures* that STIs prescribe, showing that they involve operations of *space-making* that have implications for the material, social and symbolic fabric of places (e.g., Mayer & Balázs, 2018; Phillips, 2018; Sadowski & Bendor, 2019).

However, most of these forays have been confined to more "local" matters, as questions of place, space or scale are most often addressed in studies that focus on the local or regional level. Surprisingly for a field criticized for its focus on the national level, and despite Jasanoff's emphasis on the co-production of spatial and social orders and the formation of national imaginaries, few works have systematically addressed the geographies of STIs at the national level (but see Felt, 2015; Kuchler & Bridge, 2018). While a growing body of work has documented struggles between competing STIs at the national level (e.g., Carvalho et al., 2022; Delina, 2018; Longhurst & Chilvers, 2019; Torres & Niewöhner, 2023), few have made their spatial dimensions—and consequently their *spatial partiality*—central to the analysis, and there remains scope to address them more directly and systematically.

Capturing these spatial dimensions is essential for fully understanding the production and contestation of energy futures, as energy system change involves the diffusion of "'multiple, multi-sited' social practices which are co-constitutive of normative geographical imaginaries and spatial identities" (Calvert, 2016, p. 111). Conflicting politics of space and scale, re-scaling strategies and acts of place-making are fundamental to this (e.g., Bridge, 2018; Bridge & Gailing, 2020; Calvert, 2016), and the geographical implications of wind energy deployment are well documented in particular, including reinforcing unequal socio-spatial relations between rural and urban spaces or transforming local landscapes (e.g., Avila, 2018; Pasqualetti, 2000; Rudolph & Kirkegaard, 2019).

Research has also shown that people's relationships with places influence their responses to wind projects, which can be perceived either as threats to place or, conversely, as place-making activities (e.g., Devine-Wright & Howes, 2010; Warren & McFadyen, 2010). More critical approaches have shown that constructions of place, space and scale serve as resources for groups to legitimize claims and positions related to specific projects—with objectors, for example, formulating narratives of "place-technology unfit" that draw on representations of the rural as beautiful and pristine or seascapes as restorative and open as opposed to "industrial" wind turbines (e.g., Batel et al., 2015; Devine-Wright & Wiersma, 2020; Gee, 2010; McLachlan, 2009). Socio-spatial divides, for example between cities and the countryside, also shape responses to projects and can be mobilized to construct narratives of socio-spatial injustice (e.g., Batel & Devine-Wright, 2017; Llewellyn et al., 2017; Phadke, 2011). These constructions are contested and relational, influenced by sociocultural and political histories and relations at different scales (Batel et al., 2015; Batel & Devine-Wright, 2017). This creates a need to examine their circulation across scales and groups and to understand them contextually (e.g., Batel, 2018)—moving beyond a focus that has often been too centred on local place, especially as socially dominant representations of space and place that often downplay their subjective components in favour of abstraction shape and legitimize development and siting decisions (Cowell, 2010; Devine-Wright, 2010).

Bringing these two strands of literature together, this chapter scrutinizes the spatial dimensions of the wind energy STIs struggling for traction at the national level in France. To analyze them, it uses the concept of spatial imaginaries, defined as "deeply held, collective understandings of socio-spatial relations that are performed by, give sense to, make possible and change collective socio-spatial practices" (Davoudi et al., 2018: 101) or "socially held stories, ways of representing places and spaces" (Watkins, 2015, p. 509). Imbued with implicit understandings of the spatialized social world, they contribute to shaping material geographies through their propagation and concretization (Chivallon, 2008; Davoudi et al., 2018; Watkins, 2015). In line with Chateau et al. (2021), the chapter argues that spatial and sociotechnical imaginaries are co-constituted: that spatial imaginaries are drawn upon by collectives in the construction of sociotechnical visions and feed into STIs, which are themselves underpinned by and contribute to the reinforcement of particular spatial imaginaries. STIs, as performed and materialized in discourses, practices and infrastructures, therefore impact the production of space and territory, while spatial imaginaries influence STIs and the trajectory of sociotechnical systems. The implication is that spatial imaginaries, as an analytical tool, are invaluable not only for deconstructing plans for wind energy deployment in France and the imagined orders that underpin them, but also for better understanding how and why divergent visions compete for traction.

1.2 Empirical Background

The case of wind energy in France provides an interesting example through which to illustrate the interplay between the production of desirable energy futures and geographical imaginaries. Compared to other European countries, France is still somewhat a "laggard" in terms of wind energy, ranking 17th in terms of the share of electricity demand covered by wind energy in 2024, although it is 4th in terms of installed capacity (Wind Europe, 2024).[1] It was a late start for a country that, from the 1970s to the 1990s, was the example of a "nuclear country", characterized by a modernizing and interventionist paradigm, institutional centralization and an approach to energy policy that emphasized productivism, independence and national prestige (Evrard, 2013; Evrard & Pasquier, 2018; Nadaï, 2007; Nadaï & Labussière, 2009; Poupeau, 2020). With nuclear energy accounting for 75.4% of electricity production in 1996 (International Energy Agency, 2023), renewable energy was initially met with reluctance (Evrard, 2013). Wind energy did not take off until the 2000s, when more favourable support schemes allowed projects to become profitable. This decade also witnessed an increase in disputes, as the lack of appropriate planning frameworks led to a concentration of projects in the windiest regions, creating conflictual situations (Nadaï, 2007; Nadaï & Labussière, 2009; Szarka, 2007). In 2009–2010, stricter regulations were introduced, slowing down development and prompting advocates to call for administrative simplification.

In the 2012–2015 period, the notion of energy transition was taken up by policymakers, leading to a shift in energy policy. Rather than heralding a profound turn towards a more democratic energy production system, the term lost its activist connotations as it was incorporated into a top-down discourse and came to be interpreted as the diversification and decarbonization of the energy mix and a new industrial cycle based on green growth (Aykut & Evrard, 2017; Nadaï & Wallenborn, 2019). In 2015, the Energy Transition for Green Growth Act set ambitious targets for the reduction of carbon gas emissions and the share of nuclear energy in the electricity mix. Wind energy capacity targets set in 2016 and 2020 stipulated an increase of more than 100% by 2028. Accelerating wind

[1] With 22.3 GW onshore capacity and 1.5 GW offshore capacity in 2024, see: Données et études statistiques, Ministère de la transition énergétique. (2024). Tableau de bord: Éolien—Deuxième trimestre 2024 [Dataset]. https://www.statistiques.developpement-durable.gouv.fr/publicationweb/645?type=versionimprimable

deployment became a key objective, resulting in a series of streamlining measures. At the same time, decentralization re-emerged as an issue on the French political agenda, with an increasingly diverse range of actors advocating not only for local authorities to be granted more legal powers over energy planning, but also for a broader political and cultural shift in energy practices (Evrard & Pasquier, 2018; Nadaï et al., 2015; Poupeau, 2020). In the wind energy sector, the government's attempts to increase the acceptance of projects gave rise to a localist rhetoric emphasizing local benefits and the participation of local actors and citizens. Over the period, several measures facilitated different aspects of participation, such as community energy projects and participatory financing.

However, decision-making processes remain centralized and top-down, while local authorities and citizens are only selectively involved (Aykut & Evrard, 2017; Evrard & Pasquier, 2018; Poupeau, 2020). Moreover, despite voluntarist discourses, French policymakers' attitudes towards wind energy are ambivalent, especially regarding onshore wind. In 2022, President Macron significantly scaled back onshore wind targets, while setting a highly ambitious target of more than 40GW of offshore wind by 2050[2]—an apparent shift from onshore to offshore deployment. This coincided with the resolution of long-standing ambiguities about the future of nuclear power, with the government announcing major investments in nuclear energy.[3] Wind energy has also become increasingly politicized at the national level, with conservative candidates in the 2021 (regional) and 2022 (presidential) election years surfing on anti-wind rhetoric.

This controversial context makes wind energy a relevant site for capturing STIs, as it leads to the crystallization of different visions of desirable energy futures. As the next sections will show, spatial imaginaries related to rurality and territory at different scales are a salient feature of this controversy: they constitute a resource to support antagonistic arguments about wind energy and appear to fuel competing STIs—and in this, the case of France provides a particularly relevant lens for understanding how sociotechnical and socio-spatial orders are co-produced and co-negotiated.

[2] Compared to only 1.5 GW of total installed offshore capacity and 7.8 GW at different stages of planning, development and construction in 2024.

[3] Including the launch of six nuclear European Pressurized Reactor projects, major investments in R&D for smaller nuclear reactors, and further extending the operation of existing nuclear power plants. The objective of reducing the share of nuclear in the electricity mix to 50% in 2025, introduced by the Energy Transition for Green Growth Act (2015), was also abrogated in 2023.

2 Methods

In order to investigate the interrelations between spatial imaginaries and wind energy STIs, the chapter examines the discourses of the actors involved in producing, promoting, negotiating or contesting the deployment of onshore and offshore wind energy at the national level in France between 2015—the introduction of the Energy Transition Act for Green Growth—and 2022. A sample of 170 documents from government, industry and civil society actors was analyzed. These actors were selected on the basis of their involvement in the national wind energy controversy, with the aim of collecting different perspectives in terms of activities and attitudes. The official trajectory articulated by the government is a key focus, as well as how it is contrasted by non-state actors. These include wind industry syndicates and developers, citizen energy advocates, environmental NGOs, climate activists, landscape conservation groups and anti-wind associations—as all promote specific visions of the role of wind energy in the French energy mix and whether and how it should be developed. Document analysis was used because it allowed a large amount of material to be examined, facilitating comparison across a wide range of actors. Three criteria were combined for including documents in the corpus: date of production (2015–2022), author (organizations whose main activities were related to wind energy deployment in France), and content (documents had to focus on the why, how and what of wind energy deployment). In addition, a purposive sampling strategy (Robinson, 2014) was used, following three principles: an approximately equal representation of all types of actors (civil society, government and industry); a representation of different organizations within each category; and the inclusion of different types of documents for each organization (e.g., from very formal and projective documents such as energy policy roadmaps to blog articles). The approach to policy documents was exhaustive, as these provided a context in relation to which others positioned themselves; for the rest of the material, we aimed for saturation (Saunders et al., 2018).

The material was analysed using thematic analysis (Nowell et al., 2017), with the idea that this would allow for identifying STIs and tracing their connections with spatial imaginaries, while capturing their contrasts. A deductive coding framework was created and refined throughout the exploration of the data; it was applied iteratively to each document, actor and STI, and then used to compare across STIs. Building on Longhurst and Chilvers (2019), wind energy STIs were captured as assemblages of normative framings (the *issues* that legitimize action), governance arrangements and processes (*organizings*), and technological and material commitments (*doings*) performed by actors and involving a degree of institutionalization. Attention was paid both to the visions of desirable futures that emerged and to the ways in which actors framed other STIs. To identify spatial imaginaries, we used the framework proposed by Watkins (2015), which distinguishes between place imaginaries (distinct, particular places such as London, the Middle East or Earth), idealized spaces (types of place that share generic characteristics, such as the *countryside* or various notions of *territory*) and spatial transformation imaginaries (narratives of generic processes by which places change, such as *globalization* or *gentrification*). We were interested in spatial imaginaries involving different spaces, but also different scales, including the national scale. Concurring with our scale of analysis, imaginaries of France are therefore included under the category of *place imaginary*. Finally, particular attention was paid to the traction of both sociotechnical and spatial imaginaries, by assessing the extent to which they are shared in different spheres (e.g., from advocacy to policy) and the symbolic and material instruments used to circulate them. This led to a gradient from dominant imaginaries, materialized in programmes, processes and infrastructures and supported by powerful institutions, to more minor imaginaries which remain confined to smaller groups and have less influence on policymaking and project implementation.

3 Findings: Four Competing Wind Energy STIs

Four different wind energy STIs were identified in the material (see Table 2.1). They structure and are performed by four different coalitions of actors to advocate, negotiate and/or contest the deployment of wind energy, with different levels of traction. Two of them (dominant STI and citizen energy STI) are mobilized to support the deployment of wind energy; the other two (conservative STI and anti-capitalist STI) are performed to argue against governmental wind energy policy. However, all three alternative STIs challenge national energy policy in its sociotechnical and spatial underpinnings. The following sections develop these STIs in turn and analyze their co-constitution with spatial imaginaries, while a final section draws out their implications.

Table 2.1 Four competing STIs co-constituted with spatial imaginaries[a]

	Dominant STI	*Citizen energy STI*	*Conservative STI*	*Anti-capitalist STI*
Issues	Global climate emergency National energy security, industrial competition and growth	Global climate emergency National energy security Democracy, social justice and local empowerment	Global climate emergency National energy security, sovereignty and industrial power Preserving landscape and heritage sites	Global environmental crisis Environmental and social justice Local empowerment
Organizings	Centralized decision-making Balance between state intervention and market economy	Decentralized governance and local ownership Cooperative economic processes	Centralized decision-making State and public companies vs globalization and foreign corporations	Local mobilization and decision-making; local ownership Energy as a shared common
Doings	Large-scale development and techno--economic prowess Nuclear + renewables	Small-scale, community-led projects 100% renewables	Large-scale nuclear power Small-scale or less visible renewables	Small-scale, low-tech and DIY Local savoir-faire and techniques Anti nuclear and large-scale infrastructure
Desirable futures	National economic and industrial renewal through ecological modernization	Energy, economic and political paradigm shift: Decentralization, democratization, cooperation	National industrial renewal through ecological modernization and national independence and power	Energy, economic and political paradigm shift: Local autonomy and low-tech development in secession from capitalism

(*continued*)

Table 2.1 (continued)

	Dominant STI	*Citizen energy STI*	*Conservative STI*	*Anti-capitalist STI*
Idealized spaces	Declining rural spaces Territories: Passive hosts and beneficiaries The ocean as a resource	Declining rural spaces Urban/rural solidarity Territories: Central socio-spatial and political collectives	Rural spaces: In crisis vs privileged urban spaces Bucolic countryside and heritage sites as part of France's identity	Rural spaces: Vulnerable as well as a counter-ideal for a low-tech life vs globalized urban Territories: Spaces of collective meaning; political projects
Place imaginaries	France, a powerful and virtuous nation	N/A	Nostalgic imaginary of France: a powerful nation and an attractive, heritage country	N/A
Spatial transformations	Local development: Entrepreneurial logic Rural revitalization and attractiveness	Local development: Cooperative logic Rural revitalization and empowerment	Industrialization of rural landscapes vs touristic and residential development Industrialization of coastlines	Industrialization of the rural and homogenization of territories
Socio-spatial order	Centralized space relationality (the nation above its territories) coexisting with entrepreneurial territorial development in a context of state rollout	Localist: Territorial empowerment Bottom-up and multi-level governance	Centralized space relationality (the nation above its territories) National patriots and local guardians	Localist: Bottom to bottom organization, territorial autonomy and celebration of local imaginaries

[a]This table is a simplified version of the coding framework and summarizes the findings. Issues, organizings and doings refer to the normative framings, governance and economic processes and technological commitments assembled in STIs (Longhurst & Chilvers, 2019), while desirable futures refer to the overall vision of the "good society" they fit into. Idealized spaces, place imaginaries and spatial transformations describe types of spatial imaginaries (Watkins, 2015). Socio-spatial order refers to the overall socio-spatial vision that emerges from the material

3.1 The Dominant Wind Energy STI: Territories as Contributors to the National Energy Transition

Throughout the period, government and industry actors consistently perform a STI that we characterize as dominant, because it is shared between these two types of actors concentrating economic and political resources; it is also supported by the institutional infrastructure of the state and presides over the making of wind energy policy. Wind energy is legitimized by its economic and technological prowess, in a horizon of decreasing costs and ever-increasing productivity. Offshore wind, particularly, is praised for its potential for maximizing capacity, due to lower landscape impacts, greater acceptance and fewer land constraints considering the vastness of the ocean. This connects to industrial and economic strategies, as in the "European race for [offshore] wind"[4] (France Énergie Éolienne, 2020, p. 3), it is an issue for France to become "a leader in these technologies that have strong market potential" (Ministère de la transition énergétique, 2020a, p. 21). These characterizations are underpinned by an imaginary of the ocean as offering "considerable potential for innovation and growth" (Ministère de la transition énergétique, 2017a, p. 7), with the pioneering aim of reaching "unexploited maritime areas" (Eolfi, 2018, p. 2) ... and market sectors. More generally, renewables are seen as levers for "green growth, wealth creation, sustainable jobs" (Ministère de la transition énergétique, 2015, p. 1), and a way to maintain the country's status as a "great maritime (...) [and] energy power" (Jean Castex, Premier ministre, 2022) They herald a "new world" (Ministère de la transition énergétique, 2016a, p. 3), compared to other historical paradigm shifts: "...today as in several instances in our history, a new energy paradigm is emerging, bearer of an economically, ecologically and socially promising development model, announcing a possible third industrial revolution" (Ministère de la transition énergétique, 2015, p. 4). This links to a legendary figure of the French state leading the nation in a "political voluntarism" part of the country's energy identity, with comparisons to the reconstruction and nuclear programme after the Second World War (Ministère de la transition énergétique, 2015, pp. 4–5). Here, we find that a national place imaginary of France as an industrially powerful country and strong state feeds into the dominant STI, while the energy transition

[4] All quotations have been translated by the author from French.

is simultaneously presented as a means of extending this place imaginary *into the future*.

This creates the need to scale up the deployment of wind energy. The country's lateness compared to European countries is emphasized, often linked to two concerns: cumbersome administrative procedures and growing local opposition to wind energy. This connects to how the spatialities of deployment are imagined. As an idealized space, territories are central in the empirical material. They are constructed both as the smallest scale of governance, below the national, and as more local socio-spatial collectives or communities of place, even though this construction is highly ambiguous in terms of who or what gets included. In this way, they are presented as the beneficiaries of deployment: wind projects bring "sustainable and inclusive territorial development" through job creation and tax spillover, providing funding for local services and projects (Ministère de la transition énergétique, 2017b, p. 34). In the case of onshore wind, this is linked to an idealized space of rural territories in socio-economic decline, and to a spatial transformation imaginary of rural revitalization whereby they become more attractive through the activity generated by wind projects: in "a region that has experienced deindustrialization [...] wind energy offers [...] the possibility of reviving activity, bringing life back to our countryside" (Ministère de la transition énergétique, 2021). Two logics coexist: an entrepreneurial logic (Harvey, 1989) involving competition between territories to attract capital in a context of dwindling state resources, and simultaneously a passive role of territories benefitting from spillover effects.

Territories are also considered crucial to the acceptance of wind projects. Finding space for projects and ensuring that their development is socially and spatially "harmonious" is a major concern, and territories are a *means* of resolving this (Ministère de la transition énergétique, 2020b). First, by increasing the territorial appropriation of projects—however, this is not conceptualized as a political appropriation, as reforms over the period place the onus on developers to behave virtuously and engage with locals to "take [the] specific needs" of territories into account (Ministère de la transition énergétique, 2018, p. 9), in line with a model of engagement focused on depoliticizing and reducing public concern (Barnett et al., 2012). The territory is both a context to be considered and a stakeholder to be appeased through adjustments to the location and design of projects. Second, by addressing spatial imbalances in the distribution of projects across the country and ensuring a fair contribution from all territories to achieving national targets. The “local implementation” of national objectives is a key issue (Ministère de la transition écologique, 2021, p. 5), and it can be secured through mapping different territorial potentials to “harness the resources of our territories” (Ministère de la transition énergétique, 2015, p. 6). A similar centralized perspective is apparent for offshore wind: national calls for auctions are seen as optimal to “avoid a disorderly location pattern [...] detrimental to acceptance” (Ministère de la transition énergétique, 2016b, p. 97) and, over the period, siting processes move from a project-by-project approach to more integrated spatial planning, with the setting of targets for each of the four national seaboards in line with national objectives. In both cases, this converges in a top-down construction of territories as resources and contributors to a larger national whole. We find traces of the socio-political imaginary of effective, centralized spatial planning intertwined with the national imaginary of France as the “one and indivisible” republic, a central state uniting territories behind a modernizing paradigm in the name of the general interest. It coexists ambivalently with a rhetorical emphasis on territorial empowerment and the decentralized nature of wind energy—decentralization here being understood as a physical transformation of energy grids rather than a deeper socio-political change.

3.2 *The Citizen Energy STI: Empowering Territories through Wind Projects*

The citizen energy STI is articulated by a coalition of organizations advocating for citizen- and community-led energy production models such as Energie Partagée, and on its margins it is also supported by prominent associations for environmental or climate activism. Over the last decade, it has gained legitimacy in policy circles and been appropriated by the Greens, the Left and to a lesser extent the government. This STI has similarities to the dominant STI: similar *issues* are mobilized to argue for a “war effort” to accelerate wind energy deployment, and it is also associated with national economic renewal (CLER, 2020, p. 26). However, citizen energy actors articulate both a denunciation of financialized capitalism and its impacts on energy systems, including the dominance of large operators and profit-driven logics, and a critique of centralization as a dispossession of local power. Against this background, their vision involves profound political and socio-economic change towards “a fairer, more desirable and ecological society” (Comité pour l’énergie citoyenne, 2018,

p. 4): an economic shift towards a cooperative and territorialized economy, and a political shift towards a decentralized and participatory multilevel governance. A "soft path" (Lovins, 1979) model of energy production is outlined, involving the multiplication of citizen-led energy projects, a 100% renewable energy mix, and efforts to reduce consumption.

The citizen energy STI is characterized by a very localist conception of territories: they are constructed as both the smallest scale of governance and as local communities of practice, interest and meaning, inscribed in a common socio-spatial, material context. This makes territories the only "possible space for systemic transformation" (CLER, 2020, p. 73), and the energy transition is an opportunity for them to "regain" their decision-making rights "after a 20th century (…) monopolized by large and polluting operators": from their exclusion to their return to the centre in a wider paradigm shift (Comité pour l'énergie citoyenne, 2018, p. 4). More generally, the citizen energy STI constructs the empowerment of territories as the central *issue* of wind energy deployment. National *issues* are relegated to the background, as wind projects should primarily support a territorial identity and locally shared vision of the future—as opposed to a "developer logic" dedicated to finding the most productive site regardless of context (France Nature Environnement, 2018, p. 3). This gives rise to *organizings* and *doings* that are best described by two imperatives. First, to maximize local governance, with local actors and in particular local authorities having majority control over projects to better represent the interests of the territory. Then, to ensure the territorialization of benefits through a cooperative economic ethic in which returns on capital are limited and profits reinvested locally—from "throwing money out the window" to "keeping [it] at home" (CLER, 2020, p. 27). As in the dominant STI, this is linked to an idealized space of rural territories as underprivileged and declining and a spatial transformation imaginary of rural revitalization, in which projects are levers for local resilience, reducing dependence for access to energy and finance, and ultimately leading to rural economic and political empowerment.

Combining these aspects, this territorial approach to energy outlines a qualitative development aimed at realizing a local vision, positioned against the exogenous development strategies promoted by national and European public authorities and carried out by private developers, which are "disconnected from local development (…) and social justice concerns" (Energie Partagée, 2019) and aim to "feed the competitiveness of territories", pitting them against each other (CLER, 2020, p. 51).

Inter-territorial inequalities are indeed a recurring concern: citizen energy projects are seen as opportunities for better distributing wealth between urban and rural areas, and rural energy production is in a few instances presented as a moral duty, with "each type of territory contribut[ing] to its own needs and those of others" (CLER, 2018, p. 3). While this vision is less centralized than that of dominant actors, with territories understood as relevant socio-spatial collectives in their own right, it does not imply a complete abstraction from the nation as an important scale at which the general interest is defined—the overall aim being a more multi-scalar governance in which municipalities and regions gain more influence over energy decisions.

3.3 *The Conservative STI: Nostalgia for a Glorious National Past and the Sacrifice of Rural Territories*

A conservative STI is performed by the two major anti-wind energy federations, prominent intellectuals, politicians and most anti-wind collectives at the national level, including pro-nuclear lobby groups, associations for landscape or heritage protection, and some environmental protection associations. This is the most prominent STI mobilized to oppose wind energy deployment at the national level; it is disseminated through advocacy or support to local opposition groups, and it has gained increasing media and political attention over the period. These actors reject wind energy as a way of *doing* decarbonization through a techno-economic discourse emphasizing its perceived unreliability, costs and impacts, and criticize its *organizing*, namely undemocratic siting logics, as well as opaque decision-making and funding processes. Emphasis is laid on the foreign aspects of wind energy—in terms of construction materials, *savoir faire*, workers, as well as profits going to foreign corporations. This links to a critique of the Europeanization and globalization of energy markets, seen as obscuring the general interest. Two binaries structure legitimacy: national versus global and European, and public versus private, with a conflation between national and public.

This is co-constructed with a nostalgic place imaginary of France as an influential country because of its nationally controlled nuclear industry. Central to this STI is a reconstruction of French energy and industrial history, from the heroic beginnings of the nuclear programme, leading to a peak in the country's power, to its abandonment, resulting in loss of sovereignty and political decadence. As a *doing*, nuclear energy is seen as an efficient solution for decarbonization. As for *organizing*, it is associated with a strong state enforcing the general interest through centralized decision-making and a national industry embodied by the public company EDF. Here, nuclear energy underpins a national place imaginary associated with a technopolitical identity, which it also used to materialize; the shift to another energy model signifies the loss of the country's identity and agency.

Another set of spatial imaginaries structures a denunciation of the local impacts of wind energy. An imaginary of the uncontrolled invasion of the country by wind turbines is prevalent: "…cereal plains, Provençal hills, coastlines, not an acre of land or sea is safe from them" (Causeur et al., 2020). In the case of onshore wind, this connects to an imaginary of the industrialization of the rural, as turbines transform a countryside characterized by its bucolic landscapes and heritage sites into "an industrial area" (Vent de Colère, 2020a, p. 1). Wind projects undermine the foundations of rural communities: "…the general interest of your territory is to preserve its rural […] identity and the tourist and cultural activities associated with it […] its landscape and biodiversity, which constitute its soul […] wind energy is incompatible with this" (Collectif Energie Vérité, 2020). This is reinforced by an idealization of the rural as in crisis, representing the "peripheral France" left behind by globalization (Causeur et al., 2020). Two socio-spatial binaries, between (wealthy) urban spaces and (underprivileged) rural spaces and between local (residents) and global (corporations), structure a narrative of spatial injustice and rural sacrifice, providing a local articulation of the national aspects examined above: benefits flow out of France, and out of rural territories. Although offshore wind energy is less central in their discourse, similar imaginaries are mobilized: an idealization of the French coast, the "common property of the French people" (Vent de Colère, 2020b), and an imaginary of its industrialization: "distributed" to multinationals, it will soon become an "industrial belt" (Collectif Énergie Vérité, 2021).

This feeds into a broader spatial transformation imaginary of the homogenization of French landscapes, intertwined with a place imaginary of France as "a country renowned for the diversity, variety and beauty of its landscapes" (Causeur et al., 2020). This is supported by references to controversial wind projects in sites of national importance, such as the Sainte-Victoire Mountain painted by Cézanne (e.g., Bern, 2021): iconic places that embody not only the essence of a picturesque countryside but also France's heritage and identity—suggesting that these are under threat.

Again, France's position in relation to a global outside is a concern, and this allows these actors to present themselves as both national patriots and local guardians. The local has national relevance, and the national has local incarnations; spatial imaginaries at different scales are mutually reinforcing, and an idea of the French nation bridges them.

3.4 *The Anti-Capitalist STI: Dwelling as a Political and Emancipatory Project*

The anti-capitalist STI was developed by the Amassada collective and "zone to defend,"[5] created in 2014 to oppose the construction of a large electricity transformer in the Occitanie region. This initial opposition evolved into a critique of wind energy deployment, ecological modernization and technocracy. The STI was enacted through protest and materialized in the free town of the Amassada until its forced dismantlement in 2019. It was supported by various anti-capitalist collectives, activist or academic figures, and left-wing media across France. Compared to the first three STIs, this one has received much less national resonance and attained only limited institutionalization, in part because it voluntarily sits outside traditional political arenas.

These actors' critique of wind energy development shares themes with the conservative STI, in both technological (wind energy is intermittent and impactful) and politico-economic terms (undemocratic decision-making processes create local disempowerment, and economic processes are opaque and profit-driven). However, the anti-capitalist STI articulates a deeper critique of government policy that contrasts sharply with the conservative opposition. Wind energy deployment is considered as a way of greenwashing the nuclear-centred energy system and its techno-industrial paradigm, leaving unquestioned the tenets of capitalist accumulation, industrial development and energy intensity. The contemporary sociotechnical paradigm is framed as a centralized technocracy where power is perpetuated by a network of interconnected technological devices relying on ever-increasing demands for energy: "…what is the connection between an airport […] a mega-transformer, a nuclear waste dump, open cast mines and wind farms? […] If not this very thread of a world colonized by grids […] maintained only by the extraction of […] raw materials

[5] A zone to defend (*zone à défendre*) refers to activists occupying land—usually in rural areas of ecological or agricultural value—to physically block a major development project.

and the lives it destroys?" (Amassada, 2020). A hegemonic STI is outlined, characterized by spatial, economic and political centralization and materialized by clusters of wind projects and tentacular grids connecting to European and global markets, proving that wind turbines are far from local.

Two spatial imaginaries are mobilized to denounce the out-of-placeness and uneven spatial patterns of wind energy deployment. As idealized spaces, rural territories are portrayed as vulnerable and exploited by developers. As a counter-ideal to urban spaces and an a-territorial sociotechnical system, they also embody an ideal of solidarity as well as a more ecological way of life: "…rural society was infinitely less energy-intensive, less consumerist, and more respectful of nature" (Amassada, n.d.-b). This connects to a spatial transformation imaginary in which rural territories are flattened by the industrial deployment of wind turbines and sacrificed in the name of national solidarity, prolonging their exploitation to supply urban areas: "…wind turbines homogenize territories, their distinctive features disappear […] [to] become industrial area[s] like so many in France" (Amassada, 2015b, p. 6). Wind turbines are seen here as interchangeable devices designed to produce a commodity; they materialize an abstract view of space detached from place.

These actors elaborate an alternative vision aptly summarized by the following quote: "…the solution will not come from electrification, smart networks, or connected objects […] but from low-tech inventions, radical degrowth policies, agroecology, autonomous constructions, local decisions and popular assemblies […] a new collective culture" (Amassada, 2015a, p. 3). Territories are central as an *issue*, *doing* and *organizing* in this STI. (Rural) territories are constructed as idealized spaces of collective life and relevance; as socio-spatial entities rich in a specific history, *savoir-faire*, landscape and social ties, they are the (only) appropriate scale at which to elaborate an idea of the commons. Dwelling—living and acting in territories—is a political project in secession from the logics of globalization and industrialization: "…dwelled-in places exist only to ward off the totalitarian rise of an unequivocal way of imposing a world, globalization as belligerent marketisation" (Amassada, n.d.-a, p. 10). This is linked to a broader celebration of the heterogeneity of places and their "plural imaginaries" (Ballast, 2018), and desirable sociotechnical futures are enacted in a different experience of and connection with territory.

4 Discussion

Looking across the four STIs and the spatial imaginaries that are constitutive of them (see Table 2.1), two spatial themes stand out, rurality and territories. Both play a crucial role in structuring the wind energy controversy and differentiating between STIs. They are entangled with two overlapping spatial concerns: infra-territorial concerns, i.e., the relationships between wind projects and each territory, connecting to issues such as local involvement in decision-making processes or place-technology fit; and inter-territorial concerns, i.e., the spatialization of wind energy deployment across the country, involving horizontal relationships between local territories, urban and rural, and their vertical relationship with the nation as the main scale for *organizing* energy systems. While studies have highlighted the importance of imaginaries of rurality in wind energy controversies (e.g., Batel et al., 2015; Batel & Devine-Wright, 2017; Jessup, 2010; Phadke, 2011; Woods, 2003), and others have begun to address how energy STIs mobilize specific constructions of the "local" (e.g., Burnham et al., 2017; Carvalho et al., 2022; Delina, 2018; Longhurst & Chilvers, 2019), this research is one of the first to examine both simultaneously, bringing to the fore their different roles in underpinning claims about wind energy futures. The salience of rural and territorial themes in France stems in part from their intersection with deep-rooted socio-spatial and politico-economic issues such as urban–rural inequalities, rural decline and a related sense of injustice, or the relationship between the central state and its constituents.

There are, on the one hand, structural spatial differences between the STIs mobilized in support of wind energy and those mobilized against it. The dominant STI and the citizen energy STI are both underpinned by a construction of rural areas as spaces of economic difficulty, creating space for spatial transformation imaginaries of rural revitalization, and these imaginaries are strategic for linking national and global issues to locally desirable futures. The appropriation of decentralized and localist themes by government and industry actors can also be understood in this way: articulating a depoliticized version of the citizen energy STI by removing its more transformative aspects allows them to present wind energy deployment as a vehicle for local development and democratization, thus defusing contestation on the left of the political compass. Similarly, the conservative and the anti-capitalist STIs are intertwined with an idealization of the rural as vulnerable and eminently valuable; industrialization is constructed as an undesirable rural spatial transformation, and associated with a set of values, actors and places seen as illegitimate.

On the other hand, two lines of contestation of the dominant STI emerge, involving two different visions of socio-spatial order. The first line of contestation is nationalist, incarnated in the conservative STI. Interestingly, although this STI stands in opposition to governmental energy policy, the dominant STI and the conservative STI assemble *issues*, *organizings* and *doings* that are relatively similar, valuing *hard path* development and top-down decision-making—consistent with literature showing that more dominant STIs tend to be closely shaped by existing constitutional arrangements (e.g., Carvalho et al., 2022; Delina, 2018; Jasanoff & Kim, 2015; Longhurst & Chilvers, 2019). Both STIs are underpinned by a place imaginary of France as a powerful nation and both articulate centralized visions of socio-spatial and political order. However, this place imaginary is used in different ways: conservative opponents emphasize discontinuity with a glorious national past, while government actors sketch a continuity with a desirable national future and, at the same time, emphasize the scale of the transformations to come—combining an attempt to deactivate left-wing contestation with an unrelenting proximity to the right side of the political compass. The second line of contestation is localist, incarnated in the citizen energy STI and the anti-capitalist STI. These actors negatively outline a dominant STI intertwined with national history, characterized by a management from above of energy production and a growth-oriented economy, and oppose to it two STIs decentred from this paradigm. In both, territories, as socio-spatial and political collectives, are central to the creation of more ecological ways of living through community-centred logics in which local imaginaries preside over energy production. The re-territorialization of economic and political processes is both a crucial feature of desirable futures and a means of enacting them, and the rural is constructed as a space of possible reinvention.

5 Conclusion

Spatial imaginaries are strategic for supporting the arguments of both wind energy proponents and opponents. Consistent with the literature on energy siting conflicts (e.g., Batel et al., 2015; Batel & Devine-Wright, 2017; Llewellyn et al., 2017; McLachlan, 2009), spatial imaginaries are mobilized by objectors to sustain socio-spatial and scalar divides (e.g., urban/rural, local/global) and narratives of place sacrifice, emphasizing the unfairness and destructive effects of wind energy deployment. However, extending existing literature, spatial imaginaries are here also crucial for proponents to highlight the local desirability of wind projects. More generally, their spatial dimensions are a crucial element for differentiating between STIs. They coalesce into a contrast that transcends the pro/anti divide, between more transformative and decentred STIs that value local place, and STIs centred on the national scale that reproduce dominant modes of energy provision as well as political and economic organization. The added (spatial) complexity across wind energy partisan lines speaks to the status of wind energy as a boundary object and to its interpretive flexibility: increasingly integrated into a dominant sociotechnical tradition (dominant STI), but also invested by a localist vision that develops a more socio-political understanding of decarbonization (citizen energy STI), it faces contestation on both flanks, based either on nostalgia for nuclear pasts (conservative STI), or on an even more radical challenge to energy-intensive and centralized development models (anti-capitalist STI). This shows that attention to spatial imaginaries is an asset not only for fully capturing the visions of the good society that underpin STIs, but also for understanding the dynamics of differentiation, opposition and co-optation between them. It confirms recent studies suggesting that alternative STIs tend to articulate more decentralized visions of socio-political order (e.g., Carvalho et al., 2022; Delina, 2018; Longhurst & Chilvers, 2019) but shows that challenges to dominant STIs can also come from more nationalist and centralized visions.

This is not surprising in the French context, and it can be seen as the product of a culture strongly permeated by a national imaginary articulated around a hierarchical relationship between the state and territories (e.g., Hazareesingh, 2011; Sakoun, 2022). Nevertheless, it shows how national energy pasts and identities are differently (re)constructed by actors as part of the envisioning of desirable energy futures, proposing a lesser or greater rupture. The co-constitution of national and sociotechnical imaginaries has been a central theme in the STIs literature, predominantly explored through cross-national comparisons of different state STIs (e.g., Jasanoff & Kim, 2009), case studies of individual STIs (e.g., Felt, 2015; Kuchler & Bridge, 2018), or inquiries into the transposition of a single STI across diverse contexts (e.g., Movik & Allouche, 2020), rather than through analyses of competing STIs within a single national setting (but see Torres & Niewöhner, 2023). We show here that these reconstructions of national pasts and identities are even more important as they influence prominent spatial imaginaries pertaining to both the *local* and the *national*, with visions of socio-spatial order linking the two—demonstrating the value of including a variety of spatial constructs and integrating the historical and the spatial when comparing across STIs.

The central conclusion is therefore that studying STIs at the national scale does not entail a detachment from space: sociotechnical imaginaries link to spatial imaginaries at all scales. Spatial imaginaries are not only salient in local controversies over specific projects: they inform the imagination of energy futures at the national level, and reciprocally the controversial deployment of wind energy stimulates their (re)performance. The national context, leading to the discussion of wind energy as a *general* and *nationwide* process, explains the prevalence of idealized spaces and generic imaginaries of spatial transformation, as well as the absence of more specific imaginaries of local place. This demonstrates the value of spatial imaginaries for analysing STIs: they do not presuppose a type of spatial construction, a scale or a level of specificity. Moreover, they allow scale to be captured as both an element within spatial imaginaries—the French place imaginary, for example, involves a top-down relationality constructing the national as above the local—and as a spatial imaginary in itself, as each of the STIs is characterized by a particular scalar imaginary that involves certain relations between the nation and its territories. Spatial imaginaries thus make it possible to grasp how the imagination of sociotechnical projects at the national level involves a *pre-activation* of space, which is also based on an anticipation of what might happen at the local level. This points to the temporal dimensions of sociotechnical projects and associated spatial imaginaries, from their activation at the national level to their eventual reproduction, adaptation and transformation at the local level.

Capturing these different spatialities in the making of sociotechnical change at the national level is essential, as they have material implications: the spatial imaginaries associated with the dominant STI, for example, feed into the design of wind projects, siting processes and approaches to local participation, and influence how project actors represent local contexts—they are brought down to the local, concretized in projects, and are bound to influence controversies and the positioning of local actors. Not limiting geographical analysis to the local as some of the literature has tended to do, but also interrogating the spatial imaginaries that govern technological development at the national level, is therefore necessary for fully understanding how social, technical and spatial orders are co-constituted, co-negotiated and co-contested both *at* these different scales and *across* them.

References

Amassada. (2015a). *L'éolien industriel, faussement écolo mais vraiment répressif.* Retrieved May 5, 2021, from https://douze.noblogs.org/files/2019/09/eolien.pdf

Amassada. (2015b). *Plaidoyer contre les éoliennes industrielles.* Retrieved May 5, 2021, from https://douze.noblogs.org/files/2019/09/plaidoyerA5.pdf

Amassada. (2020). *L'"économie verte" sort ses griffes.* Retrieved May 5, 2021, from https://douze.noblogs.org/files/2020/01/economie_verte.cleaned.pdf

Amassada. (n.d.-a). *Les réseaux comme champ de bataille.* Retrieved May 5, 2021, from https://douze.noblogs.org/files/2020/01/Resau_fr.cleaned.pdf

Amassada. (n.d.-b). *Non aux éoliennes industrielles.* Retrieved May 5, 2021, from http://stopeoliennes.over-blog.com/textes-%C3%A0-propos-de-l-%C3%A9olien-industriel

Avila, S. (2018). Environmental justice and the expanding geography of wind power conflicts. *Sustainability Science, 13*(3), 599–616. https://doi.org/10.1007/s11625-018-0547-4

Aykut, S. C., & Evrard, A. (2017). Une transition pour que rien ne change ? Changement institutionnel et dépendance au sentier dans les « transitions énergétiques » en Allemagne et en France. *Revue internationale de politique comparee, 24*(1), 17–49.

Ballast. (2018). Jean-Baptiste Vidalou: 'La nature est un concept qui a fait faillite'. *Ballast.* Retrieved May 16, 2021, from https://www.revue-ballast.fr/jean-baptiste-vidalou-nature-concept-a-faillite/

Barnett, J., Burningham, K., Walker, G., & Cass, N. (2012). Imagined publics and engagement around renewable energy technologies in the UK. *Public Understanding of Science, 21*(1), 36–50. https://doi.org/10.1177/0963662510365663

Batel, S. (2018). A critical discussion of research on the social acceptance of renewable energy generation and associated infrastructures and an agenda for the future. *Journal of Environmental Policy & Planning, 20*(3), 356–369. https://doi.org/10.1080/1523908X.2017.1417120

Batel, S., & Devine-Wright, P. (2017). Energy colonialism and the role of the global in local responses to new energy infrastructures in the UK: A critical and exploratory empirical analysis: Local responses to new energy infrastructures in the UK. *Antipode, 49*(1), 3–22. https://doi.org/10.1111/anti.12261

Batel, S., Devine-Wright, P., Wold, L., Egeland, H., Jacobsen, G., & Aas, O. (2015). The role of (de-)essentialisation within siting conflicts: An interdisciplinary approach. *Journal of Environmental Psychology, 44*, 149–159. https://doi.org/10.1016/j.jenvp.2015.10.004

Bern, S. (2021). Stéphane Bern: 'Madame Pompili, les éoliennes sont une négation de l'écologie !' *Le Figaro*. Retrieved September 25, 2021, from https://www.lefigaro.fr/vox/societe/stephane-bern-madame-pompili-les-eoliennes-sont-une-negation-de-l-ecologie-20210530

Bridge, G. (2018). The map is not the territory: A sympathetic critique of energy research's spatial turn. *Energy Research & Social Science, 36*, 11–20. https://doi.org/10.1016/j.erss.2017.09.033

Bridge, G., & Gailing, L. (2020). New energy spaces: Towards a geographical political economy of energy transition. *Environment and Planning A: Economy and Space, 52*(6), 1037–1050. https://doi.org/10.1177/0308518X20939570

Burnham, M., Eaton, W., Selfa, T., Hinrichs, C., & Feldpausch-Parker, A. (2017). The politics of imaginaries and bioenergy sub-niches in the emerging northeast U.S. bioenergy economy. *Geoforum, 82*, 66–76. https://doi.org/10.1016/j.geoforum.2017.03.022

Calvert, K. (2016). From 'energy geography' to 'energy geographies': Perspectives on a fertile academic borderland. *Progress in Human Geography, 40*(1), 105–125. https://doi.org/10.1177/0309132514566343

Carvalho, A., Riquito, M., & Ferreira, V. (2022). Sociotechnical imaginaries of energy transition: The case of the Portuguese roadmap for carbon neutrality 2050. *Energy Reports, 8*, 2413–2423. https://doi.org/10.1016/j.egyr.2022.01.138

Causeur et al. (2020). *Monsieur le président de la République, mettez un terme à l'implantation des éoliennes !* Retrieved November 5, 2021, from https://www.change.org/p/pr%C3%A9sident-de-la-r%C3%A9publique-stopper-l-implantation-d-%C3%A9oliennes-en-france-c59f118e-6dbb-4da3-aae1-a48e1eba8397

Chateau, Z., Devine-Wright, P., & Wills, J. (2021). Integrating sociotechnical and spatial imaginaries in researching energy futures. *Energy Research & Social Science, 80*, 102207. https://doi.org/10.1016/j.erss.2021.102207

Chivallon, C. (2008). L'espace, le réel et l'imaginaire: A-t-on encore besoin de la géographie culturelle ? *Annales de géographie, 660–661*(2), 67. https://doi.org/10.3917/ag.660.0067

CLER. (2018). *Nouvelles solidarités urbain/rural: Une condition de la transition énergétique nationale*. Retrieved November 16, 2021, from https://cler.org/wp-content/uploads/2018/11/Etude-nouvelles-solidarites-urbain-rural.pdf

CLER. (2020). *La transition énergétique territoriale: Créatrice de valeur(s) et moteur de développement*. Retrieved October 18, 2021, from https://cler.org/

wp-content/uploads/2020/09/CLeR_TePOS-Transition-e%CC%81nerge%CC%81tique-territoriale-BD.pdf

Collectif Energie Vérité. (2020). *Analyser une étude d'impacts: Les points de vigilance*. Retrieved December 11, 2021, from https://www.energieverite.com/post/analyser-une-%C3%A9tude-d-impacts-les-points-de-vigilance

Collectif Énergie Vérité. (2021). *Eolien en mer: Le carcan de fer et de béton du littoral français*. Retrieved January 16, 2022, from https://www.energieverite.com/post/eolien-en-mer-le-carcan-de-fer-et-de-b%C3%A9ton-du-littoral-fran%C3%A7ais

Comité pour l'énergie citoyenne. (2018). *PPE: Cahier d'acteur*. Retrieved October 18, 2021 from https://cpdp.debatpublic.fr/cpdp-ppe/cahier-dacteur-ndeg41-collectif-energies-citoyennes.html

Cowell, R. (2010). Wind power, landscape and strategic, spatial planning—The construction of 'acceptable locations' in Wales. *Land Use Policy, 27*(2), 222–232. https://doi.org/10.1016/j.landusepol.2009.01.006

Davoudi, S., Crawford, J., Raynor, R., Reid, B., Sykes, O., & Shaw, D. (2018). Policy and practice spatial imaginaries: Tyrannies or transformations? *Town Planning Review, 89*(2), 97–124. https://doi.org/10.3828/tpr.2018.7

Delina, L. L. (2018). Whose and what futures? Navigating the contested coproduction of Thailand's energy sociotechnical imaginaries. *Energy Research & Social Science, 35*, 48–56. https://doi.org/10.1016/j.erss.2017.10.045

Devine-Wright, P. (2010). From backyards to places: Public engagement and the emplacement of renewable energy technologies. In *Renewable Energy and the Public*. Routledge.

Devine-Wright, P., & Howes, Y. (2010). Disruption to place attachment and the protection of restorative environments: A wind energy case study. *Journal of Environmental Psychology, 30*(3), 271–280. https://doi.org/10.1016/j.jenvp.2010.01.008

Devine-Wright, P., & Wiersma, B. (2020). Understanding community acceptance of a potential offshore wind energy project in different locations: An Island-based analysis of 'place-technology fit'. *Energy Policy, 137*, 111086. https://doi.org/10.1016/j.enpol.2019.111086

Eaton, W. M., Gasteyer, S. P., & Busch, L. (2014). Bioenergy futures: Framing sociotechnical imaginaries in local places: Bioenergy futures. *Rural Sociology, 79*(2), 227–256. https://doi.org/10.1111/ruso.12027

Energie Partagée. (2019). Retrieved October 10, 2021, from *Menaces sur la transition énergétique citoyenne: Il est temps d'agir*. https://energie-partagee.org/menaces-sur-la-transition-energetique-citoyenne-il-est-temps-dagir/.

Eolfi. (2018). *PPE: Cahier d'acteur*. Retrieved June 16, 2021, from https://cpdp.debatpublic.fr/cpdp-ppe/cahier-dacteur-ndeg81-eolfi.html

Evrard, A. (2013). Chapitre 7 / La France, trajectoire instable d'un pays en retard. In *Contre vents et marées. Politique des énergies renouvelables en Europe* (pp. 189–230). Presses de Sciences Po. https://shs.cairn.info/contre-vents-et-marees--9782724613353-page-189

Evrard, A., & Pasquier, R. (2018). Territorialiser la politique de l'éolien maritime en France. *Gouvernement et action publique, 7*(4), 63–91.

Felt, U. (2015). Sociotechnical imaginaries and the formation of Austria's Technopolitical identity. In *Dreamscapes of modernity: Sociotechnical imaginaries and the fabrication of power*. The University of Chicago Press.

France Énergie Éolienne. (2020). *L'éolien, pilier du monde d'après*. Retrieved June 18, 2021, from https://fee.asso.fr/wp-content/uploads/2020/05/plan-de--relance_13mai_def-def.pdf

France Nature Environnement. (2018). *PPE: Cahier d'acteur*. Retrieved October 21, 2021, from https://cpdp.debatpublic.fr/cpdp-ppe/cahier-dacteur--ndeg31-france-nature-environnement.html

Gee, K. (2010). Offshore wind power development as affected by seascape values on the German North Sea coast. *Land Use Policy, 27*(2), 185–194. https://doi.org/10.1016/j.landusepol.2009.05.003

Harvey, D. (1989). From managerialism to entrepreneurialism: The transformation in urban governance in late capitalism. *Geografiska Annaler: Series B, Human Geography, 71*(1), 3–17. https://doi.org/10.1080/04353684.1989.11879583

Hazareesingh, S. (2011). L'imaginaire républicain en France, de la Révolution française à Charles de Gaulle. *Revue historique, 659*(3), 637–654. https://doi.org/10.3917/rhis.113.0637

International Energy Agency. (2023). *Energy Statistics Data Browser—France* [Dataset]. Retrieved December 12, 2024, from https://www.iea.org/data-and-statistics/data-tools/energy-statistics-data-browser?country=FRANCE&fuel=Energy%20supply&indicator=ElecGenByFuel

Jasanoff, S., & Kim, S.-H. (2009). Containing the atom: Sociotechnical imaginaries and nuclear power in the United States and South Korea. *Minerva, 47*(2), 119–146. https://doi.org/10.1007/s11024-009-9124-4

Jasanoff, S., & Kim, S.-H. (Eds.). (2015). Dreamscapes of modernity: Sociotechnical imaginaries and the fabrication of power. The University of Chicago Press.

Jasanoff, S., & Simmet, H. R. (2021). Renewing the future: Excluded imaginaries in the global energy transition. *Energy Research & Social Science, 80*, 102205. https://doi.org/10.1016/j.erss.2021.102205

Jean Castex, Premier ministre. (2022). *Déclaration de M. Jean Castex, Premier ministre, sur la dépendance énergétique de la France, le développement des énergies renouvelables et notamment l'installation de cinquante parcs éoliens en mer d'ici* 2050, *Port-la-Nouvelle (Aude)*. Retrieved January 6, 2023, from https://www.vie-publique.fr/discours/284518-jean-castex-14032022-installation-de-50-parcs-eoliens-en-mer

Jessup, B. (2010). Plural and hybrid environmental values: A discourse analysis of the wind energy conflict in Australia and the United Kingdom. *Environmental Politics, 19*(1), 21–44. https://doi.org/10.1080/09644010903396069

Kuchler, M., & Bridge, G. (2018). Down the black hole: Sustaining national socio-technical imaginaries of coal in Poland. *Energy Research & Social Science, 41*, 136–147. https://doi.org/10.1016/j.erss.2018.04.014

Lambert, C. E. (2022). Beneath your feet and in your place: Multi-scalar imaginaries of energy, place, and local geothermal development. *Energy Research & Social Science, 94*, 102856. https://doi.org/10.1016/j.erss.2022.102856

Levenda, A. M., Richter, J., Miller, T., & Fisher, E. (2019). Regional sociotechnical imaginaries and the governance of energy innovations. *Futures, 109*, 181–191. https://doi.org/10.1016/j.futures.2018.03.001

Llewellyn, D. H., Rohse, M., Day, R., & Fyfe, H. (2017). Evolving energy landscapes in the South Wales valleys: Exploring community perception and participation. *Energy Policy, 108*, 818–828. https://doi.org/10.1016/j.enpol.2017.04.028

Longhurst, N., & Chilvers, J. (2019). Mapping diverse visions of energy transitions: Co-producing sociotechnical imaginaries. *Sustainability Science, 14*(4), 973–990. https://doi.org/10.1007/s11625-019-00702-y

Lovins, A. (1979). *Soft energy paths: Toward a durable peace*. Harper.

Marquardt, J., & Delina, L. L. (2019). Reimagining energy futures: Contributions from community sustainable energy transitions in Thailand and The Philippines. *Energy Research & Social Science, 49*, 91–102. https://doi.org/10.1016/j.erss.2018.10.028

Mayer, M., & Balázs, D. (2018). Modern silk road imaginaries and the co-production of space. In M. Mayer (Ed.), *Rethinking the silk road* (pp. 205–226). Springer Singapore. https://doi.org/10.1007/978-981-10-5915-5_13

McLachlan, C. (2009). 'You don't do a chemistry experiment in your best China': Symbolic interpretations of place and technology in a wave energy case. *Energy Policy, 37*(12), 5342–5350. https://doi.org/10.1016/j.enpol.2009.07.057

Ministère de la transition écologique. (2021). Projet de loi portant lutte contre le dérèglement climatique et renforcement de la résilience face à ses effets. Exposé des motifs. Retrieved February 18, 2022 from https://www.assemblee--nationale.fr/dyn/15/textes/l15b3875_projet-loi#

Ministère de la transition énergétique. (2015). Projet de loi relatif à la transition énergétique pour la croissance verte. Exposé des motifs. Retrieved February 2, 2021, from https://www.ecologie.gouv.fr/sites/default/files/documents/0-_Expose_des_motifs.pdf

Ministère de la transition énergétique. (2016a). La loi de transition énergétique pour la croissance verte en actions: Territoires, citoyens, entreprises. https://

enerulco.univ-littoral.fr/wp-conTent/uploads/2016/10/16172_loi-TE-en-action_DEF_light-21.pdf.
Ministère de la transition énergétique. (2016b). *Programmation Pluriannuelle de l'Énergie*. Retrieved March 7, 2020, from https://www.ecologie.gouv.fr/sites/default/files/documents/PPE%20int%C3%A9gralit%C3%A9.pdf
Ministère de la transition énergétique. (2017a). *La France exemplaire: Les territoires en action*. Retrieved March 7, 2020, from https://www.ecologie.gouv.fr/sites/default/files/publications/15140-8_france-exemplaire-territoires-action_DEF_Web_Page-%2B%C3%A1-page_0.pdf
Ministère de la transition énergétique. (2017b). *Stratégie nationale pour la mer et le littoral*. Retrieved March 8, 2020, from https://mer.gouv.fr/sites/default/files/2021-03/17094_Strategie-nationale-pour-la-mer-et-le-littoral_fev2017.pdf
Ministère de la transition énergétique. (2018). *Conclusions du groupe de travail éolien*. Retrieved March 10, 2020, from https://www.ecologie.gouv.fr/sites/default/files/documents/DP_Groupe_Travail_eolien_2018.pdf
Ministère de la transition énergétique. (2020a). *Développement harmonieux de l'éolien terrestre*. Retrieved January 15, 2021, from https://www.ecologie.gouv.fr/sites/default/files/documents/Fiche%20com%20%C3%A9olien%20VDEF.pdf
Ministère de la transition énergétique. (2020b). Synthèse. Programmation pluriannuelle de l'énergie. Retrieved January 15, 2021, from https://www.ecologie.gouv.fr/sites/default/files/documents/20200422%20Synthe%CC%80se%20de%20la%20PPE.pdf
Ministère de la transition énergétique. (2021). *Déclaration de Mme Barbara Pompili, ministre de la transition écologique, sur le développement de l'éolien en mer, à Dunkerque*. Retrieved December 10, 2021, from https://www.vie-publique.fr/discours/280444-barbara-pompil-10052021-eolien-en-mer
Molden, O. C., & Meehan, K. (2018). Sociotechnical imaginaries of urban development: Social movements around "traditional" water infrastructure in the Kathmandu Valley. *Urban Geography, 39*(5), 763–782. https://doi.org/10.1080/02723638.2017.1393921
Movik, S., & Allouche, J. (2020). States of power: Energy imaginaries and transnational assemblages in Norway, Nepal and Tanzania. *Energy Research & Social Science, 67*, 101548. https://doi.org/10.1016/j.erss.2020.101548
Nadaï, A. (2007). "Planning", "siting" and the local acceptance of wind power: Some lessons from the French case. *Energy Policy, 35*(5), 2715–2726. https://doi.org/10.1016/j.enpol.2006.12.003
Nadaï, A., & Labussière, O. (2009). Wind power planning in France (Aveyron), from state regulation to local planning. *Land Use Policy, 26*(3), 744–754. https://doi.org/10.1016/j.landusepol.2008.10.018

Nadaï, A., Labussière, O., Debourdeau, A., Régnier, Y., Cointe, B., & Dobigny, L. (2015). French policy localism: Surfing on 'positive Energie territories' (Tepos). *Energy Policy, 78*, 281–291. https://doi.org/10.1016/j.enpol.2014.12.005

Nadaï, A., & Wallenborn, G. (2019). Transformations énergétiques sous contrainte écologique forte. *Multitudes, n° 77*(4), 43–53.

Nowell, L. S., Norris, J. M., White, D. E., & Moules, N. J. (2017). Thematic analysis: Striving to meet the trustworthiness criteria. *International Journal of Qualitative Methods, 16*(1), 1609406917733847. https://doi.org/10.1177/1609406917733847

Pasqualetti, M. J. (2000). Morality, space, and the power of wind-energy landscapes. *Geographical Review, 90*(3), 381. https://doi.org/10.2307/3250859

Phadke, R. (2011). Resisting and reconciling big wind: Middle landscape politics in the new American west. *Antipode, 43*(3), 754–776. https://doi.org/10.1111/j.1467-8330.2011.00881.x

Phillips, A. K. (2018). *Infrastructural imaginaries: Highways and the sociotechnical production of space in Baltimore*. Virginia Polytechnic Institute and State University.

Poupeau, F.-M. (2020). Everything must change in order to stay as it is. The impossible decentralization of the electricity sector in France. *Renewable and Sustainable Energy Reviews, 120*, 109597. https://doi.org/10.1016/j.rser.2019.109597

Robinson, O. C. (2014). Sampling in interview-based qualitative research: A theoretical and practical guide. *Qualitative Research in Psychology, 11*(1), 25–41. https://doi.org/10.1080/14780887.2013.801543

Rudolph, D., & Kirkegaard, J. K. (2019). Making space for wind farms: Practices of territorial stigmatisation in rural Denmark. *Antipode, 51*(2), 642–663. https://doi.org/10.1111/anti.12428

Sadowski, J., & Bendor, R. (2019). Selling smartness: Corporate narratives and the Smart City as a sociotechnical imaginary. *Science, Technology, & Human Values, 44*(3), 540–563. https://doi.org/10.1177/0162243918806061

Sakoun, J.-P. (2022). L'imaginaire français et l'esprit des lieux. Territoires, Nation, Europe. Entretien avec Stéphane Rozès. *Humanisme, 334*(1), 76–83. https://doi.org/10.3917/huma.334.0076

Saunders, B., Sim, J., Kingstone, T., Baker, S., Waterfield, J., Bartlam, B., Burroughs, H., & Jinks, C. (2018). Saturation in qualitative research: Exploring its conceptualization and operationalization. *Quality & Quantity, 52*(4), 1893–1907. https://doi.org/10.1007/s11135-017-0574-8

Schelhas, J., Hitchner, S., & Brosius, J. P. (2018). Envisioning and implementing wood-based bioenergy systems in the southern United States: Imaginaries in everyday talk. *Energy Research & Social Science, 35*, 182–192. https://doi.org/10.1016/j.erss.2017.10.042

Smith, J. M., & Tidwell, A. S. (2016). The everyday lives of energy transitions: Contested sociotechnical imaginaries in the American west. *Social Studies of Science, 46*(3), 327–350. https://doi.org/10.1177/0306312716644534

Szarka, J. (2007). Why is there no wind rush in France? *European Environment, 17*(5), 321–333. https://doi.org/10.1002/eet.460

Torres, I., & Niewöhner, J. (2023). Whose energy sovereignty? Competing imaginaries of Mexico's energy future. *Energy Research & Social Science, 96*, 102919. https://doi.org/10.1016/j.erss.2022.102919

Trencher, G., & van der Heijden, J. (2019). Contradictory but also complementary: National and local imaginaries in Japan and Fukushima around transitions to hydrogen and renewables. *Energy Research & Social Science, 49*, 209–218. https://doi.org/10.1016/j.erss.2018.10.019

Vent de Colère. (2020a). *Lettre à Mme Elisabeth Borne.* Retrieved October 15, 2021 from https://www.ventdecolere.org/communique/VdC%20-%20Lettre%20de%20couverture%20%c3%a0%20la%20Ministre%20de%20la%20transition%20ecologie.pdf

Vent de Colère. (2020b). *Website.* Retrieved October 20, 2021 from https://www.ventdecolere.org/

Warren, C. R., & McFadyen, M. (2010). Does community ownership affect public attitudes to wind energy? A case study from south-West Scotland. *Land Use Policy, 27*(2), 204–213. https://doi.org/10.1016/j.landusepol.2008.12.010

Watkins, J. (2015). Spatial imaginaries research in geography: Synergies, tensions, and new directions: Spatial imaginaries. *Geography Compass, 9*(9), 508–522. https://doi.org/10.1111/gec3.12228

Wind Europe. (2024). Wind energy in Europe: 2023 statistics and the outlook for 2024–2030 (p. 56). Wind Europe. Retrieved February 23, 2025 from https://windeurope.org/data/products/wind-energy-in-europe-2023-statistics-and-the-outlook-for-2024-2030/

Woods, M. (2003). Conflicting environmental visions of the rural: Windfarm development in mid Wales. *Sociologia Ruralis, 43*(3), 271–288. https://doi.org/10.1111/1467-9523.00245

CHAPTER 3

Beyond Infrastructural Populism: Rural Energy Infrastructures as Emancipatory Imaginaries of the Rural

Matthias Naumann and David Philipp Rudolph

1 Introduction

In a joint debate article published in September 2022 in Denmark's largest daily newspaper, the conservative *Jyllands Posten*, the chairmen of the National Council for Rural Development and the Climate, Environment and Planning Committees of the Association of Danish Municipalities called for "the energy transition to become a turning point for the development of rural areas" (Jyllands Posten, 2022; own translation). In this call, the authors describe the expansion of infrastructure for the use of renewable energy, which at first glance appears to be incompatible with "good life in the countryside" (ibid.), as a unique opportunity for the fight against climate change and for the future of rural areas. They are

M. Naumann (✉)
Julius Maximilian University of Würzburg, Würzburg, Germany
e-mail: matthias.naumann@uni-wuerzburg.de

D. P. Rudolph
Technical University of Denmark, Roskilde, Denmark
e-mail: dpru@dtu.dk

S. Becker, B. Fladvad (eds.), *Contested Imaginaries of Future Technologies*, https://doi.org/10.1007/978-3-032-11497-6_3

calling on the Danish government to come up with serious solutions that serve rural development, that provide the added value of renewable energy to the affected communities instead of the infrastructure operators, and, last but not least, that involve rural citizens in order to avoid undemocratic decision-making processes and strengthen social cohesion in Denmark. The appeal calls for "solutions" that "develop" local communities "instead of phasing [them] out" (ibid.).

This chapter points to two key aspects. Firstly, and similar to other European countries, rural areas in Denmark, as well as in Germany, are affected by the severe consequences of structural change, whereby the expansion of renewable energies to date appears to have been insufficiently or not at all associated with rural development. Secondly, there exist two visions for the expansion of renewable energies indicated. One vision in which energy infrastructures contribute to the quality of life in rural areas, and one vision in which the massive expansion of renewable energies is contrary to *good life* in the countryside, jeopardizing or even displacing it.

The example from Denmark illustrates how political conflicts over infrastructure in rural areas raise questions about infrastructural futures, about infrastructural utopias as well as socio-technical imaginaries. Utopian as well as dystopian imaginaries of rural futures always have an infrastructural and thus socio-technical dimension. We explain this on the basis of three points. Firstly, the term infrastructural peripheralization stands for regional disadvantages along the lines of factually missing, deficient or even undesirable infrastructures in rural areas. Infrastructural and regional disadvantages can reinforce each other and lead to a permanent and literal *decoupling*. Secondly, these political problems are linked to current developments of an *infrastructural* populism. Infrastructural deficits may not only be a reason for the above-average support for right-wing populist parties and movements in rural areas. Right-wing populists also develop their own positions on infrastructure policy as well as imaginaries of regional and technological development in rural settings. Thirdly, we counter these planning and political challenges for rural areas with utopian infrastructural imaginaries —counter-designs for socially and ecologically just and democratic rural futures.

In our chapter, we combine socio-technical imaginaries and imaginaries of the rural as well as rural development in two ways. Firstly, we see infrastructural detriments as a reason for the emergence of right-wing populism in rural areas—a dystopian perspective on rural infrastructure futures. Secondly, convincing alternatives to right-wing populist endeavours as well as utopian imaginaries also require ideas about how rural areas and their infrastructures can be shaped in the future. In the following, we refer to current literature as well as to empirical illustrations from Denmark, which are based on previous work. These relate in particular to contested development of renewable energy infrastructures in rural areas (Elkjær et al., 2023) and their integration into rural development strategies (Rudolph & Clausen, 2021).

2 Infrastructural Peripheralization in Rural Areas

The crisis in rural areas is an infrastructural crisis in several respects. Economic structural change is leading to the financialization or *assetization* (Stirling et al., 2023) of rural properties and land, partly with the aim of exploiting them for energy supply (Alonso Serna, 2022; Kirkegaard et al., 2023a). In some rural areas in the Global North, demographic change is leading to an overload of infrastructure, such as health care, on the one hand, and underutilization, for example of schools or water infrastructure, on the other (Naumann, 2009). Climate change is calling into question the existing energy and water supply, but increasingly also transport in rural areas, making comprehensive transformations necessary. Finally, digitization is not only leading to new technical possibilities, but also to new social divisions in rural areas (Li et al., 2020). Infrastructure, previously a key instrument of structural policy in efforts to balance out spatial disparities, threatens to become an element of the *peripheralization* of rural areas. This primarily affects regions at a greater distance from urban centres, away from transport routes and tourist attractions. These rural areas are at risk of *infrastructural peripheralization* (see Naumann & Reichert-Schick, 2013; Pike et al., 2023; Sykes, 2018; Tomaney et al., 2024), which encompasses three aspects:

- Dismantling without replacement: this can be seen in food retailing, medical care and school locations.
- Thinning out and reduction: a significant reduction in services can be observed, particularly in public transport, but also in socio-cultural services. In many places, for example, bus services only continue to operate as school transport.
- Expansion and extension: This is characterized by the expansion in the area of wastewater disposal, but currently in particular by

infrastructure for the use of renewable energy sources. However, this expansion is repeatedly met with local protests (Naumann & Reichert-Schick, 2013).

The current transformation of infrastructures in these regions goes hand in hand with peripheralization and threatens to exacerbate existing disadvantages. The difficulty of maintaining facilities and services of public interest is thus becoming a key characteristic of peripheralized rural areas. In scientific as well as political publications such as the *Deutschlandatlas* of the Federal Ministry for Housing, Urban Development and Building (2023), questions of infrastructure, such as broadband coverage, accessibility of public transport or health care, are key indicators for determining regional disparities—and therefore also starting points for their political consideration. Similarly, the interactive Danish Neighbourhood Atlas (*NabolagsAtlas*) launched by the Department of the Built Environment at Aalborg University in 2023 (Department of the Built Environment, 2025) provides detailed insights into the livelihoods and social and economic development of thousands of neighbourhoods based on various indicators, such as housing, demographics, mobility and prosperity, and offers a decision-support tool for potential intervention.

The overlap of economic and demographic problems with infrastructural issues is also illustrated by examples of rural areas in Denmark. Since the 1990s, peripheral municipalities in rural areas of Denmark have been labelled *Outskirts-Denmark* (*Udkantsdanmark*), whereby the original terminology arose due to the peripheral location, remoteness and distance of the municipalities from central infrastructural services. However, the term *Outskirts-Denmark*, which initially did not have negative connotations, also increasingly insinuated a division and unequal development of the country in public discourse, with one part being seen as progressive and prosperous and the other as backward in terms of income, education, infrastructural provision and quality of life and, accordingly, being treated as a poor relation by the national government. This already stigmatizing description of rural areas away from urban growth centres has also found expression in the dystopian spatial imagination of *the rotten banana* (*den rådne banan*)—or to put it more charitably: *the overripe banana*. This expression can be traced back to the geographical location of the disadvantaged peripheral areas stretching from West Jutland to the islands of Lolland and Falster in the south, which produce a banana-like outline on a map.

Over the last three decades, these rural communities have been severely affected by economic changes, infrastructural decline, migration and the centralization of public services. However, due to their coastal and peripheral location, these areas also offer advantages for the use of renewable energy sources, particularly favourable wind resources and comparatively inexpensive land use. It is therefore not surprising that greater utilization of renewable energies in marginalized areas is cited as the basis for structural change and economic upturn. On the other hand, this offers the opportunity to counteract persistent stigmatization and highlights the usefulness of rural areas for Denmark's pioneering role in the energy transition. However, contrary to the vision of linking the siting of renewable energy infrastructure with rural development opportunities, some wind farm operators have mobilized and seized on the territorial stigma of *Outskirts-Denmark*, not only to justify the construction of wind farms in marginalized areas, but also to make room for them by buying up houses on the outskirts of neglected and structurally weak villages (Rudolph & Kirkegaard, 2019). This practice serves to comply with distance regulations between wind turbines and residential buildings, to increase the profitability of wind farms and to counteract local opposition forces. The paradoxical argumentation of the wind farm operators for this practice refers to an infrastructural revitalization of rural areas and support for municipalities in their limited efforts to develop settlements that have already been abandoned (ibid.). However, the prospect of private-sector companies taking on the future of selected, dependent areas and replacing state action harbours the risk of a new cycle of unequal development. In this scenario, the further development of structurally weak areas would be even more dependent on the interests of private companies, and state intervention to reduce spatial disparities would become even less important.

However, infrastructural disadvantages as an element of regions being *left behind* (Rodríguez-Pose, 2018) also provide an explanation for the success of right-wing populist movements and parties, which are discussed in the next section.

3 Infrastructural Populism in Rural Areas

In the last two decades, right-wing populist parties have been able to establish themselves in the political system in many countries of the Global North and in some cases, such as in Poland, Hungary and recently Finland, become part of governments. In many cases, right-wing populist parties and movements have been able to capitalize on dissatisfaction with social and spatial divisions. For example, a number of studies show a connection between support for right-wing populist parties and *places that don't matter* (Rodríguez-Pose, 2018). Likewise, research has also identified links between right-wing populist rhetoric and the perceived implications of energy infrastructure developments in remote and peripheral communities (Batel et al., 2024). Furthermore, energy transition efforts in rural areas were addressed by right-wing populist rhetoric in an ambivalent way, by either advancing nationalist and modernist imaginaries in the global race of expanding renewable energy infrastructures or by lamenting the misrecognition of impacts of the energy transition on *pure people* in rural communities and an alleged corrupt urban elite benefitting from the green transition (Valquaresma et al., 2024). As already indicated, infrastructure is an element of *being left behind*.

The term *left behind place* has become a leitmotif in geographical and planning-related debates to understand spatial disparities and discuss their social, economic and political implications. While the spatial imaginaries of left behind places have been variously used to draw attention to inequalities, disparities and divisions (Pike et al., 2024), discussions about left behind places and regions have ventured beyond economic-geographic perspectives of economic decline, deprivation and infrastructural decay, and explicitly include issues such as political discontent, expressions of negligence, and sense of loss and perceived marginalization (e.g. MacKinnon et al. 2024; Tomaney et al., 2024). In particular, the melange of these material and affective conditions has been described as being prone to co-optation by right-wing populist movements, especially in rural areas (Rodríguez-Pose et al., 2023).

In her study of German media discourses, Deppisch (2019) sees infrastructure decay as a cause of feelings of being left behind, which may be a reason for the electoral success of the far-right Alternative for Germany (AfD).

The term *infrastructural populism* (Beveridge et al., 2024) refers firstly to infrastructural disadvantages as an explaining factor for the above-average support for right-wing populist parties and movements in rural areas. This is also illustrated by empirical observations from Denmark, where the right-wing populist Dansk Folkeparti (DF, Danish People's Party) is of particular importance.

The DF was founded in 1995 and has played a decisive role in shaping political decisions in Denmark over the last two decades. It worked together with the right-wing conservative minority government between 2001 and 2011 and supported the right-wing liberal minority government between 2015 and 2019 as the second-strongest parliamentary group, gaining greater support in rural and suburban areas in particular (Bächler & Hopmann, 2016). Unlike the AfD in Germany, for example, the DF was not excluded from day-to-day politics by a *firewall* of other parties after its initial successes and was therefore able to have a significant influence on the political discourse (Kosiara-Pedersen, 2019). However, the DF's approval rating plummeted in the last parliamentary elections in 2019 (8.7%) and the early elections in 2022 (2.6%). The DF's current decline appears to be due to a general shift to the right in Denmark, with the ruling Social Democratic Party in particular pursuing similar goals to the DF in terms of maintaining a national welfare state and adopting a restrictive immigration policy towards non-Western immigrants and asylum seekers (Nedergaard, 2018; Wiggen, 2023). It was not only in its heyday that the DF discovered the interests of rural areas for itself and pursued a policy of national equalization and convergence.

> I don't like using the word 'Outskirts-[Denmark]'. It already makes the areas outside the big cities into something distant and intangible. However, we in the Danish People's Party attach great importance to rural areas. We must ensure a balanced Denmark. (Dansk Folkeparti leader in: Jyllands Posten, 2017; own translation)

To achieve this balance, the party is also explicitly focusing on infrastructure:

> Good infrastructure is important in all parts of the country. (Dansk Folkeparti, 2021, p. 34; own translation)

> We need to ensure that not all the funds for infrastructure end up on public rail connections and the development of bicycle parking in the large university cities. (Dansk Folkeparti in Altinget, 2020; on support for transport infrastructure and tensions between private car mobility and public transport provision, own translation)

These highlights from Denmark clearly show how the topic of infrastructure is used by right-wing populist parties to argue that rural areas should not be abandoned, while reproducing divisions between mobility requirements of rural areas and progressive urban lifestyles.

Secondly, *infrastructural populism* therefore also understands infrastructure as a field for the development of right-wing populist positions. This applies above all to the energy and transport sectors as policy areas in which right-wing populist parties are active. One example of this is the political disputes surrounding local or regional transformations of the energy supply. Under keywords such as *energy populism* (Dechézelles & Scotti, 2022) or *climate nationalism* (Kashwan et al., 2023), current research describes the *political ecologies of the far right* (Atkins & Menga, 2022). The energy policy of the Dansk Folkeparti is an empirical example of this.

After initially rejecting the utilization and expansion of renewable energies, the DF is now also unable to ignore the growing importance of this economic sector in Denmark. This applies not only to the export of renewable energy technologies, but also to the expansion of the domestic market in order to achieve national climate targets, improve the nationwide infrastructure and benefit citizens.

> The Danish People's Party supports the expansion of green energy production in Denmark. It just has to be done in line with the fact that there are consumers who buy the electricity produced. For the Danish People's Party, the most important task is therefore to ensure that the green energy we produce ourselves is better utilized than it is today and reaches those parts of society that are still kept alive by fossil fuels. Otherwise, we will just build solar panels, wind turbines etc. for the benefit and pleasure of our neighbours – and that makes no sense. (Dansk Folkeparti, 2023; own translation)

In a contribution on the situation in Denmark's peripheral areas, a DF member of parliament denounces in particular the unequal provision and promotion of infrastructure measures by the political elites between rural and urban regions. The contribution to the discussion even conjures up a spatial division in Danish society along dividing lines in the provision of infrastructure.

> While the state is constantly willing to increase growth in the capital region and the larger cities with university hospitals, concert halls, metros, light rail and other infrastructure, it is as if Danish society has rallied against the part of the population that lives in the peripheral areas and who would otherwise be equal citizens. (Member of Parliament for Dansk Folkeparti, in: Jyllands Posten, 2015; own translation)

Thirdly, ***infrastructural populism*** also stands for the creation of their own infrastructures by right-wing populists. For example, the rejection of public or established bourgeois media has led to right-wing populist parties and movements being very active on social media and developing their own channels there (Naumann, 2021, p. 217f.). This was evident, for example, in the protests against the measures to contain the Covid-19 pandemic, where messenger services such as Telegram, but also social media such as Facebook and YouTube, played a decisive role in mobilization. In addition to these primarily digital infrastructures, institutional infrastructures such as foundations, event spaces and companies that support right-wing populist activities have also emerged. The infrastructures created by right-wing populist actors are of particular importance in rural areas, where, as described above, public infrastructures have been reduced in recent years. This is also illustrated by examples from Denmark, where social networks have become more important than the previously established media and can act as *echo chambers* for right-wing populist positions. Examples of this include the right-wing populist, or self-described as nuanced and politically incorrect, Internet news portals *Den Korte Avis* or *24nyt*, whose Facebook pages have several tens of thousands of followers (Mayerhöffer, 2021), whereby the online presence of *24nyt* was blocked on Facebook due to criticism for misleading journalism.

The various infrastructural dimensions of right-wing populism in rural areas raise the question of what alternative or progressive imaginaries of infrastructures for rural areas could be.

4 Alternative Infrastructural Imaginaries for Rural Areas

Finally, we contrast the pessimistic accounts of rural areas, which are characterized by a deficient provision of infrastructure and increasingly being appropriated by right-wing populist actors, with alternative imaginaries of rural infrastructures. We propose a mutually constitutive relationship between imaginaries of rurality and infrastructural imaginaries: on the one hand, imaginaries of infrastructures are important elements of rural imaginaries (and material living conditions) today; on the other hand, infrastructural imaginaries are inscribed into imaginaries of the rural futures. Infrastructural imaginaries can thus be considered as a form of "spatial imaginaries" (Watkins, 2015).

There are various examples of the maintenance or expansion of infrastructure in rural areas, such as the citizen bus linked to an app, the village shop run with civic engagement that also offers postal services, the reopened village school, the establishment of energy cooperatives, or the development of mobile services in the areas of health and care. Many of these examples are based on technological and social innovations, incremental practices, flexible adaptation of specifications and standards, and the voluntary commitment of people in rural regions (e.g. Olmedo et al., 2023; Vercher et al., 2023). The de-carbonization of rural areas can represent concrete infrastructural imaginaries for rural areas, even if more radical and transformative imaginaries emerging at the local level tend to be suppressed by techno-optimist and growth-oriented rationales of climate action and energy transition (Marquardt and Nasiritousi, 2022).

This imaginary of *eco-localization* (North, 2010) is followed by numerous initiatives in the energy sector, such as the NGO *Wind People* in Denmark. This was a grassroots organization founded in 2008 in response to deteriorating conditions for community energy projects in order to break new ground in the energy transition by combining the construction of renewable energy with the promotion of the common good in rural communities. Unlike locally anchored and operating grassroots initiatives, the activities of the *Wind People* were not geographically limited and included both support for the implementation of specific energy projects and cross-location energy policy lobbying. Their goals were geared towards greater financial participation of citizens in infrastructure facilities and fundamental changes in the tendering criteria for energy projects in order to partially remove them from the market or to readjust existing market mechanisms. After initial success in the implementation of some citizen energy projects, the *Wind People* initiative ultimately failed in its efforts to structurally change the competitive regulations and restrictions of the renewable energy market and subsequently disbanded in 2019 (Kirkegaard et al., 2023b).

> Wind People cannot in good conscience stand aside and watch a small community being overrun by a company that works primarily for its own profits without taking the local community into account. (Wind People in: Nibe Avis, 2017; own translation)

Wind People called for a stronger local economic anchoring of wind and solar parks, mainly through new planning processes and hybrid ownership structures for the plants, in which citizens have a greater share in the infrastructure and profits, as well as the establishment of local development funds whose deposits should go directly to the affected communities.

> There can be two end products in energy planning. An external project developer sets up wind turbines in a local community, adheres to the legal requirements, and there is a hell of a lot of trouble because the end users end up with a huge mast that they have no idea at all that it is producing renewable energy, and they only see the impairments. In the second project, where they first set out with the vision, involved the community, identified the values in their local community, etc., then technically they achieved exactly the same solution, but the end product is a completely different one. Because there is a huge mast here which is a nuisance but which also leads to welfare improvements in the local community that are so much more significant and can be felt here and now. (Interview, Wind People, 2016)

As the call described at the beginning makes clear, state and private initiatives for rural energy transitions should be brought together. However, the example of *Wind People* also shows that (supra)national regulation can penetrate and limit the mobilization of existing imaginaries of rural infrastructure. Despite the abandonment of their activities, *Wind People* have exemplified imaginaries of rurality outside of the hegemonic energy policy discourse and significantly advanced alternative forms of organization for rural infrastructure.

Beyond the existing imaginaries of rural infrastructure, another paradigm shift in infrastructure planning and policy is therefore necessary—the social appropriation of infrastructure. The term *social appropriation* stands for a comprehensive decommodification of infrastructure and thus goes beyond questions of legal or material ownership. Infrastructure provision is therefore not based on goals of economic efficiency, but is committed to social balance, sustainability and democratic participation. This results in both a fundamental orientation towards public welfare of those responsible for rural infrastructure provision and concrete projects in various infrastructural areas.

Examples of this are approaches to energy or mobility justice (Jenkins et al., 2016; Pereira et al., 2017). Another fundamental challenge lies in the creation of new infrastructural rationalities; further conceptual references can provide impulses for this, such as *alliance technology* (Bloch, [1959] 1985) and *convivial technology* (e.g. Arora et al., 2020), which provoke a rethinking of socio-technological relationships, or ideas about anti-capitalist rural spaces (Halfacree, 2007). The approach of *prefigurative politics* (Springer, 2016) also attempts to use concrete, emancipatory practices to promote fundamental changes in the here and now and to model utopias, while *technoregions of insurrection* (Brennan, 2023) build on this and encourage insurgent practices specifically for the development of decentralized energy infrastructures. However, the realization of these emancipatory and alternative imaginaries of rural infrastructural provision leads to new contradictions. The implementation of new energy infrastructures involves, oftentimes, a renunciation of neoliberal and state-led solutions and the orientation towards self-dependent and autonomous strategies that are based on solidary practices and mutual aid, jointly driven by local actors. These approaches not only bring together conceptual, argumentative and practical requirements for infrastructural imaginaries that are necessary for the realization of progressive, solidarity-based and insurgent alternatives to the organization and use of infrastructure in rural areas. A combination of various elements of these approaches can also provide guidance for explicitly evoking these imaginaries to counter a right-wing populist appropriation of the countryside by not only designing alternatives but also exemplifying them in the midst of an infrastructure policy shaped by the neoliberal *Zeitgeist*.

Nevertheless, there is a greater need for exploring the amalgamation of rural and infrastructural imaginaries to shed light on fundamental questions of their interpretation, strategic implementation, geographical anchoring and institutionalization, as well as their emancipatory potential. For a more flourishing and critical debate on socio-technical imaginaries, the rural provides a useful lens for understanding infrastructural pasts, transformations and futures, as well as their contestations in specific spatial contexts. How do the provision of infrastructure, its underlying ambitions and its inherent conflicts contribute to the rurality of places and regions? What kind of rural infrastructure is desirable, and for whom? What different imaginaries of the rural and understandings of infrastructural *progress* exist, and how do they relate to each other? Addressing these questions from an emancipatory perspective can help point to practical levers for unravelling right-wing populist rhetoric and countering the appropriation of rural imaginaries.

5 Conclusion

In this chapter, we have discussed different infrastructure imaginaries and their contested relation to imaginaries of rural development. By drawing on spatial representations of peripheral rural areas in Denmark, we have detected tensions between established, populist and alternative imaginaries. The development of infrastructural imaginaries in rural areas is the subject of political debates in which, for example, the following questions are negotiated:

- Scalability: Is the lowest spatial level necessarily best suited to achieve social balance, sustainability and democratic participation? How can locally adapted solutions become models for other regions?
- Institutionalisation: In which organizational forms of infrastructure provision does social appropriation manifest itself? What does *public* ownership mean—public legal forms such as self-owned businesses, special-purpose associations, etc. or civil society-supported cooperatives?
- Conflicts of objectives and competing imaginaries: The negotiation and prioritization of the various demands on rural infrastructure is the subject of continuous debate and is linked to questions of time horizons when implementing the respective goals in infrastructure provision. A central question here is whose infrastructure imaginaries we are talking about. Imaginaries can also be determined by local governments, while imaginaries supported by grassroots movements can be marginalized.

Dealing with these—as well as other—questions helps to conceptually define infrastructural imaginaries more precisely and to gradually realize them. Essentially, this implies making rural infrastructures—their presence or absence—visible. With their claim to social balance, sustainability and democratic participation, alternative infrastructural imaginaries contradict current developments of peripheralization and right-wing populism. In addition, the conceptual definition and practical development of infrastructural imaginaries also contributes to a realization of a *right to the countryside*, the creation of rural commons and thus also spatial justice. Infrastructural utopias are therefore a step on the way to rural imaginaries.

References

Alonso Serna, L. (2022). Land grabbing or value grabbing? Land rent and wind energy in the isthmus of Tehuantepec, Oaxaca. *Competition and Change, 26*(3–4), 487–503. https://doi.org/10.1177/10245294211018966

Altinget. (2020). Debat. DF: Kollektiv trafik og privatbilisme er ikke modparter. Altinget Retrieved December 16, 2020, from https://www.altinget.dk/transport/artikel/df-kollektiv-trafik-og-privatbilisme-er-ikke-modparter

Arora, S., van Dyck, B., Sharma, D., & Stirling, A. (2020). Control, care, and conviviality in the politics of technology for sustainability. *Sustainability: Science. Practice and Policy, 17*(S2), 247–262. https://doi.org/10.1080/15487733.2020.1816687

Atkins, E., & Menga, F. (2022). Populist ecologies. *Area, 54*(2), 224–232. https://doi.org/10.1111/area.12763

Bächler, C. M., & Hopmann, D. N. (2016). Denmark: The rise of the Danish people's party. In T. Aalberg, F. Esser, C. Reinemann, J. Stromback, & C. de Vreese (Eds.), *Populist political communication in Europe* (pp. 29–41). Routledge.

Batel, S., Valquaresma, A., & Alba, M. (2024). Rural communities' energy metabolisms in Portugal: Between territorial injustices and far-right populism. *Journal of Rural Studies, 111*, 103425. https://doi.org/10.1016/j.jrurstud.2024.103425

Beveridge, R., Naumann, M., & Rudolph, D. (2024). The rise of 'infrastructural populism': Urban infrastructure and right-wing politics. *Geography Compass, 18*(2), e12738. https://doi.org/10.1111/gec3.12738

Bloch, E. ([1959]1985). *Das Prinzip Hoffnung*. Suhrkamp.

Brennan, R. (2023). Technoregions of insurrection: Decentralizing energy infrastructure and manifesting change at scale. In M. Nadesan, M. J. Pasqualetti, & J. Keahey (Eds.), *Energy democracies for sustainable futures* (pp. 41–49). Academic Press.

Dansk Folkeparti. (2021). Livet leves også i provinsen. Nærhedsreform. Marts 2021. Retrieved September 15, 2023, from https://danskfolkeparti.dk/medie/Landdistriktsudspil.pdf

Dansk Folkeparti. (2023). *Et grønnere Danmark*. Retrieved September 15, 2023, from https://danskfolkeparti.dk/politik/et-groennere-danmark/

Dechézelles, S., & Scotti, I. (2022). Wild wind, social storm: "Energy populism" in rural areas? An exploratory analysis of France and Italy. *Rural Sociology, 87*(S1), 784–813. https://doi.org/10.1111/ruso.12399

Department of Built Environment (2025). NabolagsAtlas. Detaljeret indblik i mere end 13.000 danske nabolag. Aalborg University. Retrieved May 5, 2025, from https://www.nabolagsatlas.dk/dk/

Deppisch, L. (2019). „Wo sich menschen auf dem land abgehängt fühlen, hat der Populismus freie Bahn"—Eine analyse des populär-medialen Diskurses zu der Bedeutung von Infrastrukturverfall, Abstiegsangst und rechten (extremistischen) Werten für den Zuspruch zum Rechtspopulismus. Johann Heinrich von Thünen Institute, Institute of Rural Studies.

Elkjær, L. G., Rudolph, D., & Horst, M. (2023). Different pasts, contested presents and desired futures: Local narratives and identities in the co-production of a shared wind energy ownership model. *Local Environment, 28*(12), 1515–1533. https://doi.org/10.1080/13549839.2023.2238746

Federal Ministry for Housing, Urban Development and Building. (2023). *Deutschlandatlas*. Retrieved August 10, 2023, from https://www.deutschlandatlas.bund.de/DE/Karten/_node.html

Halfacree, K. (2007). Trial by space for a 'radical rural': Introducing alternative localities, representations and lives. *Journal of Rural Studies, 23*(2), 125–141. https://doi.org/10.1016/j.jrurstud.2006.10.002

Jenkins, K., McCauley, D., Heffron, R., Stephan, H., & Rehner, R. (2016). Energy justice: A conceptual review. *Energy Research & Social Science, 11*, 174–182. https://doi.org/10.1016/j.erss.2015.10.004

Jyllands Posten. (2015). *Udkantsdanmark skal blomstre igen*. Retrieved September 18, 2023, from https://jyllands-posten.dk/debat/kronik/ECE7452984/udkantsdanmark-skal-blomstre-igen1/

Jyllands Posten. (2017). *Det mener partierne om Udkantsdanmark*. Retrieved October 17, 2023, from https://jyllands-posten.dk/debat/breve/ECE10005120/det-mener-partierne-om-udkantsdanmark/

Jyllands Posten. (2022). *Lad den grønne omstilling blive et vendepunkt for vores landdistrikter*. Retrieved September 18, 2023, from https://jyllands-posten.dk/debat/breve/ECE14381112/lad-den-groenne-omstilling-blive-et-vendepunkt-for-vores-landdistrikter/

Kashwan, P., Chung En-Liu, J., & Das, J. (2023). Climate nationalisms: Beyond the binaries of good and bad nationalism. *WIREs Climate Change, 14*(2), e815. https://doi.org/10.1002/wcc.815

Kirkegaard, J. K., Nyborg, S., Georg, S., & Horst, M. (2023b). Towards failed renewable energy communities? Activist attempts to change market conditions in the Danish wind energy market. *Energy Research & Social Science, 102*, 103152. https://doi.org/10.1016/j.erss.2023.103152

Kirkegaard, J. K., Rudolph, D., Nyborg, S., & Cronin, T. (2023a). The landrush of wind energy, its socio-material workings, and its political consequences: On the entanglement of land and wind assemblages in Denmark. *Environment and Planning C: Politics and Space, 41*(3), 548–566. https://doi.org/10.1177/23996544221143657

Kosiara-Pedersen, K. (2019). Stronger core, weaker fringes: The Danish general election 2019. *West European Politics, 43*(4), 1011–1022. https://doi.org/10.1080/01402382.2019.1655920

Li, R., Chen, K., & Wu, D. (2020). Challenges and opportunities for coping with the smart divide in rural America. *Annals of the American Association of Geographers, 110*(2), 559–570. https://doi.org/10.1080/24694452.2019.1694402

MacKinnon, D., Beal, V., & Leibert, T. (2024). Rethinking 'left-behind' places in a context of rising spatial inequalities and political discontent. *Regional Studies, 58*(6), 1161–1166. https://doi.org/10.1080/00343404.2023.2291581

Marquardt, J., & Nasiritousi, N. (2022). Imaginary lock-ins in climate change politics: The challenge to envision a fossil-free future. *Environmental Politics, 31*(4), 621–642. https://doi.org/10.1080/09644016.2021.1951479

Mayerhöffer, E. (2021). How do Danish right-wing alternative media position themselves against the mainstream? Advancing the study of alternative media structure and content. *Journalism Studies, 22*(2), 119–136. https://doi.org/10.1080/1461670X.2020.1814846

Naumann, M. (2009). Neue Disparitäten durch Infrastruktur? Der Wandel der Wasserwirtschaft in ländlich-peripheren Räumen. oekom.

Naumann, M. (2021). Infrastruktureller Populismus. Infrastruktur als agenda, instrument und Erklärung rechter Raumproduktionen. *Geographische Zeitschrift, 109*(4), 208–226. https://doi.org/10.25162/gz-2021-0004

Naumann, M., & Reichert-Schick, A. (2013). Infrastructure and Peripheralization: Empirical evidence from North-eastern Germany. In A. Fischer-Tahir & M. Naumann (Eds.), *Peripheralization. The making of spatial dependencies and social injustice* (pp. 145–167). Springer VS.

Nedergaard, P. (2018). *Zurück zu den Wurzeln: Warum fordert die dänische Sozialdemokratie eine restriktive Einwanderungspolitik?* Retrieved October 17, 2023, from https://library.fes.de/pdf-files/bueros/budapest/14497.pdf

Nibe Avis. (2017). *Opfordring til udviklingsfond i Nørrekær Enge.* Retrieved September 18, 2023, from https://nibeavis.dk/norrekaerenge/4038-opfordring-til-udviklingsfond-i-norrekaer-enge

North, P. (2010). Eco-localisation as a progressive response to peak oil and climate change—A sympathetic critique. *Geoforum, 41*(4), 585–594. https://doi.org/10.1016/j.geoforum.2009.04.013

Olmedo, L., van Twuijver, M., & O'Shoughnessy, M. (2023). Rurality as context for innovative responses to social challenges—The role of rural social enterprises. *Journal of Rural Studies, 99*, 272–283. https://doi.org/10.1016/j.jrurstud.2021.04.020

Pereira, R., Schwanen, T., & Banister, D. (2017). Distributive justice and equity in transportation. *Transport Reviews, 37*(2), 170–191. https://doi.org/10.1080/01441647.2016.1257660

Pike, A., Beal, V., Cauchi-Duval, N., Frankling, R., et al. (2024). 'Left behind places': A geographical etymology. *Regional Studies, 58*(6), 1167–1179. https://doi.org/10.1080/00343404.2023.2167972

Rodríguez-Pose, A. (2018). The revenge of the places that don't matter (and what to do about it). *Cambridge Journal of Regions, Economy and Society, 11*(1), 189–209. https://doi.org/10.1093/cjres/rsx024

Rodríguez-Pose, A., Terrero-Davila, J., & Lee, N. (2023). Left-behind versus unequal places: Interpersonal inequality, economic decline and the rise of populism in the USA and Europe. *Journal of Economic Geography, 23*(5), 951–977. https://doi.org/10.1093/jeg/lbad005

Rudolph, D., & Clausen, L. T. (2021). Ländliche Entwicklung auf der basis erneuerbarer Energien? Emanzipatorische Potenziale zwischen radikaldemokratischer und neoliberaler Logik. *PROKLA. Zeitschrift für kritische Sozialwissenschaft, 51*(3), 497–516. https://doi.org/10.32387/prokla.v51i204.1959

Rudolph, D., & Kirkegaard, J. K. (2019). Making space for wind farms: Practices of territorial stigmatisation in rural Denmark. *Antipode, 51*(2), 642–663. https://doi.org/10.1111/anti.12428

Springer, S. (2016). *The anarchist roots of geography*. University of Minnesota Press.

Stirling, P., Gallent, N., & Purves, A. (2023). The assetisation of housing: A macroeconomic resource. *European Urban and Regional Studies, 30*(1), 15–35. https://doi.org/10.1177/09697764221082621

Sykes, O. (2018). Post-geography worlds, new dominions, left behind regions, and 'other' places: Unpacking some spatial imaginaries of the UK'S 'Brexit' debate. *Space and Polity, 22*(2), 137–161. https://doi.org/10.1080/13562576.2018.1531699

Tomaney, J., Blackman, M., Natarajan, L., Panayotopoulos-Tsiros, D., Sutcliffe-Brathwaite, F., & Taylor, M. (2024). Social infrastructure and 'left-behind places'. *Regional Studies, 58*(6), 1237–1250. https://doi.org/10.1080/00343404.2023.2224828

Valquaresma, A., Batel, S., Afonso, A. I., Guerra, R., & Silva, L. (2024). The renewable energy transition and "the people"—Exploring the intersections of right-wing populism and the renewable energy transition in Portuguese media discourses. *Environmental Communication, 18*(7), 847–861. https://doi.org/10.1080/17524032.2024.2326423

Vercher, N., Bosworth, G., & Esparcia, J. (2023). Developing a framework for radical and incremental social innovation in rural areas. *Journal of Rural Studies, 99*, 233–242. https://doi.org/10.1016/j.jrurstud.2022.01.007

Watkins, J. (2015). Spatial imaginaries research in geography: Synergies, tensions, and new directions. *Geography Compass, 9*(9), 508–522. https://doi.org/10.1111/gec3.12228

Wiggen, M. (2023). The shift to the right in Denmark. In K. Kondor & M. Littler (Eds.), *The Routledge handbook of far-right extremism in Europe* (pp. 202–213). Routledge.

CHAPTER 4

The EU's Green Energy Transition: Contested Imaginaries of Fossil Fuel Futures

Les Levidow

1 Introduction: The European Union's Green Energy Transition to What?

In 2019 the European Commission (EC) launched the European Green Deal, extending its long-time claims for global environmental leadership. This "new growth strategy" set out to strengthen economic efficiency so that Europe would become the "world's first climate-neutral continent by 2050". It would mobilize macroeconomic means to put citizens' well-being at the centre of economic policy, and "put the Sustainable Development Goals at the heart of the EU's policymaking and action" (EC, 2019, pp. 2, 3). Yet there had been long-time warnings that sustainable development is undermined by economic growth, especially if equated with GDP. In that same year, the European Environmental Agency warned that the EU would not achieve its sustainable vision of living well within the limits of the planet's resources by continuing to promote economic growth (EEA, 2019, p. 2).

L. Levidow (✉)
The Open University, Milton Keynes, UK
e-mail: les.levidow@open.ac.uk

S. Becker, B. Fladvad (eds.), *Contested Imaginaries of Future Technologies*, https://doi.org/10.1007/978-3-032-11497-6_4

Nevertheless, European institutions have aimed to reconcile economic growth with sustainability through technoscientific innovation, with a decarbonized energy supply as one cornerstone of this development. This agenda has relied on market incentives, portrayed as technologically neutral, even as politically neutral: "…it is essential to ensure that the European energy market is fully integrated, interconnected and digitalized, while respecting technological neutrality". The European Green Deal advocated "smart infrastructure", in particular: "…innovative technologies and infrastructure, such as smart grids, hydrogen networks, carbon capture, storage and utilization, energy storage, also enabling sector integration" (EC, 2019, p. 6). Feeding into a geo-economic grand strategy, the EU would become "a global leader" against climate change by innovating low-carbon, eco-efficient technologies, and exporting them globally.

Powerful economic actors have sought to seize the flexibilities available in this framework by framing energy transition pathways in their interest. Notably, the fossil fuel industry promoted three pathways, portraying their character as merely technical. First, renewable energy would expand in mainly centralized forms. Second, natural gas would provide a climate-friendly partner for renewable energy (Haas, 2019, pp. 71–72). In this new framework, gas would complement renewables, together offering an eventual long-term decarbonization. Third, the industry has promoted "clean hydrogen" as a techno-market fix that could credibly complement renewable energy. In particular, Carbon Capture Usage and Storage (CCUS, sometimes just CCS) would decarbonize natural gas into "blue hydrogen", supposedly as a crucial technological step towards water-electrolysis producing zero-carbon "green hydrogen". The lobby demanded market incentives for such technological solutions to achieve Net Zero carbon emissions. Oil companies have embraced this aim, partly because they lead CCUS development, which can help justify more gas.

Thus the term "green energy transition" has had rival, contested meanings. This chapter theorizes rival narratives and imaginaries regarding European energy futures and the roles of natural gas and hydrogen therein. It will discuss how rival imaginaries around the energy transition have emerged and impacted the European Green Deal's policy framework. First, the chapter will examine how the natural gas industry has built partnerships and established the hegemonic imaginary of extending natural gas as a transitional fuel source, aided by the decarbonization promises around future applications of CCUS and hydrogen. Second, the chapter will discuss two cases in the future hydrogen imaginary materializes in real-world settings. In Malta, a "hydrogen-ready" gas pipeline was devised in the face of civil society opposition to fossil fuel lock-in. In Germany, the need to feed a to-be-established *Hydrogen Autobahn* system results in offensive geopolitics, potentially transforming the countries international relations around energy. Third, the chapter will take a brief look at the alternative agenda counterposed by industry-critical civil society organizations (CSOs). Each of these competing future visions will be analysed as a sociotechnical-spatial imaginary, i.e., as a socially shared vision of a feasible, desirable future, as summarized in Table 4.1. The theoretical concept underlying this analysis is explained in the next section.

Table 4.1 EU's green energy transition: rival imaginaries

	Hegemonic imaginary	*Alternative imaginary*
Alliance components	EU, transnational energy companies and EC advisory bodies: IOGP, OGA, CCUS Forum, ICM Forum	Industry-critical CSOs: CEO, FoE, GNDE, BUND, Klima Allianz, Iberian NGOs, ReCommon
Green energy transition	Natural gas can undergo low-carbon innovation and complement renewables to accommodate rising demands for clean energy Develop clean hydrogen initially via CCUS (blue H) and later via water electrolysis (green H). Provide market incentives to drive clean breakthrough technologies	Demand full switch to renewables, while decreasing overall energy consumption Incentives and subsidies for energy efficiency upgrades can improve well-being and welfare. Public-sector role should link economic aims with environmental justice: decarbonizing the economy, reversing biodiversity loss, and tackling inequalities
Natural gas	EU will continue to need natural gas for decades Locking out CCUS-hydrogen would delaydecarbonization: No CCUS, no net-zero. Sites lacking clean H remain isolated from new technology, so they must be connected by H highways, etc.	Natural gas brings energy insecurity, fuel poverty, stranded assets, corporate capture, distraction from alternatives, etc. CCUS-hydrogen fix risks locking in natural gas, delaying a low-carbon transition and raising energy costs Gas phase-out would encourage cheap and effective alternatives of renewable energy, yielding health benefits

(*continued*)

Table 4.1 (continued)

	Hegemonic imaginary	*Alternative imaginary*
Energy market and infrastructure	Facilitate CCUS value chain to incentivize low-carbon energy: initially from natural gas and biomass, later from electrolysis. Fund facilities to import synthetic e-methane from green H Create markets for H supply and CO2 storage Need for integrated, interconnected, and digitized EU-wide energy market	EU further liberalizes Europe's energy markets, but fails to use regulation to decarbonize energy suppliers by eliminating fossil fuels. Risks driving up European prices, even as renewable energy costs fall Alternative: Decommission gas infrastructure Flexible energy systems via demand response, greater storage capacity and integrated sources of renewable energy
EC energy programmes	Financial incentives should de-risk investment for clean H, enabling no-regrets infrastructure development for energy production and transport, initially from natural gas	Programmes socialize the risks and privatize benefits. They extend the corporate capture of EU energy policy. Fossil fuel companies become subsidy-harvesters
Idealized spaces, clean hydrogen backbones, and valleys	EU becomes a global leader for overcoming climate change. Hydrogen backbone (H-ready gas pipelines) provides a durable widespread linkage for low-C future. Hydrogen valleys and connectors will spread the benefits	EU plan for CCUS-hydrogen is incompatible with climate protection EU agenda frames marginal sites as empty spaces lacking their own capacity for low-carbon development. Global South to face a hydrogen curse
Place imaginaries around, e.g., Malta's TransGas pipeline	Malta's energy isolation and dependence on oil imports must be overcome via LNG terminal and hydrogen-ready gas pipelines Blue hydrogen will provide a transition to zero-carbon green hydrogen	TransGas pipeline threatens the Mediterranean's lungs and reinforces corporate corruption Malta must invest in the country's resilience and autonomy, e.g. energy savings, local renewables, and community energy projects
Spatial transformations, e.g. Germany's H Autobahns	Market incentives and state investments will drive new infrastructure with clean H towards a green energy transformation. H valleys will enable knowledge exchange and accelerate region-wide adoption Germany will become C-neutral through more H production and import via corridors, with distribution via H Autobahns. Benefits to exporting countries will avoid a new energy imperialism	EU shows a disconnect between extraction and consumption zones, allowing injustices to continue. Shift to low-carbon imports from private *green enclaves* promise green H, but more plausibly will impose blue hydrogen Germany's CCUS-hydrogen plan is a dangerous pseudo-solution perpetuating fossil fuel Alternative future: Expand domestic production and use of renewable energy

2 Techno-Innovation Agendas as Imagined Futures: Analytical Perspectives

From 2005 onwards, the EU's green transition policy was gradually narrowed. Originally meaning sustainable development through the entire economy, it increasingly focused on decarbonizing the energy system, emphasizing carbon metrics. This policy shift opened or extended opportunities for previously controversial sources such as nuclear energy, "clean coal", and eventually CCUS to decarbonize natural gas (Morata and Solorio Sandoval, 2012, 2013). Underlying such policy frameworks, future societal visions related to specific technologies can be illuminated by the theoretical concept of sociotechnical imaginaries (STIs). These capture what constitutes the public good or a good life; they are "collectively imagined forms of social life and social order reflected in the design and fulfilment of nation-specific scientific and/or technological projects", potentially shaping political institutions (Jasanoff & Kim, 2009, p. 120). Such a vision is considered "an important cultural resource that enables new forms of life by projecting positive goals and seeking to attain them" (Jasanoff & Kim, 2009, p. 122).

An imaginary may serve to mobilize various organizations and resources, shaping "the hearts and minds of human agents and institutions" (Jasanoff, 2015, p. 17). The concept helps to understand "why different moral valences attach to new scientific ideas and technological inventions", and likewise "how actors with authority to shape the public imagination construct stories of progress in their programmatic statements, and how they blend into these their expectations of science and technology" (Jasanoff, 2015, p. 337). Any national debate thereby, reinforces "patterns of public reason, evidence production and knowledge uptake that constitute a nation's political culture" (Jasanoff and Kim, 2009, p. 140). Sociotechnical imaginaries are neither monolithic nor uncontested; instead, "...[m]ultiple imaginaries can coexist within a society in tension or in a productive dialectical relationship" (Jasanoff & Kim, 2015, p. 4). To fulfil the analytical potential of the approach, as argued here, it is important to carve out these tensions between hegemonic and alternative imaginaries as they compete and manifest through policy frameworks.

As one recurrent, dominant policy framework, green innovation policies have been linked to a techno-market imaginary. This assumes that environmental issues are manageable through appropriate economic incentives and technological innovation, without fundamentally undermining lifestyles or economic growth. This imaginary claims to reconcile economic and environmental concerns (Levy & Spicer, 2013, p. 666). Based on neoliberal environmentalism, market incentives aim to stimulate more eco-efficient practices that reduce environmental burdens, especially through technoscientific innovation. The latter has extended the EU's ecological modernization agendas since the 1990s, seeking capital-intensive eco-efficient resource extraction and use (Levidow, 2023: Chapter 2; Levidow & Raman, 2020).

Illustrating how the techno-market imaginary underlies policy, the 2009 Renewable Energy Directive mandated quotas for renewable transport fuel, thus guaranteeing a European market for biofuels for the next decade. In the hegemonic narrative, the mandate would stimulate technoscientific innovation for *sustainable biofuels*, especially second-generation biofuels that avoid edible feedstock. Yet this innovation hadn't materialized a decade later. By default, the quota stimulated a new industry for conventional biofuels, based on edible feedstock, whose production caused environmental degradation, especially in Southeast Asia (Levidow, 2013, 2023: Chapter 4). The techno-market framework helped key actors to inflict harm, while avoiding any responsibility. Consequently, for at least a decade it perpetuated carbon-intensive transport fuel, dependent on the internal combustion engine.

Alongside sociotechnical imaginaries, spatial imaginaries envisage new beneficial arrangements within or across places. Such spatial imaginaries have been theorized by Watkins (2015) as belonging to three types: *Place imaginaries* define a distinct space and its characterization. *Idealized spaces* are descriptions of places sharing generic characteristics, such as the "global city" or the "ghetto". *Spatial transformation* imaginaries are narratives about the processes by which spaces and places change, for better or for worse; examples here include "gentrification" and "globalization". These kinds of imaginaries are inter-related and can become strategically linked (ibid.). Combining both strands, struggles around rival future visions link technoscientific and spatial change.

Additionally, energy sources of different kinds were connected to various spatial imaginaries justifying new trajectories and investments. Fossil energy has been imagined as a stable, secure, flexible energy source for industrial sites, most recently revoked in justifications for liquified natural gas (e.g. West, 2025). By contrast, renewables have been imagined as a driver of rural economic renewal (Cloke et al., 2017; Zhong, 2024).

For the EU's energy transition plan towards climate neutrality, such imaginaries have been grounded in ecological modernization, i.e. capital-intensive eco-efficient resource extraction and use for a *green economy*. Extractivism entails an imaginary of spatial transformation, extending Europe's long-time designs on the Global South since the colonial period. Recently this imaginary has been combined with a greening narrative, linking resource extraction with economic growth and environmental sustainability, as putative benefits for the exporters and importers alike. While critical materials are exported as a surplus from seemingly empty spaces, green colonialism reproduces an unjust global division of labour, "...now dyed green, and spur[ring] a new global commodity supercycle" (Dietz, 2024, p. 29).

3 EU's Green Energy Transition Becomes a Corporate Agenda for *Clean Hydrogen*

3.1 The Rival Narratives of Energy Transition

For several decades, civil society groups and experts have invoked imperatives for a renewables transition, especially warning that fossil reserves would lose their financial value and so become *stranded assets*. To replace the EU's fossil energy regime, civil society groups linked a full transition to renewable energy with less hierarchical social relations such as community-based and decentralized energy projects. Lower electricity prices and decarbonization policies were potentially turning oil reserves into stranded assets, while renewable energy sources had declining costs and greater take-up (Haas, 2019, p. 70). By the second decade of the twenty-first century, some governments could plausibly restrict fossil fuels, thus politically stranding some of the fossil industry assets.

Facing these developments as threats, industry counter-strategies sought structural, discursive, and policy changes to ensure a long-term future for fossil reserves as functional capital assets (Carton, 2019; Malm & Carton, 2024, pp. 16–17). As a structural change, fossil-based energy companies began to take over large renewable players, promoting investments in large-scale, centralized renewable facilities and shifting their narratives towards a complementary relation with fossil fuels (Haas, 2019, p. 71). One major element in the discursive strategy was to perpetuate natural gas by framing it as a *transition fuel*, as a *companion* complementing fluctuating renewable energy supply. Paradoxically, despite becoming cheaper, renewable energies were obstinately blamed for being too expensive, within a hostile narrative towards state investment as a burden. A zero-carbon energy system would remain an eventual long-term destination, rather than a transition in the commonplace sense.

This narrative underwent widespread criticism (CEO, 2017) and was contradicted by the guidelines of the European Green Deal, potentially strengthening pressures to end the EU's dependence on natural gas (EC, 2019). Nevertheless, EC policy has witnessed recurrent tensions and alternations between the two visions of transition. In particular, Russia's invasion of Ukraine quickly stimulated more long-term infrastructure for the EU's natural gas supplies (EC, 2022).

The agenda to perpetuate natural gas was supported by several arguments: that gas is lower-carbon than other fossil fuels, that the natural gas infrastructure can be readily upgraded (or newly designed) as "hydrogen ready", that it complements renewable energy, and that it can be decarbonized by CCUS generating hydrogen. The gas lobby successfully relabelled the latter as "clean, low carbon blue hydrogen", long before its production might even have become commercially viable (CEO, 2020, p. 6). This *clean hydrogen imaginary*, transitioning through the different colours of hydrogen (see below), has justified market-type incentives and state funds for new infrastructure.

In 2023, the European Green Deal was updated by the *Green Deal Industrial Plan for the Net-Zero Age*. This economic policy plan has promoted the green transition as "a new industrial revolution aimed at ending the age of fossil fuels", thanks to "clean breakthrough technologies", especially "fossil-free renewable hydrogen". These technologies would facilitate a "net-zero industrial transformation" (EC, 2023). Against this, critics argued that CCUS technology "will enable oil to be extracted from declining fields and unconventional shale oil and gas reservoirs that would have otherwise been unrecoverable" (Hanieh, 2024, p. 225). However, the EU was already approving and subsidizing industry plans for greatly expanding natural gas infrastructure and liquefied natural gas (LNG) imports, supposedly crucial for CCUS-hydrogen. Let us see how the emerging clean hydrogen imaginary further shifted and shaped EU policy frameworks.

3.2 *Sociotechnical-Spatial Imaginaries of Clean Hydrogen*

Hydrogen fuel has three main types (grey, blue, and green), whose roles have been causally linked in innovation imaginaries, as explained next. So far, nearly all hydrogen production has been *grey hydrogen*. As the main industry motive, it is used for Enhanced Oil Recovery, as well as for oil refining, both carbon-intensive processes. It is also used for making ammonia fertilizers and chemicals such as methanol. Grey hydrogen is produced from natural gas or methane through steam methane reformation. During this process, carbon dioxide (CO_2) is released into the atmosphere as a waste product. For every tonne of hydrogen extracted, roughly 10 tonnes of CO_2 are produced. Therefore, the greenhouse gas (GHG) footprint is at least 20% higher than natural gas (Howarth & Jacobson, 2021).

For at least two decades, technological development has sought to capture carbon from natural gas reformation in order to generate so-called *blue hydrogen*, supposedly much lower-carbon than natural gas per se. Yet its GHG emissions are nearly as high when accounting for its total emissions. As a consequence, blue hydrogen promotion can arguably be considered as less about decarbonizing the economy than about perpetuating natural gas and capturing any future hydrogen market for the fossil fuel companies. This future pathway has also been favoured by the EU's regulatory criteria (CEO, 2020; Szabo, 2021).

EC policy has portrayed blue hydrogen as a market prerequisite for later investment in zero-carbon *green hydrogen* from electrolysis, powered by a renewable energy source (EC, 2020, p. 4). Large-scale green hydrogen production would require vast amounts of land, water, and renewable energy, the sources of which are generally left vague. This renders green hydrogen production energy-inefficient, relative to directly using the electricity. Last, new infrastructure for natural gas has been promoted as *hydrogen-ready*. This denotes energy-related infrastructure such as metres, junctions, recompressing facilities, and pipelines. The term hydrogen-ready holds the promise of low-carbon hydrogen but more readily extends natural gas, thus blurring any distinction between energy sources.

Reinforced by CCUS, the *clean hydrogen imaginary* has proliferated spatial metaphors evoking faster decarbonization alongside stronger societal bonds and benefits. Current and future gas pipelines have been rebranded a European Hydrogen Backbone as a durable, secure, desirable future. This justified support for EU policy, given its structural dependence on CCUS: "As European gas infrastructure companies, we fully support the European Green Deal and we are willing to play our part in facilitating the scale up of renewable and low carbon gas" (EHB, 2020, p. iii). The report showed how current pipelines could be repurposed for hydrogen, initially blue hydrogen produced by CCUS, eventually extending to green hydrogen (EHB, 2020).

Indeed, the EU has planned to expand its hydrogen pipelines from 2000 km (in 2023) to 53,000 by 2040, many of which would be partly retrofitted fossil gas infrastructure. These have been metaphorically called *hydrogen valleys* for internal linkages, alongside hydrogen imports via three *Hydrogen Corridors*: from the Mediterranean, North Sea, and eventually Ukraine (EC, 2022). Hydrogen valleys "link all stages in the hydrogen value chain" from production to use. They "would reduce hydrogen costs and enable the scale-up of clean hydrogen production faster than if production is dependent on renewables generation alone", according to promoters (CATF 2023, p. 9). By developing hydrogen valleys on either side of national borders, the industry aims "to facilitate the exchange of knowledge, technologies, and resources"; this would accelerate adoption of hydrogen across a region and across frontiers (EOG, 2024, p. n.p.).

In mid-2024, the EC announced plans for at least 50 hydrogen valleys, *local industrial or transport clusters where renewable hydrogen supply feeds local demand* (DG R&I, 2024). The connected spatial metaphors leave flexible the local interlinkages and the specific local forms, such as eventual hydrogen production and use. As an idealized spatial imaginary, the hydrogen valley helps to stabilize local versions that reflect (and obscure) the sunk investments of the companies whose core activity involves the supply or use of fossil fuels, but which are now under pressure vis a vis the climate imperative (Upham and Maristany, 2025). However, it also marginalized a more feasible, plausible trajectory, namely that truly renewable energy generation with appropriate infrastructure could have a faster scale-up, without converting energy to green hydrogen. But this route would undermine the fossil economy and so has remained politically awkward for the EU elite.

3.3 *Techno-Market Imperatives for Policy Support*

Alongside political lobbying, fossil gas companies have funded expert groups to elaborate their CCUS-hydrogen imaginary for the Net Zero targets of the European Green Deal. To promote market-based policy incentives, they emphasize the necessity of building up European hydrogen and biomethane value chains. An industry study, *Gas Decarbonisation Pathways 2020 to 2050*, anticipated a large quantity (1700 TWh) of hydrogen being produced within the EU by 2050 and so reducing GHG emissions (Gas for Climate, 2020). Its fulfilment would remain contingent on appropriate incentives, especially market quotas and direct investment, which thereby become policy imperatives. In particular, these should "make gas infrastructure future proof in an integrated energy system", a euphemism for locking in natural gas.

Under the European Green Deal, the Commission soon sponsored the European Clean Hydrogen Alliance (ECHA), which has promoted CCUS-hydrogen imaginaries alongside such policy agendas. Its launch event included three European energy ministers and CEOs of several multinational companies. It has emphasized the *transitional* character of natural gas:

> This includes hydrogen produced from renewable sources and, during a transition period, low-carbon hydrogen (fossil-based with carbon capture as well as electricity-based hydrogen) with significantly reduced full life-cycle greenhouse gas emissions compared to existing hydrogen production. (ECHA, 2020)

Before 2020, many potential CCUS projects had been cancelled and dismissed as wasteful. Early promotional programmes have included the European Energy Programme for Recovery (EEPR) and the NER300 programme (DG Clima, 2017). The European Court of Auditors (ECA, 2018, p. n.p.) found that "neither of the programs succeeded with the deployment of CCS in the EU". Given such failures, the transitional period could continue indefinitely. "CCS failed to live up to its potential during the previous investment cycle (2009–2015)", the industry lobby group International Organization of Oil and Gas Producers (IOGP) acknowledged to the Commission, but gave reassurance that future efforts would show success (IOGP, 2020; cited in CEO, 2020, p. 16). Such efforts featured the industry-driven Zero Emissions Platform, likewise advocating priority funds for CO_2 transport and CCUS.

In 2020, the Commission allocated €130m from its Connecting Europe Facility towards CO_2 transport projects. Despite earlier critiques on subsidies for renewables, reports urged state support for the expensive infrastructure necessary to create novel markets for both hydrogen and CO_2 storage. In the words of Deloitte Finance, "…[t]hese investments need to start in a timely manner to ensure demand and supply grow in lockstep, avoid technology lock-outs and mitigate risk of stranded assets" (2021, p. 9). The imaginary here emphasized a dual risk of lock-out: losing the market value of fossil reserves and likewise of a hypothetical value chain, i.e. a lucrative trajectory for CO_2 storage. Many more projects followed under the banner of blue hydrogen.

The Commission also sponsored the Carbon Capture Usage and Storage (CCUS) Forum, which likewise justified market incentives for CCUS-hydrogen. The Forum welcomed the European Innovation Fund grant for novel demonstration projects:

> However, experience has shown that new low-carbon technologies require sustained support through several deployment iterations, just as many years of power-price incentives and other mechanisms have supported the maturation of wind and solar energy. Similarly sustained support…will likewise be necessary for developing various applications of CCUS to commercial prospects that can attract large volume, low-risk finance, and be driven by market incentives alone. (CCUS Forum, 2021, p. 19)

Therefore, the Forum said, demonstration projects must be expanded, especially Backbone Pipelines for both CO_2 and hydrogen, as well as "solutions for dispersed emitters using all transport modes available" (ibid., p. 25). When updating the Renewable Energy Directive, it mandated specific targets and promotional measures necessary to "facilitate the ramping-up of the hydrogen industry", and likewise for "promoting the European hydrogen market" (EU, 2023, p. n.p.). These were meant as a self-fulfilling prophecy for a market which hardly existed. Hence, imperatives for policy support inverted the climate risk of locking in natural gas, now turned into a future financial benefit by perpetuating it for hydrogen fuel.

3.4 Implementing the Natural Gas Lock-In Via Hydrogen Backbones

In those imaginaries, future low-carbon energy would initially extend natural gas, which therefore warrants new infrastructure, state subsidy, and other market incentives. This imaginary was quickly taken up by the European Green Deal. Under that banner, the EC approved new gas pipelines which had been delayed on grounds of climate harm and/or financial unviability.

For many years Wintershall Dea had been developing BlueHyNow, a CCS-hydrogen project at the so-called Wilhelmshaven Energy Hub on the German North Sea coast. In the original plan, the CO_2 generated during production would be captured and then shipped to Norway and Denmark for storage (Pekic, 2022). This long-term plan ultimately justified a large-scale import terminal for liquefied natural gas (LNG). This was granted a regulatory exemption from open market regulations, i.e. authorized to set its own tariffs and thus shape its own market. As a key rationale for this market advantage, the project espoused the aim to produce and import e-methane made from green hydrogen. The project was developed by Tree Energy Solutions, which critics denounced as a "subsidy harvester" (Parks, 2024).

Another contentious case was the Franco-Spanish-Portuguese proposal for a MidCat fossil gas pipeline across Catalonia. Here the hydrogen-readiness of the pipeline was disputed between Spain and France. While Spain anticipated a growing domestic green hydrogen production and favoured a hydrogen line from the start, France was sceptical about hydrogen eventually replacing natural gas. As one expert stated, "France has no plan to undertake this investment because green hydrogen will have a smaller number of consumers because its use is limited and investment in networks for its transport will be difficult to recuperate" (cited in Keeley, 2022). Nevertheless, thanks to the low-carbon imaginary alongside political lobbying, the earlier decision was reversed. The EU allocated enormous budgets to stimulate investment in new gas pipelines including MidCat. In these ways, the policy has funded infrastructure and products which otherwise would have no market or would not exist (Iberian NGOs, 2024).

Alongside the CCUS-hydrogen lobby, expert groups raised the policy stakes for the EU to fulfil its target. A key slogan raised a threat: "no CCUS, no net zero". It was "not possible to wait until the demand develops to build the pipelines and storage required", as an imperative for the EU to create the demand and so stimulate investment (CCUS Forum, 2023, pp. 3, 4). Having invited industry experts to serve as advisors, the Commission soon accepted their advice that the EU must scale up the CCUS value chain through various incentives.

By 2024, the EC had approved ever-more "clean" hydrogen proposals as Projects of Common Interest, making them eligible for faster permits and grants (H Insight, 2024a). From the EU's Innovation Fund, 10 European clean hydrogen projects were among recipients of €4.8bn in grants (H Insight. 2024b). To ensure a CCUS-hydrogen value chain, the lobby further requested support measures for CO_2 storage and a "carbon removals market". This would allow ongoing GHG emissions by purchasing carbon removal credits from "offsetting projects" dependent on CCUS. Moreover, such credits were meant to be included in the EU's Emissions Trading System (CEO, 2024a) as a substitute for the energy system to reduce its own carbon emissions. Accommodating this, the European Commission proposed the Carbon Removal Certification Framework, expanding a market in carbon credits as another substitute (RZE, 2024).

The European Commission also promoted an Industrial Carbon Management Strategy (ICMS) through the ICM Forum, successor to the CCUS Forum. This has proposed various measures to massively scale up CCUS-hydrogen. Likewise, CO_2 transport infrastructure had the aim to create a *single market* for CO_2, alongside technological carbon removals dependent on CCUS. Since 2021, the ICM Forum has promoted agendas similar to the fossil fuel industry (CEO, 2024b; CCUS Forum, 2023).

Such agendas have sought broad acceptance by engaging CSOs, especially through the CCUS Forum. According to its 2023 report on public perception, "...it is crucial to establish the legitimacy of CCUS technology among the public" (cited in CEO, 2024a, p. 17). Mainstream environmental CSOs had been participating in those advisory groups, meanwhile advocating market incentives for green hydrogen. One such group, Transport & Environment, initially sought "to move hydrogen from hype to hope", especially in the fields of aviation and shipping (T&E, 2020). Later, this body became more critical of the hegemonic framework. For example:

> To truly decarbonize transport, we should not use fossil gas to produce hydrogen and other e-fuels. Switching away from oil as transport fuel to use

> fossil gas to produce hydrogen (using technologies like carbon capture and storage) will leave transport dependent on fossil fuels and its infrastructure. (T&E, 2024)

For several decades, environmentalist groups and experts had warned that fossil fuels would become stranded assets, as a self-interested basis for their owners to plan an energy transition. The natural gas lobby strategically inverted the warning to CCUS-hydrogen technology as a saviour. It would become "stranded" unless it gained state support, initially by policies maintaining the asset value of natural gas reserves.

The political contest over the EU's hydrogen imaginary has been played out in national contexts, always involving international forces. Rival agendas have devised sociotechnical-spatial imaginaries espousing an energy transition, as shown in the next two sections. Malta illustrates especially an idealized space, while Germany illustrates a potential spatial transformation of North–South relations.

4 Melita TransGas Pipeline: Malta as an Idealized, Contested Space

Within European Commission strategies, the Mediterranean has been depicted as a leader in the clean hydrogen economy. These idealizations meet frictions when they are set to materialize in real-world places.

In Malta, contested imaginaries of energy transitions are exemplified by rival agendas for decarbonizing the energy system. The oft-cited goal has been to overcome the island state's dependence on oil imports through closer connections with the continental EU energy system, initially through natural gas pipelines. Malta's main source of energy has been heavy fuel oil, so the state-owned company Interconnect Malta, directed by the Energy Ministry, proposed Melita TransGas: a gas pipeline from Sicily that would help to substitute oil by a lower-carbon fuel.

However, the European Green Deal from 2020 prevented the allocation of EU funding to fossil fuel projects, including gas. Funding could now only be spent on electricity projects, including interconnectors and smart grids, as well as infrastructure for potentially *renewable* gases such as biogas, biomethane, and hydrogen. On these grounds the Maltese gas pipeline was originally excluded from funding through the Connecting Europe Facility, both in 2020 and 2021 (Vella, 2021).

But this exclusion ended, once hydrogen was established as a building block of the European Union's energy transition strategy. Under the EU's External Engagement Strategy and REPowerEU Plan (EC), the EU intends to import tens of millions of tonnes of renewable hydrogen into the EU in future years: "Not only can the Mediterranean directly contribute to the production of these molecules, but it is also an ideal transit region for molecules coming from further afield" (cited in Kneebone, 2022).

According to the Malta and Cyprus governments, moreover, the two island states risked energy isolation by, lacking a connection to the trans-European gas network. In 2022, a new list rebranded the Melita TransGas pipeline as a "hydrogen-ready" pipeline, thanks to a derogation from the original rules: the gas pipeline would be built also to flexibly transport hydrogen in the future. The European Commission agreed to allow "blending projects" during a transitional period that ends in 2029. As an extra condition, the European Council declared that such funding will exclude entities connected to fraud, corruption, or conduct related to criminal organizations, a proviso implicitly referring to suspected links between Maltese Electrogas and the 2017 assassination of the journalist Daphne Caruana Galizia (Vella, 2023).

Reinforcing the fossil fuel lobby, the Maltese Government advocated the H-ready pipeline for natural gas from Sicily, alongside an LNG terminal. Both infrastructures supposedly became an imperative to avoid the stated risk of energy isolation. "Without this interconnector, Malta will be locked out of this emerging sector" (Malta Govt, 2022, p. n.p.). According to Melita Transgas, the project would help integrate the gas and future hydrogen market and improve the security of energy supply, given that presently the island depends on LNG supply through shipping (Melita TG, 2022). In effect, the hydrogen promise helped to justify the gas pipeline.

The pipeline initiative provoked opposition on many grounds. Critics upheld that it would lock Malta into a fossil fuel future and signify a climate-incompatible investment, leading to stranded assets, as in the EU overall. The pipeline construction would also impact the seagrass beds of Posidonia oceanica around Delimara. Known as the *lungs of the Mediterranean*, this seagrass can capture up to 15 times as much carbon dioxide as the same area of rainforest (Keeley, 2022). Therefore, it should be protected as a carbon sink and wildlife reserve.

Friends of the Earth (FoE) Malta and the Daphne Caruana Galizia Foundation jointly published an Open Letter highlighting the corrupt politics that led to her assassination. The Open Letter was part of EU-wide actions demanding #PeopleOverPolluters, led by the Fossil Free Politics Coalition. Together they opposed the gas pipeline for undermining Malta's sustainable energy goals, including the EU's proposed shift away from internal combustion engine vehicles towards hybrid and electric vehicles (FoE Malta. 2023a). As Friends of the Earth (FoE) Malta's report further argued, investment in new gas projects diverts funds away from cleaner, renewable energy sources and further locks Malta into a fossil-based energy system. EU funds, therefore, *risk ending up in the pockets of ElectroGas shareholders* (FoE Malta, 2023a, p. n.p.; also 2023b; Vella, 2021, 2023). Moreover, the proposal would underestimate the real GHG emissions of gas usage in Malta. The opposition campaign gave the pipeline many ominous place meanings; it anticipated new links between high-carbon fossil systems, energy dependence, and the island's corporate corruption.

5 Germany's Hydrogen Autobahn: A New Infrastructure With Global North–South Links

In line with the hegemonic CCUS-H imaginary, Germany's 2020 hydrogen strategy had emphasized zero-carbon green hydrogen as crucial for achieving Net Zero. Chancellor Olaf Scholz declared in 2022: "Hydrogen technologies determine the success of the energy transition and thus the entire transformation of our economy towards climate neutrality" (cited in CEO, 2023). Why such an agenda from Germany? As one motive, Germany continued to face high energy prices, impeding industrial investment. As a widespread expert view, "...electricity prices in Germany are unlikely to decline any time soon as the adoption of electric cars and the planned expansion of hydrogen production will significantly increase future electricity demand" (Loch-Temzelides, 2024, p. n.p.). In the hegemonic agenda, parallel remedies combine hydrogen distribution for transforming the industrial base and greater import of supposedly pretended low-carbon energies.

For domestic transportation, a Hydrogen Core Network was devised, largely mirroring existing gas distribution infrastructure. These hydrogen highways (even called a *Hydrogen Autobahn*) would distribute lower-cost energy wherever needed by industrial users (BMWK, 2024a, 2024b). But this grand future soon morphed into a process of several stages, starting with blue hydrogen from natural gas as a first step, which today remains the most plausible endpoint. According to the Ministry, until sufficient green hydrogen is available, there will be a need "to also use low-carbon hydrogen produced from…natural gas in combination with CCS" (BMWK. 2023; cited in CEO, 2023, p. 22).

This positive reference to CCS marks another recent shift in Germany's energy policy: after long-term rejection, the German government in May 2024 approved offshore CO_2 storage and the construction of a carbon pipeline network connecting inland carbon producers with the North Sea storage site. In principle, natural gas plants would also be allowed to use CCUS technologies (BMWK, 2024c). This decision was jointly denounced by several environmental groups. According to WWF Germany, "CO2 capture in power plants requires high initial investments, which are only worthwhile for the operators if they can generate electricity from natural gas in the long term", hence undermining Germany's ambition for an energy transition and incompatible with Germany's climate targets (Klima Allianz, 2024).

The second leg of Germany's hydrogen strategy regards international agreements on importing green hydrogen. Germany has been the strongest advocate of the EU's hydrogen agenda and has been the most active country in seeking agreements for hydrogen sources abroad. According to the then Federal Ministry for Economic Affairs and Climate Action, initial purchase agreements for green hydrogen are "an important step towards transforming Germany as an industrial base, achieving our climate targets and safeguarding sustainable jobs in our country" (BMWK, 2024a, p. n.p.). The Ministry also emphasized the long-term need to import evermore products storing renewable energy, generically known as Power-to-X (PtX), e.g. in gaseous condition or as synthetic liquid fuel. So did the Ministry for Development Cooperation:

> Germany's potential for power production from renewable sources will likely be insufficient. Germany will therefore have to import PtX products on a large scale over the medium to long term. Making such products will offer countries in the Global South a broad range of opportunities for economic development…. (BMZ, 2024)

Germany's Hydrogen Acceleration Act 2023 mandated the speedy construction of new terminals and other port infrastructure to import natural gas. Against this, environmental organizations denounced any plans to import products of fossil fuels, as threatening the energy transition in the exporter countries as well as in Germany (CEW, 2024). Germany's Ministry for Development gave assurances that such energy imports would benefit the exporters through economic diversification, energy security, and job creation. "The production of green hydrogen…provides new opportunities for economic development, especially for developing and emerging economies that have a wealth of renewable energy sources" (BMZ, 2024). The latter phrase implied that such resources could provide a cornucopia, readily available to address local needs in the Global South, if only EU countries help governments there to do so. When Economy Minister Robert Habeck went on a hydrogen mission to Namibia in December 2022, he stated: "The last thing we can accept is a kind of new energy imperialism". Hydrogen exports to Germany should benefit people in Namibia, he emphasized (CEW, 2022; cited in CEO, 2023. p.24).

To realize green hydrogen, large-scale import would require vast tracts of land to generate solar power and new infrastructure for transporting the fuel. Indeed, such plans were emerging by 2023. According to critics:

> German-backed green hydrogen projects abroad follow colonial patterns. Resources are ap-propriated while negative impacts like ecological damage and energy scarcity are conveniently outsourced. Conflicts over land and water use are already becoming apparent and could intensify over the next years. There are also concerns about the livelihoods of fishing communities as a result of mega ports and other export infrastructure, as well as pollution from the waste of the desalination plants that are needed to obtain water for green hydrogen production in arid regions. (CEO, 2023, p. 5)

This policy relegates green hydrogen to a long-term prospect, both in Europe and the Global South. It helps to normalize potentially enormous energy imports from the Global South. But again, this potential reshaping of North–South relations was contested.

6 Critical Civil Society and Alternative Imaginaries

As stated in the previous two sections, national conflicts have international resonances, variously drawing on and shaping EU-wide conflicts around fossil fuel futures. These involve rival imaginaries of sociotechnical-spatial solutions. Industry-critical groups have promoted an alternative imaginary, while seeking to undermine the hegemonic one.

Opposing the European Green Deal, the pan-EU Diem25 party formed a broader coalition, the Green New Deal for Europe (GNDE). According to its report, the EU has a historical obligation to drive the global green transition, but this is undermined by its market-driven policy framework:

> Public-sector roles should link economic aims with a broader vision of environmental justice: decarbonizing Europe's economy, reversing biodiversity loss and tackling inequalities in Europe and around the world. (GNDE, 2019, p. 27)

> Europe's energy systems must be grounded in public investment and ownership across energy generation, transmission, distribution, management and conservation — a vision that is incompatible with the EU's heavily market-driven reform strategy. (GNDE, 2019, p. 62)

As mentioned above, the hegemonic market-driven imaginary resulting in feasible options for blue hydrogen was criticized early on by EU-wide civil society organizations. For example:

> This hydrogen bubble draws oxygen away from important conversations on how to implement the solutions needed for Europe's energy transformation. Energy efficiency, replacing fossil fuels in the power, heating and transport sectors with renewable alternatives, and electrifying as much of our heating and transport as possible. (FoE, 2020, p. n.p.)

> Hydrogen is a hoax that distracts from the real solutions, which include increasing the energy efficiency of buildings (rather than heating homes inefficiently with hydrogen), transitioning to agroecological farming (rather than just greening synthetic fertilizers) and reducing traffic (instead of wasting energy on hydrogen-powered cars). (CEO, 2023, p. 33)

When the industry more specifically advocated policies to create new markets for "the hydrogen value chain", this attracted sarcastic comments: in other words, industry wants the Commission to artificially create markets for a so far non-existent commodity—CO_2—as a feedstock for chemicals, fertilizers, plastics, building materials, and synthetic fuels. This in turn would incentivize the creation of so far non-existent CCUS infrastructure. This folly rests on the back of an even bigger folly, the major shortcoming of Carbon Capture and Utilization (CCU): Captured CO_2 is often released back into the atmosphere at the end of a product's or material's life (CEO, 2023, p. 14).

As opponents warned, the anticipated CCUS-H fix may lock in natural gas, delay a low-carbon transition, and keep energy costs artificially high. Perpetuating natural gas would yield energy insecurity, fuel poverty, stranded assets, corporate capture, sacrificing of human rights, distraction from alternatives, etc. As FoE (2024, p. 6) commented, "...the disconnect between extraction and consumption zones cannot be used as a veil allowing such injustices to happen out of sight and out of mind". Critics demanded incentives and subsidies for renovations and energy efficiency upgrades for better well-being and welfare, coupled with a switch to renewables, while decreasing overall energy consumption (FoE, 2024).

As the broader context of this conflict, Net Zero as a major block in European Green Deal strategies has been increasingly greenwashed and so contested. Arithmetically, it means balancing the GHG released with those removed. By whom or what? Strictly speaking, by a specific activity. Politically speaking, it originally meant credible plans for companies to significantly reduce their own emissions, especially by phasing out fossil fuels; carbon removal could deal with minor residual emissions.

By contrast, however, many companies have been seeking or claiming to offset most emissions by purchasing carbon credits, even within their own value chain (CMW, 2023). And some have been making speculative promises that techno-market incentives would stimulate decarbonization sometime in the future. As a strategic response, many European critics have jointly counterposed an agenda of Real Zero Emissions (RZE, 2024).

7 Conclusion: Hegemonic, Contested Imaginaries of Hydrogen

For several decades the EU has developed a techno-market policy framework, whereby market incentives with R&D subsidies will stimulate technoscientific innovation enabling more efficient resource usage, thus reducing environmental burdens. As a policy concept, market-driven innovation has been framed as a politically neutral pathway towards societal progress. Jointly with the European Commission, industry lobby groups have elaborated specific agendas that maintain their political-economic hegemony. This ostensibly sought to stimulate "advanced biofuels" from non-edible biomass, meant to substitute for oil more sustainably than conventional biofuels. But the mandate helped perpetuate the internal combustion engine; it protected the "investment climate" for techno-innovation rather than the biospheric climate through GHG savings (Levidow 2013, 2023).

An analogous strategy emerged to shape the hegemonic interpretation of the EU's green energy transition. The European green energy framework has undergone tensions and alternations between two core positions, namely: either renewable energy would soon replace fossil fuels. or else fossil fuels would provide a companion to renewables as an eventual destination. The latter frame gained political strength, especially for natural gas as a "transition fuel". EU policy for an energy transition had already been narrowed from sustainable development to energy decarbonization (Morata & Solorio Sandoval, 2013; Haas, 2019). This exemplifies a global strategy of fossil fuel companies transforming themselves into part of the solution: "...they not only hide their ongoing centrality to the fossil economy, but aim to frame and determine the societal response to climate change" (Hanieh, 2024, p. 223).

Transnational energy companies therefore also advocated *grey hydrogen*, crucial for Enhanced Oil Recovery, yet supposedly a step towards lower-carbon blue hydrogen. Critics discredited this agenda for perpetuating an obsolete high-carbon fuel, thus weakening its political support. As a new agenda, resonating with ecological modernization, "clean hydrogen" would enable natural gas to indefinitely complement renewable energy for a green energy transition. According to the hegemonic sociotechnical imaginary, EU policy must create market incentives for Carbon Capture and Storage (CCUS) to produce blue hydrogen from natural gas. Further innovation would eventually produce green, zero-carbon hydrogen from water electrolysis powered by renewable energy, imagined as abundantly available. CCUS as part of smart infrastructures must accompany hydrogen-ready gas pipelines in order to fulfil the market potential.

From 2020 onwards, the fossil fuel industry and EC jointly sponsored new expert advisory bodies elaborating *clean hydrogen* as a feasible, desirable future. Some mainstream environmentalist organizations regularly participated, accommodating and internalizing the hegemonic imaginary, despite any doubts. This future would depend on support measures, especially to incentivize markets for hydrogen supply and CO2 storage. Otherwise, the green energy transition faced the risk of locking out the crucial technological means: "No CCUS, no net zero", the advocates warned. This techno-market framework has reshaped the green energy transition to protect the fossil fuel industry.

Accordingly, by 2023 the European Green Deal was updated by the *Green Deal Industrial Plan* for the Net-Zero Age. This plan has promoted the green transition as "a new industrial revolution aimed at ending the age of fossil fuels", thanks to "clean breakthrough technologies", especially "fossil-free renewable hydrogen"; these technologies would facilitate a "net-zero industrial transformation" (EC, 2023, p. n.p.). In the same period, the EU was approving and subsidizing industry plans for greatly expanding natural gas infrastructure and LNG imports, supposedly crucial for CCUS-hydrogen, as a critical trajectory for decarbonization. To justify support measures for CCUS-hydrogen infrastructure and markets, the hegemonic imaginary initially emphasized the eventual aim to produce green hydrogen. This would go beyond dependence on fossil fuels, even though advocates sought to protect their financial value. But by 2024 the imaginary downplayed or postponed green hydrogen, instead emphasizing decarbonization via blue hydrogen, especially imports from outside the EU. This spatial shift provoked greater dissent from CSOs (civil society organizations) about potential harm in the Global South.

Those hegemonic sociotechnical imaginaries have also featured spatial imaginaries. They have idealized specific infrastructures, places, and their spatial transformations as eventually decarbonizing the energy system. A European Hydrogen Backbone would extend, upgrade, and rename natural gas pipelines as hydrogen-ready. Likewise, hydrogen valleys, corridors, and connectors imagine bringing together places for their mutual benefit, especially through and for technoscientific innovation; otherwise, those places would lose out.

In such ways, the sociotechnical imaginary of clean hydrogen has legitimized policies to create a new market and various pipeline projects with EU funding. It was linked to the spatial imaginary of valleys of low-carbon transitions transforming specific sites and regions, justifying regulatory approval and large investments with state subsidy. As a pattern, valley projects promise new value chains for zero-carbon green hydrogen but facilitate blue hydrogen as the more plausible scenario.

In response, industry-critical CSOs have contested this hegemonic agenda. They have warned that CCUS investment risks locking in natural gas, alongside major energy companies marginalizing renewable energy as a potential competitor. They warn that the hegemonic agenda socializes the risks and privatizes the gains. The EU hydrogen agenda would risk green extractivism continuing to plunder the Global South, appropriating land and resources to benefit multinational companies.

Accordingly, opponents have elaborated alternatives to transform the EU for a socially just decarbonization. They have advocated several measures, such as decommissioning gas infrastructure, expanding renewable energy, strengthening public-sector roles, and reducing energy poverty. New infrastructures should facilitate renewable energy via more flexible systems, demand response, greater storage capacity, and diverse sources using available technologies and their integration across the supply chain. Together such measures should ensure that low-carbon sources truly replace fossil fuels, as means to achieve Net Zero under the European Green Deal. Linking various critical groups, this alternative imaginary provided an EU-wide basis to contest the hegemonic one (FoE, 2024; GNDE, 2019; Iberian NGOs, 2024). The contest has been played out around site-specific spatial imaginaries, conferring place meanings in Malta and Germany, here summarized in turn.

Advocates of new gas infrastructure have promised to save Malta and Cyprus from energy isolation, eventually via clean hydrogen. A "hydrogen-ready" pipeline would help Malta to overcome dependence on oil imports. Opponents have warned that such new infrastructure would degrade the Mediterranean seaweed field as a carbon sink, as well as create dependence on natural gas companies, which have been implicated in murderous corruption. These rival agendas imagine a future Malta as an ideal place for green energy—in highly divergent ways.

Germany has been planning to extend its own domestic distribution through more pipelines, renamed Hydrogen Autobahns, and to access *clean hydrogen* from North Africa and overseas other places. The hegemonic state-industry imaginary has emphasized benefits to supplier countries, whose empty spaces need economic development. This exemplifies a potential spatial transformation of German North–South relations. Opponents warn against such plans as green colonialism, i.e. privatizing land and resources overseas. They counterpose public-sector narratives to link economic aims with environmental justice, e.g. by decarbonizing Europe's economy, reversing biodiversity loss, and overcoming inequalities in the Global South.

In all those ways, the European Green Deal has been a contested agenda for a green energy transition: the hegemonic state–industry partnership has promoted natural gas as a transition fuel. Its expansion and infrastructure would facilitate a low-carbon transition, basing decarbonization on market incentives for future technological means. This has successfully mobilized policy and financial support for its techno-market framework perpetuating natural gas. Beneficent sociotechno-spatial imaginaries have sanitized or obscured the EU's land and resource plunder as a partnership relation. By contrast, opponents have counterposed infrastructure for expanding and integrating renewable energy, while reducing energy consumption. Underlying these rival agendas are sociotechnical-spatial imaginaries of feasible, desirable futures, likewise along divergent lines.

Acknowledgements Helpful comments were received from: Sören Becker (University of Marburg), Pascoe Sabido (Corporate Europe Observatory), and Paul Upham (University of Groningen).

References

BMWK. (2023, February 24). Überarbeiteter Entwurf für die Weiterentwicklung der Nationalen Wasserstoffstrategie (NWS) nach erfolgter Ressortabstimmung (Revised draft for the further development of the National Hydrogen Strategy following interdepartmental coordination). Berlin: Federal Ministry for Economic Affairs and Climate Action (BMWK).

BMWK. (2024a, July 11). Important step for global hydrogen ramp-up: Germany will work with H2Global to import green hydrogen products on a large scale from 2027. Federal Ministry for Economic Affairs and Climate Action (BMWK). https://www.bmwk.de/Redaktion/EN/Pressemitteilungen/2024/07/20240711-h2global.html

BMWK. (2024b). Germany's new Autobahn for green hydrogen. https://www.youtube.com/watch?v=rleGiZRPCwM

BMWK. (2024c). Cabinet clears path for CCS in Germany, 29 May, https://www.bundeswirtschaftsministerium.de/Redaktion/EN/Pressemitteilungen/2024/05/20240529-cabinet-clears-path-for-ccs-in-germany.html

BMZ. (2024). Green hydrogen and power-to-X products – how it works. Berlin: Federal Ministry for Development and Economic Cooperation. https://www.bmz.de/en/issues/green-hydrogen

Carton, W. (2019). 'Fixing' climate change by mortgaging the future: Negative emissions, spatiotemporal fixes, and the political economy of delay. *Antipode, 51*(3), 730–769.

CATF. (2023). A roadmap for the deployment of EU hydrogen valleys, Clean Air Task Force (CATF). https://cdn.catf.us/wp-content/uploads/2023/11/02155931/roadmap-deployment-eu-hydrogen-valleys.pdf

CCUS Forum. (2021). A vision for carbon capture, utilisation and storage in the EU. Clean Air Task Force. Prepared for the European Union, CCUS Forum by the CCUS Vision Working Group.

CCUS Forum. (2023). Towards a European cross-border CO2 transport and storage infrastructure: Recommendations ahead of the EU industrial carbon management strategy; Report of the CCUS Forum Working Group on CO2 infrastructure.https://circabc.europa.eu/ui/group/75b4ad48-262d-455d-997a-7d5b1f4cf69c/library/435ae9cd-1cb6-49a9-9311-f77c21c64d82/details

CEO. (2017). *The great gas lock-in: Industry lobbying behind the EU push for new gas infrastructure.* Corporate Europe Observatory. https://corporateeurope.org/sites/default/files/the_great_gas_lock_in_english_.pdf

CEO. (2020). The hydrogen hype: Gas industry fairy tale or climate horror story? https://corporateeurope.org/en/hydrogen-hy

CEO. (2023). Germany's great hydrogen race: The corporate perpetuation of fossil fuels, energy colonialism and climate disaster. https://corporateeurope.org/sites/default/files/2023-03/Executive%20EN%20summary_Germany%20great%20hydrogen%20race_0.pdf

CEO. (2024a). The Carbon Coup: How corporate capture is locking Europe into a fossil-fuelled future, https://corporateeurope.org/en/carboncoup

CEO. (2024b, October 9). The Carbon Coup revisited: The little-known 'forum' locking Europe into a fossil-fuelled future. https://corporateeurope.org/en/CarbonCoupRevisited

CEW. (2022, December 6). Germany must avoid "energy-imperialism" in hydrogen deal with Namibia. *Clean Energy Wire.* https://www.cleanenergywire.org/news/germany-must-avoid-energy-imperialism-hydrogen-deal-namibia-minister

CEW. (2024, July 24). German govt adopts import strategy for g reen hydrogen. *Clean Energy Wire.* https://www.cleanenergywire.org/news/german-govt-adopts-import-strategy-green-hydrogen

Cloke, J., Mohr, A., & Brown, E. (2017). Imagining renewable energy: Towards a Social Energy Systems approach to community renewable energy projects in the Global South. *Energy Research & Social Science, 31*, 263–272. https://www.sciencedirect.com/science/article/pii/S2214629617301895

CMW. (2023). Zeroing in on Greenwashing: How corporations misuse net zero pledges.https://carbonmarketwatch.org/2023/03/09/zeroing-in-on-greenwashing-how-corporations-misuse-net-zero-pledges/

Deloitte Finance. (2021). Hydrogen4EU. https://www.hydrogen4eu.com/_files/ugd/2c85cf_a3c72fe01d0744959ee03e8472fd2b2e.pdf

DG Clima. (2017). European innovation fund, co-funded by the New Entrants' Reserve (NER) programme of the European Union. Brussels: Commission of the European Communities. https://climate.ec.europa.eu/document/download/ce9a2f0a-d6b7-482b-9b5d-29652b792b0d_en?filename=ner300_factsheet_en.pdf

DG R&I. (2024, June 25). Repowering the EU with hydrogen valleys: Commission presents progress towards a European hydrogen economy. Directorate-General for Research and Innovation. https://research-and-innovation.ec.europa.eu/news/all-research-and-innovation-news/repowering-eu-hydrogen-valleys-commission-presents-progress-towards-european-hydrogen-economy-2024-06-25_en

Dietz, K. (2024). Global energy transitions and green extractivism. In *The geopolitics of green colonialism: Global justice and eco-social transitions* (pp. 27–39). Pluto.

EC. (2019). The European Green Deal, Communication from European Commission COM (2019) 640 final. https://commission.europa.eu/strategy-and-policy/priorities-2019-2024/european-green-deal_en

EC. (2020). A hydrogen strategy for a climate-neutral Europe, COM 301 (2020).

EC. (2022). REPowerEU: A plan to rapidly reduce dependence on Russian fossil fuels and fast forward the green transition. https://ec.europa.eu/commission/presscorner/detail/en/IP_22_3131

EC. (2023). Green deal industrial plan for the net-zero age. https://ec.europa.eu/commission/presscorner/detail/en/ip_23_510

ECA. (2018). Demonstrating carbon capture and storage and innovative renewables at commercial scale in the EU: Intended progress not achieved in the past decade. European Court of Auditors. https://www.eca.europa.eu/Lists/ECADocuments/SR18_24/SR_CCS_EN.pdf

EEA. (2019). European Environment Agency, The European Environment – State and outlook 2020: Executive summary. Publications Office of the European Union, Luxembourg. https://bit.ly/3oGogrk

EHB. (2020). European Hydrogen Backbone. https://ehb.eu/files/downloads/2020_European-Hydrogen-Backbone_Report.pdf

EOG. (2024, April 10). The EU's hydrogen-powered future of Europe unveiled. *Europa Oil & Gas Magazine*. https://energy-oil-gas.com/news/the-eus-hydrogen-powered-future-of-europe-unveiled/

EU. Renewable Energy Directive 2023/2413 amending Directive (EU) 2018/2001. https://eur-lex.europa.eu/legal-content/EN/TXT/PDF/?uri=OJ:L_202302413

FoE. (2020). Why the hydrogen bubble could burst in Europe's face. https://friendsoftheearth.eu/news/why-hydrogen-bubble-burst-europes-face/

FoE. (2024). Shaping a fossil-free future. https://friendsoftheearth.eu/wp-content/uploads/2024/11/Shaping-a-Fossil-Free-Europe_full-briefing.pdf

FoE Malta. (2023a). #NoGasPipeline to Malta! Sign the letter to decision makers. https://foemalta.org/climate-change/nogas/

FoE Malta. (2023b). Fossil-Free Malta: A report on the energy system in Malta, its climate impacts, and a vision for the future. https://foemalta.org/download/climate-report-towards-a-fossil-free-malta/; also https://foemalta.org/download/wur_euw2024_synthesisreport/

Gas for Climate. (2020). Gas decarbonisation pathways 2020 to 2050. https://gasforclimate2050.eu/wp-content/uploads/2023/12/Gas-for-Climate-Gas-Decarbonisation-Pathways-2020-2050.pdf

GNDE. (2019). Blueprint for Europe's just transition: The green new deal for Europe. www.gndforeurope.com

Haas, T. (2019). Struggles in European Union energy politics: A Gramscian perspective on power in energy transitions. *Energy Research & Social Science, 48*, 66–74. https://doi.org/10.1016/j.erss.2018.09.011

Hanieh, A. (2024). *Crude capitalism: Oil, corporate power, and the making of the world market*. Verso.

Howarth, R. W., & Jacobson, M. Z. (2021, August 12). How green is blue hydrogen? *Energy Science & Engineering*. https://doi.org/10.1002/ese3.956

Hydrogen Insight. (2024a, April). EU to fast-track 65 hydrogen projects after signing energy infrastructure list into law. *Hydrogen Insight*. https://www.hydrogeninsight.com/policy/eu-to-fast-track-65-hydrogen-projects-after-signing-energy-infrastructure-list-into-law/2-1-1623079?

Hydrogen Insight. (2024b, October 23). Ten European clean hydrogen projects were among recipients of €4.8bn in grants from EU's innovation fund. *Hydrogen Insight*. https://www.hydrogeninsight.com/production/ten-european-clean-hydrogen-projects-among-recipients-of-4-8bn-in-grants-from-eu-s-innovation-fund/2-1-1728851

Iberian NGOs. (2024). Los peligros del «gasoducto verde» H2Med: ONGs ibéricas se unen y alertan sobre los ries-gos del proyecto H2Med [The dangers behind the "green pipeline" H2Med: Iberian NGOs join forces and raise awareness about the risks of the H2Med project]. https://docs.google.com/document/d/1XEwdI5fpyD_jqLiPov9FzfOJ29M7xkMn/edit

IOGP. (2020). New and old CCS projects in Europe: What's different this time? International Association of Oil & Gas Producers (IOGP), document obtained by Corporate Europe Observatory using freedom of information rules, Ares 2002055, https://www.asktheeu.org/es/alaveteli_pro/info_requests/access_to_documents_related_to_t_2

Jasanoff, S. (2015). Imagined and invented worlds. In S. Jasanoff & S. H. Kim (Eds.), *Dreamscapes of modernity: Sociotechnical imaginaries and the fabrication of power* (pp. 321–342). The University of Chicago Press.

Jasanoff, S., & Kim, S. (2009). Containing the atom: Sociotechnical imaginaries and nuclear power in the United States and South Korea. *Minerva, 47*(2), 119–146.

Keeley, G, (2022, November 4). New pipeline between France and Spain unlikely to solve energy problems, experts say. *Euronews*. https://www.

euronews.com/my-europe/2022/11/04/new-pipeline-between-france-and-spain-unlikely-to-solve-energy-problems-experts-say

Klima Allianz. (2024, May 30). Kein roter Teppich für die fossile Industrie: Einige Mitglieder kritisieren Kohlendioxidspeicherungsgesetz. https://www.klima-allianz.de/mitglieder/detail/kein-roter-teppich-fuer-die-fossile-industrie-ccs

Kneebone, J. (2022). The Mediterranean as a leader in the clean hydrogen economy: Production, transmission, end-use. https://fsr.eui.eu/the-mediterranean-as-a-leader-in-the-clean-hydrogen-economy-production-transmission-end-use/

Levidow, L. (2013). EU criteria for sustainable biofuels: Accounting for carbon, depoliticising plunder. *Geoforum, 44*(1), 211–223. https://doi.org/10.1016/j.geoforum.2012.09.005

Levidow, L. (2023). *Beyond climate fixes: From public protest to system change.* Bristol University Press. https://bristoluniversitypress.co.uk/beyond-climate-fixes

Levidow, L., & Raman, S. (2020). Sociotechnical imaginaries of low-carbon waste-energy futures: UK techno-market fixes displacing public accountability. *Social Studies of Science, 50*(4), 609–641. https://journals.sagepub.com/doi/pdf/10.1177/0306312720905084

Levy, D. L., & Spicer, A. (2013). Contested imaginaries and the cultural political economy of climate change. *Organization, 20*(5), 659–678.

Loch-Temzelides, T. (2024, August 22). So much for German efficiency: A warning for green policy aspirations? https://www.bakerinstitute.org/research/so-much-german-efficiency-warning-green-policy-aspirations

Malm, A., & Carton, W. (2024). *Overshoot: How the world surrendered to climate breakdown.* Pluto.

Malta Govt. (2022). Malta's hydrogen-ready pipeline. https://www.euractiv.com/wp-content/uploads/sites/2/2022/10/mc-Fact-sheet-Melita.pdf

Melita TransGas. (2022). https://melitatransgas.com.mt/

Morata, F., & Solorio Sandoval, I. (2012). *European energy policy: An environmental approach.* Edward Elgar. https://www.researchgate.net/publication/298490018_European_energy_policy_An_Environmental_Approach

Morata, F., & Solorio Sandoval, I. (2013). When 'green' is not always sustainable: The inconvenient truth of the EU energy policy. *Carbon Management, 4*(5), 555–563. https://www.tandfonline.com/doi/full/10.4155/cmt.13.42

Parks, R. (2024, March 28). Hydrogen-derived e-methane import terminal moves a step closer to FID after exemption. *Hydrogen Insight.* https://www.hydrogeninsight.com/policy/hydrogen-derived-e-methane-import-terminal-moves-a-step-closer-to-fid-after-exemption/2-1-1618530

Pekic, S. (2022, August 4). Wintershall Dea and NWO to work on BlueHyNow hydrogen production plant. *Offshore Energy*. https://www.offshore-energy.biz/wintershall-dea-and-nwo-to-work-on-bluehynow-hydrogen-production-plant/

RZE. (2024). Real Zero Europe, https://www.realzeroeurope.org/#our-statement

Szabo, J. (2021). Fossil capitalism's lock-ins: The natural gas-hydrogen nexus. *Capitalism Nature Socialism, 32*(4), 91–110.

T&E. (2020, February 5). Moving hydrogen from hype to hope. Transport & Environment https://www.transportenvironment.org/articles/moving-hydrogen-hype-hope

T&E. (2024, March 13). Batteries vs hydrogen. Transport & Environment. https://www.transportenvironment.org/topics/energy/hydrogen-efuels

Upham, P., & Maristany, P. C. (2025). The global yet local nature of energy imaginaries: The cases of Dutch and Spanish hydrogen valleys. *Energy Research & Social Science, 123*, 104028. https://doi.org/10.1016/j.erss.2025.104028

Vella, M. (2021, June 12). Dalli secures derogation for €400 million gas pipeline to be eligible for EU funding. *Malta Today*. https://www.maltatoday.com.mt/environment/energy/110202/dalli_secures_derogation_for_400_million_gas_pipeline_to_be_eligible_for_eu_funding#.ZDQZhi8Rpaq

Vella, M. (2023). Pipeline cash benefits Yorgen Fenech, NGOs say in petition to decision-makers. *Malta Today*. https://www.maltatoday.com.mt/environment/energy/125700/pipeline_cash_benefits_yorgen_fenech_ngos_say_in_petition_to_decisionmakers

Watkins, J. (2015). Spatial imaginaries research in geography: Synergies, tensions, and new directions: Spatial imaginaries, geography. *Compass, 9*(9), 508–522. https://doi.org/10.1111/gec3.12228

West, K. (2025). How LNG is helping to deliver responsible energy security. World Economic Forum. https://www.weforum.org/stories/2025/01/lng-gas-energy-security/

Zhong, Q. (2024). Impact of renewable resources on economic development in rural areas. *International Journal of Social Sciences and Public Administration, 5*(2), 147–151. https://doi.org/10.62051/ijsspa.v5n2.18

PART II

Digital Promises

CHAPTER 5

Envisioning the Future of Water in the UK: Exploring Digital Water, Its Imaginaries, and Spatial Implications

Christina Walter

1 Introduction

Water, as well as our relationship with it, is being transformed to react to climate change, rising water demand, and quality issues (Sarni, 2020). This transformation coalesces with the increasing implementation of digital technologies in the water sector, comprising both hardware and software. Hardware includes, for example, smart pumps, water meters, and sensors to measure different aspects of water quality. New software solutions process data for monitoring water flows throughout the networks using artificial intelligence (AI) or machine learning, and are able to model and predict water demand in an area. These technological developments are discursively tied to specific visions of the future as "the future of water is digital" (Sarni, 2020). Recent developments in the English water sector promote the application of digital technologies as exemplified in the Strategic Pipeline Alliance (SPA). The Strategic Pipeline Alliance (SPA),

C. Walter (✉)
University of Augsburg, Augsburg, Germany
e-mail: christina.walter@geo.uni-augsburg.de

S. Becker, B. Fladvad (eds.), *Contested Imaginaries of Future Technologies*, https://doi.org/10.1007/978-3-032-11497-6_5

located in the East of England, is one of the biggest water infrastructure projects in the UK and aims to address future water shortages by transporting water from "wetter to drier areas of the region" (Anglian Water, 2023a; Mann, 2020). By realizing this project, pertinent visions of the future have strong implications and effects on the production of space.

With the increasing adoption of digital water technologies, their role in the production of space increases, above all by creating new regions of water exchange and management. In this contribution, I want to sketch out some of these spatial reconfigurations that are constituted through the construction of the Strategic Pipeline Alliance Project. For this chapter, a discourse analysis around the topic of digital water was conducted. It identified technological solutionism and sociotechnical imaginaries as the two central strands of argument (Walter, 2024). On the one hand, there is a prevailing technological solutionism (Morozov, 2013) in the discourse, presenting digital technologies as the only viable solution to challenges within the water sector. On the other hand, sociotechnical imaginaries (Jasanoff, 2015) of the future constitute digital tools of water management as a new technical and economic pathway within the water sector, resulting in positive and optimistic future outlooks for the sector and beyond. I assess these two main lines of argument to critically examine the Strategic Pipeline Alliance project.

At first, the Science and Technology perspective of sociotechnical imaginaries is introduced. This is followed by a section on the concept of technological solutionism and the sociotechnical imaginaries which are deeply embedded within the digital water discourse and its practices. Then, the Strategic Pipeline Alliance project and the infrastructural and spatial implications of the related future visions are highlighted before the main findings are concluded.

2 Sociotechnical Imaginaries of the Future

Claims, promises, and descriptions of possible futures have been studied from the perspective of Science and Technology Studies (STS), among others (e.g., Future Studies). Statements regarding the future are performative as they not only describe what the future may bring, but also how the expectations, visions, and anticipations expressed influence what might happen (Konrad et al., 2017). Narratives about the future legitimize research, policies, or technologies in different sectors and guide the general societal discourse on how the grand challenges of the twenty-first century should be addressed (ibid.). STS has investigated the future from different vantage points such as expectations, visions, and sociotechnical imaginaries. Sociotechnical imaginaries are defined by Jasanoff (2015, p. 4) as:

> collectively held, institutionally stabilized, and publicly performed visions of desirable futures, animated by shared understandings of forms of social life and social order attainable through, and supportive of, advances in science and technology.

These futures are generally rooted in positive visions of progress; thus the term *desirable futures* is often used (Jasanoff, 2015). Studies on sociotechnical imaginaries have, hence, concentrated on how imaginaries legitimize or delegitimize certain future pathways; thus current power relations are deeply embedded within them and modify expectations and visions (Konrad et al., 2017). Multiple imaginaries can simultaneously prevail within a society, either in a productive dialectal relation or in opposition to each other as counter-imaginaries (Jasanoff, 2015). Powerful actors such as courts, institutions, or the media then define or promote the dominant imaginary supporting their position and thus shape the broader societal future discourse (Jasanoff, 2015). Generally, sociotechnical imaginaries need to align with existing cultural norms, values, and structures, as well as with the material infrastructure, and economic and political systems to be implemented successfully (Sadowski & Bendor, 2019). Jasanoff (2015, p. 4) emphasizes that imaginaries "encode not only visions of what is attainable through science and technology, but also of how life ought, or ought not, to be lived; in this respect they express a society's shared understandings of good and evil."

Studying sociotechnical imaginaries reveals the intertwining and complex sociotechnical arrangements between society and technology (Fouché, 2017). Thereby, technology is often considered from two different vantage points. Firstly, how the development of new technologies is influenced by humans, and secondly, how humans are impacted by the development of technologies, e.g., infrastructures, networks, or technological systems (Fouché, 2017). For the case of water infrastructures, Furlong (2010) studied the introduction of water efficiency technologies serving as *mediating technologies* in Canadian water utilities. Furlong (2010, p. 460) defines mediating technologies as "small devices that can be added to an infrastructural network with the intention of modifying its performance (e.g. efficiency technologies)." She showed that the integration of mediating technologies into infrastructure networks leads to shifts in both the sociotechnical and environmental relations within the cities. Thus, digital water technologies such as sensors, digital water meters, pumps, or software solutions can be understood as mediating technologies. Coutard et al. (2005, p. 1) argue that water infrastructures are "well-developed and long-lasting infrastructures" and are therefore one of the least flexible infrastructures. Adopting digital water technologies can alter the relations between the technical network and other actors such as consumers, institutions, or nature within an (urban) water system in planned and unforeseen ways.

3 Technofixes and Technological Solutionism in Digital Water

The critical debate around the concept of the technological fix criticizes the common mindset that social and ecological problems can be solved using technologies (Dickel, 2021). For example, solutions claiming to create a sustainable future through the adoption of digital innovations such as smart metering or remote interactions with virtual technologies are suspected of merely being technological fixes (Dickel, 2021). The term *technological fix* originated as a positively connoted concept of rational problem-solving and was coined by Alvin Weinberg, who characterizes a technological fix as the transformation of a social problem into a technological one. Once the problems are framed technologically, they are easier to define, which in turn also limits the space for solutions, as due to the redefinition only certain technical means are possible to solve the problem (Dickel, 2021; Johnston, 2018).

Since the early 1970s the term *technological fix* has been used more critically (Rosner, 2004). According to Rosner (2004, p. 3), the phrase has since then been "seen as partial, ineffective, unsuccessful, threatening; one-sided as opposed to holistic; mechanical as opposed to ecological." Today, if something is regarded as a technological fix, it typically implies a separation of the domains of technology, nature, and society (Dickel, 2021). In the field of Urban Planning and Architecture, the strong belief in positive outcomes of technological solutions was termed "solutionism" (Murphy, 2012). Solutionism can be defined as the idea that there is a technological fix to every social problem (Morozov, 2013). For Morozov

(2013), the ideology of technological solutionism legitimizes and sanctions actions that presuppose rather than investigate the problems they seek to solve. Technology, as a generalized interpretation and practice of modernity, allows technical applications to appear as solutions to major social problems (Dickel, 2021). Moreover, technological fixes would ensure stability, indicating that it was not necessary for society to change their way of life and individual behavior as technical innovations secured the current mode of existence (Lyons, 2011).

David Harvey (2001), who coined the notion of the *spatial fix*, deliberately aligned it with the idea of the *technological fix*. The *fix*—regardless of whether if it is spatial or technological—is a structural process producing power relations. It temporarily acts as a solution or stabilizer for the observed case, but later generates new problems (Ekers & Prudham, 2017; Svarstad et al., 2018). Importantly, these solutions in technological fixes tend to address the symptoms rather than the social and economic causes of environmental pollution and resource consumption (Dickel, 2021). This is also the case in the field of digital water: while digital technologies (e.g., sensors, AI models, meters) might allow for better knowledge and monitoring of the water quantity in a region, they still do not solve the underlying causes of water scarcity. Rather, they stabilize and conserve the dominant power relations around water provision.

4 Future Imaginaries of Digital Water

Constructions of the future have notably been studied in STS by Jasanoff and Kim (2015) as well as Beckert (2016). Both criticize the prominent notion of path dependency for being historically deterministic, and both argue against individualistic conceptions of imaginaries (Hajer & Pelzer, 2018). Both propose that imaginaries should be analyzed from a performativity perspective and highlight the necessity to investigate the institutional and sociotechnical context or practice from which shared future visions arise (Hajer & Pelzer, 2018). Beckert (2016) examines how imaginaries of shared economic futures are constructed through specific knowledge instruments. He detects that most major social-theoretical concepts apply the concept of path dependency to explain the present from the past (Beckert, 2016). In contrast to the historically deterministic perspective applied by Beckert (2016), Jasanoff and Kim (2015) analyze socio-technological systems, by relating imagination to both wider material and social dimensions, with a strong perspective on "desirable futures" stimulating sociotechnical developments in the present (ibid., p. 2). Imaginaries of the future are also prominently transported within the discourse of digital water, generally linked to a positive outlook for the water sector in general. The implementation of digital technologies, for instance artificial intelligence, is instrumental for this, as "AI has an increasingly important role in the water sector and it is likely to increase in the future"[1] (Guida, 2020). New technologies are seen as the way to improve the water sector and ensure that the sector will be set for the future.

Future imaginaries within the discourse on digital water are not neutral as they convey a modernization trajectory (Anand, 2017; Gupta, 2015; Howe et al., 2015). Modernization trajectories conceptualize the future through notions of innovation, progress, and improvement, presuming the future will imply improvements compared to the present, as the present itself is full of improvements compared to the past (Delanty, 2021; Wagner, 2016). This also solidifies the collective belief in the desirability of technologies and their power to solve our current problems in the future. However, Adloff and Neckel (2019) argue that the future encompasses multiple trajectories and can also be envisioned in another way. Doubt as to what the future may hold for society is expressed in many spheres of our everyday lives (Oomen et al., 2021). This uncertainty is especially common regarding the impending threats of ecological catastrophes and social inequalities (Krznaric, 2019). Thus, future visions of those risks are intertwined in the public imagination along with visions promoting and evaluating specific technologies (Oomen et al., 2021).

This, again, can also be observed in the general discourse on digital water. Salguero (2021) states that "[t]here are many threats ahead for utilities, such as [...] escalating demand for water, [...] due to a growing population; [...] overexploited, finite resources, and inefficient and ageing infrastructures. The only tool that companies can rely on to achieve efficient management is the use of new technologies." This further emphasizes arguments for uncertainty due to global challenges and specific risks in the water sector, with technologies as the way to achieve this desirable vision of the future. The imaginaries conveyed through the discourse on digital water as well as the anticipated establishment of digital water infrastructures result in new forms of power, shaped through standards, rules, and regulations that are institutionalized by technology companies,

[1] Stated by Professor Kapelan in an interview with the International Water Association.

utilities, or other influential actors (Björkman, 2018; Carse & Lewis, 2017; Cousins, 2019; Picon, 2018).

5 Case Study and Methodology

The Strategic Pipeline Alliance aims to secure water supplies for future generations as well as to improve drought resilience in the East of England, achieved by moving water from the "wettest areas in the north of our region to the driest areas in the south and east, where water isn't as easily sourced" (Anglian Water, 2023b).

Construction for the SPA started in the summer of 2021 and the network is expected to be completed by the summer of 2027 (Kanaris, 2024; Pashby, 2024). However, the end date of the project has been delayed multiple times due to the pandemic, the 2023/2024 winter turning out to be the wettest on record, as well as steel supply issues (Anglian Water, 2024; Pashby, 2024). Within the SPA project, 330 km of pipeline are being built, stretching from North Lincolnshire to Essex in the south, with pumping stations and storage reservoirs throughout the region. This network will be accompanied and monitored by a digital twin (Anglian Water, 2024; Anglian Water Services, 2025; Gregor & Stirland, 2019; Gregory, 2022). Figure 5.1 shows the route of the pipeline in the East of England as well as the pumping stations and water storage tanks. After completion, the SPA is expected to address a water shortage of 30 million liters a day, estimated for the East of England in the future (Chambers, 2021). James Crompton, the SPA director for Anglian Water, argues that "[t]he strategic pipeline is vital in addressing the predicted *jaws of death* moment for water availability in the East of England – the point at which demand for water greatly outstrips the available supply" (Taylor, 2022). Due to population growth in the region, this prediction could prove true as soon as 2030 without the SPA project (Anglian Water, 2023c).

The discourse analysis conducted examined 89 web texts from international websites[2] specifically targeted toward professionals working in the water sector or related sectors such as infrastructure provision or civil engineering. As keywords, *digital water*, *digitalization of water*, *digitalization of the water sector*, *digitalization of the water industry*, and *AI for water* were used to find suitable texts. The selected texts were coded and

[2] Such as aquatechtrade.com, iwa-network.org, smartwatermagazine.com, or waterworld.com

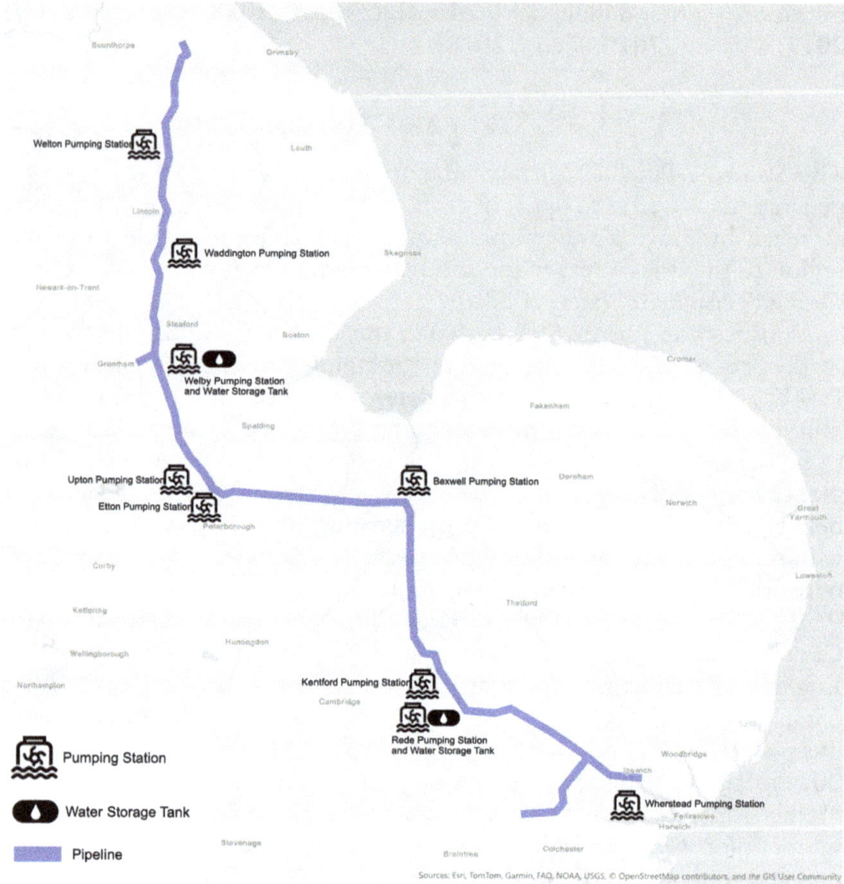

Fig. 5.1 Map of the Anglian Waters Strategic Pipeline project. Source: Author's own representation according to Anglian Water, 2024

analyzed to gain insights into the topics, the argumentative and narrative structure, as well as the typical linguistic terms utilized within.[3] The discourse analysis around the topic of digital water identified technological solutionism and sociotechnical imaginaries as the two central strands of

[3] For more information on the discourse analysis of digital water, see the 2024 publication "Digital Technologies for the Future of the Water Sector? Examining the Discourse on Digital Water" published in Geoforum 148, 103918.

argument (Walter, 2024), as presented in the previous sections. These two strands of the discourse were critically examined and applied to the Strategic Pipeline Alliance (SPA) case study, which consisted of an analysis of the SPA's promotional materials, and online posts, as well as expert interviews with SPA stakeholders, to reveal the spatial implications that can unfold from visions enmeshed in large-scale infrastructure projects.

6 Solutionism and Spatial Fixes in SPA

Solutionist thinking is prevalent in the discourse around the SPA project, establishing an infrastructure network the success of which "is fundamental to supplying free flowing water throughout the region, making us more resilient to risks of drought" (Anglian Water, 2023b). Here, the pipeline project is being directly linked as a solution to address the looming future threats of drought in the East of England. It is portrayed that the future challenge of drought or water shortages in the region will be solved or at least reduced, as the SPA "is one of the largest infrastructure projects in Europe [...] [and] will help tackle future water shortages" (Anglian Water, 2023b).This will be supported by the introduction of "cutting-edge digital infrastructure — a digital twin — which will mirror the physical infrastructure, providing real-time data to drive insight, helping us to monitor and optimize the Anglian Water network" (Anglian Water, 2022, p. 13). In framing infrastructures and digital technologies as the only solution to current and/or future water challenges, the discourse consolidates techno-optimist positions, rendering alternative solutions or ways to overcome them more difficult to implement or even think about. Through these statements, technology is, on the one hand, directly associated with a socio-natural phenomenon (e.g., the hydrosocial nature of water), while, on the other, it is understood as the only solution to current natural and social problems (e.g., climate change, increasing water demand). Therefore, this solutionist thinking entails a depoliticizing element. Popartan et al. (2022, p. 7) argue that the introduction of AI decision-making algorithms in the water sector "may consolidate the already reductionist and depoliticized water governance perspective that is dominant nowadays." It is important to understand that managing water is not just a technical field, concerned with the provision of water infrastructure, but also a political field as it entails human values, behaviors, and organizations.

When completed, it can be argued that the SPA project will represent a new spatial fix (Harvey, 2001), connecting regions of different water availability with each other. Anglian Water (2023a) states that "the pipeline will allow us to move water from areas of surplus to areas in deficit," resulting in pumping water from the North to the South, as the northern part of the region is generally wetter than the South. Additionally, licenses issued by the Environment Agency regulate water abstraction to make sure not to over-abstract from groundwater bodies. Thus, Anglian Water "must reduce the amount of water [they] take from sensitive areas like chalk streams in the south and east of [their] region" (Anglian Water, 2024). This further increases the dependence of the southern region on the North. Furthermore, storage reservoirs—holding around 20 million liters of water—will be built to ensure continuous water flow and supply for the growing region, without imposing drastic behavior changes regarding water use by the local population (Anglian Water Services, 2025).

7 Infrastructural and Spatial Implications of the SPA's Future Vision

Visions of the future are materialized through large-scale infrastructure projects. New infrastructures are considered as "future proof" by their designers (Edwards et al., 2009, p. 371) as well as "promises made in the present about our future" (Appel et al., 2018, p. 27). Therefore, infrastructures are the material manifestation of future visions and anticipations (Cousins, 2019; Howe et al., 2015; Larkin, 2018). Visions of water futures are created and distributed through the discourse around digital water, constructing a dominant trajectory for advancing the water sector. According to Delanty (2021, p. 2), the future can be seen as the "product of the present and the choices made in the present"; thus "the future is now". Within the SPA project, this path is apparent in statements such as "Future proofing our water supplies" (Anglian Water, 2023b). The way to achieve this future is through implementing digital technologies—in the case of the SPA, it is the digital twin that combines hardware and software and is seen as a powerful tool to monitor and manage water transfers throughout the region when and where needed.

At the same time, infrastructures preserve the social and cultural settings of the time they were first created and are thus always historically rooted (Howe et al., 2015). This applies not only to building infrastructures but likewise to "more liquid-like channels of infrastructures [such as] digital flows [...] as technology and demands for data [...] ebb and flow" (Howe et al., 2015, p. 8). Today, code is everywhere; thus Kitchin and Dodge (2014) introduced the concept of code/space where software and the spatiality of everyday life co-constitute each other. Ash et al. (2016) argue that this results in the blending of space and code. Technological processes link the digital and physical spaces and their relations (Maciej, 2024). In the following, two spatial implications are discussed, (1) the establishment of new physical water infrastructures and (2) the creation of digital spaces and their spatial impacts.

(1) Physical water infrastructures—especially pipes—often go unnoticed, as they are buried underground and not visible on a daily basis. Only if a disruption, such as leaks or pipe bursts, occurs and maintenance is needed do their existence and importance for our everyday lives become apparent. In the case of the SPA project, a new pipeline is being built and during this process, the infrastructure is visible, until it will (mostly) become *invisible* again after completion. While the pipeline itself will be completely underground, the pumping stations will be visible overground. The SPA project is envisioned as a *spine* holding together the region and leaving "a green and social legacy" (Anglian Water, 2024). The pipeline itself is made from a mix of steel pipes and polyethylene pipes, catering to different expected volumes and water pressures. While steel pipes are used in the northern section between Elsham and Peterborough, the smaller polyethylene pipes are installed in the southern section (Kanaris, 2024). As the construction process disrupts natural spaces and often occurs close to local communities, Anglian Water openly communicates about the project and its importance for the overall vision of a water-secure future. To reach this goal, Anglian Water is engaging its pipeline workers in various community projects. As part of these, Anglian Water has "donated more than 2,500 books to primary schools and proactively work[ed] with children on literacy development, planted thousands of trees to boost biodiversity, built special *commuter* fences to help bats with their navigation and donated life-saving defibrillators to communities" (Anglian Water, 2024) throughout the region. They also made sure that the projects were communicated in a positive way to convey a positive water future and build trust in the project to solve future drought issues in the region. Therefore, these community projects are mainly carried out in close spatial proximity to the current building sites.

(2) The digital technologies employed create new digital spaces—physically residing in data centers located around the globe—in which the

monitoring and decision-making processes take place (Data Centers World Map, 2025). The vast amounts of data collected are stored in *the cloud*. This allows remote and *real-time* access to the data (Mackenzie, 1997, 2007).[4] However, cloud computing relies on infrastructures such as data centers, cables, as well as energy and water infrastructure and so much more. Wiig (2013, p. 22) demonstrates that while "[T]he last leg of the infrastructural support is wireless and immaterial [...] the rest of the system exists as distinct spaces of network equipment embedded within the landscape." The material infrastructure of the cloud is located in spaces with distinct characteristics which provide "particular political, historical, and geographical conditions"; these include, for instance, energy, a suitable climate, water, fiber optic connections, tax breaks, and security (Pickren, 2018, p. 231). The need for vast amounts of energy and water clearly illustrates the extractive and resource-intensive nature of the data industry and highlights that "computing and data are far from *virtual* and immaterial" (Pickren, 2018, p. 236).

This material dimension of cloud infrastructures is often forgotten as the resulting environmental impacts are spatially distanced from the location of the end-user and the resource "flows hidden at the point of consumption" (Monserrate, 2022, pp. 3–4; Pickren, 2018, pp. 226, 236). Thus, the digital infrastructure is largely invisible, and this invisibility is central to normalizing or *black-boxing* the sociotechnical system (Pickren, 2018, p. 229). Black-boxing is defined by Hinchliffe (1996, p. 665) as a "(temporary) stability, so much so that the controversies surrounding their adoption have to a large extent been erased." The connection between invisibility and normalization is particularly true for digital technologies as their algorithms and codes operate behind the screens while the material domain is masked by intangible metaphors such as *the cloud* (Pickren, 2018, p. 229). Therefore, digital infrastructures like other infrastructures play a crucial role in shaping possible futures through path-dependencies (Jackson et al., 2007; Pickren, 2018, pp. 229–230). Turnbull et al. (2022, p. 10) argue that examining digital technologies through a *material lens* allows for the inclusion of the immense material

[4] Mackenzie (1997, 2007) considered "real-time" as a temporal condition that is fabricated, as computational operations take time to process the data. This "machine time" can be divided into "seek time, run time, read time, access time, available time, real time, polynomial time, time division, time slicing, time sharing, time complexity, write time, processor time, hold time, execution time, compilation time, and cycle time" (Mackenzie, 2007, pp. 89–90). See also Kitchin (2017) on the realtimeness of smart cities.

infrastructures of digital devices, providing the material basis for digitization, and unveiling the extractive economies they rely on (Kuntsman & Rattle, 2019). As a consequence, "... the promise of digital technologies for environmentally-positive futures is debatable" (Turnbull et al., 2022, pp. 10). This shows, for instance, that the SPA project should not only consider the local effects but also the global effects that are hidden behind the screens and sensors and make the digital twin model possible in the first place.

This becomes even clearer when targeting water use in data centers to cool the server racks more efficiently and reduce the carbon footprint in comparison to air cooling (Monserrate, 2022, pp. 9–10). Needless to say, global climate change increases the average global temperature and also the uncertainty about water resources. In response to the growing awareness of data center impact on water-scarce communities like Mesa and Bluffdale in the Western United States, companies like Google have promised to become "water positive by 2030" and "replenish 120 percent"[5] of the water used in their facilities and offices (Brandt, 2021; Monserrate, 2022, p. 10).

Yet, the water consumption of data centers does not align well with the SPA vision that digital technologies are introduced to "combat the risk of shortages, boosting resilience and securing water supplies" as the focus is only on their own supply region (Anglian Water, 2024). However, the consequences for communities and water bodies close to data centers are not accounted for. This creates a spatial divide between the location where the data is sourced (UK) and where it is processed (data center). This divide is only bridged through the virtual space, which connects those places through the digital infrastructure. However, due to the volatile nature of *the cloud*, the SPA team doesn't know where in the world their data is stored and processed, as the data infrastructure is provided by Microsoft's cloud-based software Azure (Costain, 2021). This further detaches the environmental and spatial implications of the data center sites, where the virtual spaces for monitoring, augmenting, and analyzing water availability in the East of England are located, from the region itself.

[5] According to Googles Chief Sustainability Officer Kate Brand (2021), this is achieved by "enhancing our stewardship of water resources across Google office campuses and data centers, replenishing our water use and improving watershed health and ecosystems in water-stressed communities; sharing technology and tools that help everyone predict, prevent and recover from water stress."

8 Conclusion

This chapter discussed the spatial implications of the Strategic Pipeline Alliance Project in the East of England. The SPA envisions a drought-secure future achieved through the implementation of digital water technologies as part of their new water infrastructure—a 330 km pipeline transporting water through the region (Anglian Water Services, 2025). Based on the discourse analysis around the topic of digital water, technological solutionism and sociotechnical imaginaries were identified as the two main lines of argument (Walter, 2024). These are also visible in the SPA project. Solutionist thinking is noticeable as the pipeline project is conveyed as the solution to address the looming threats of future drought in the East of England, while sociotechnical imaginaries of the future are illustrated through the implementation of digital technologies such as the digital twin, which aims to secure the region's water supply by transferring water from areas of surplus to those with shortages. Thus, the application of digital technologies as seen through the SPA promotes visions of a drought-free future and has implications for the production of space. The vision conveyed by the SPA creates new hybrid spaces between the physical and digital. Visions and projections of the (near) future are understood as a necessity within the project as potential water shortages need to be known in advance to enable water transport along the pipeline. So, imaginaries and projections of the (near) future are seen as essential to prevent drought conditions in the East of England.

Future visions and technological solutionism in the SPA project become spatially manifest through the establishment of new water infrastructures and virtually, through the creation of digital spaces. The SPA project is envisioned as the spine of the region. While the pipeline itself will be completely underground after construction is finished, the pumping stations will be visible, both spatially fixing this vision of a water-secure future which is achieved through digital technologies—like the digital twin which is intended to "provid[e] real-time data to drive insight[s], helping [...] to monitor and optimise the Anglian Water network" (Anglian Water, 2022, p. 13). To ensure that the vision of a water-secure future also reaches the residents and to build trust in Anglian Water as a reliable water provider in the future, community projects are carried out near current construction sites. Due to the digital technologies involved, new digital spaces are created which also have distinct spatial impacts (e.g., water and energy consumption). These digital spaces reside around the globe, existing in data centers and operating through codes and algorithms. As these digital spaces created for monitoring and data analysis also rely on material infrastructures with consequences for physical spaces, the SPA project should not only be considered regarding its local effects, but in terms of externalized spatial effects caused by the digital processes in the data centers. The pipeline and the digital twin are currently under construction, and at the same time, the visions of a water-secure future are established in space. The new relations forming between physical and virtual spaces, as well as among diverse stakeholders, will only manifest once the project is finished. Thus, further investigation of the spatial consequences emerging in the physical as well as the digital space is needed in the future.

Acknowledgments Thank you to Sören Becker and Benno Fladvad for your insightful comments and for inviting me to contribute to this book project, as well as to Tabea Bork-Hüffer and Jacqueline Kowalski for your valuable feedback on an earlier version of this chapter.

Parts of this chapter have previously been published in the article "Digital Technologies for the Future of the Water Sector? Examining the Discourse on Digital Water" published in 2024 by Geoforum in Volume 148, 103918. DOI: https://doi.org/10.1016/j.geoforum.2023.103918

References

Adloff, F., & Neckel, S. (2019). Futures of sustainability as modernization, transformation, and control: A conceptual framework. *Sustainability Science, 14*, 1015–1125.

Anand, N. (2017). *Hydraulic City: Water and the infrastructure of citizenship in Mumbai*. Duke University Press.

Anglian Water. (2022). *Anglian Water's five-point plan for innovation acceleration. How we're dressing tomorrow's challenges today.*

Anglian Water. (2023a). *Our strategic pipelines*. Anglian Water. Retrieved September 6, 2023, from https://www.anglianwater.co.uk/about-us/our-strategies-and-plans/new-water-pipelines/

Anglian Water. (2023b). *Strategic Pipeline Alliance*. Anglian Water. Retrieved September 6, 2023, from https://www.anglianwater.co.uk/environment/investing-in-the-future-of-water/strategic-pipeline-alliance/

Anglian Water. (2023c). *Huge new water main network opens new pipelaying front*. Anglian Water. Retrieved September 6, 2023, from https://www.anglianwater.co.uk/news/pipelaying-has-started-on-another-section-of-anglian-waters-huge-new-multi-million-pound-water-main-network/

Anglian Water. (2024). *Our strategic pipelines.* Retrieved September 18, 2024, from https://www.anglianwater.co.uk/corporate/strategies-and-plans/new-water-pipelines/

Anglian Water Services. (2025). *Strategic Pipeline Linkedin update.* Retrieved April 2, 2025, from https://www.linkedin.com/posts/anglianwater_our-strategic-pipeline-activity-7310598938766499842-DT63?utm_source=share&utm_medium=member_desktop&rcm=ACoAAEFZfggBKlAXV9CHn-5uWeVnRBuxtUgT-Io

Appel, H., Anand, N., & Gupta, A. (2018). Introduction: Temporality, politics, and the promise of infrastructure. In N. Anand, A. Gupta, & H. Appel (Eds.), *The promise of Infrastructure* (1st ed., pp. 1–38). Duke University Press.

Ash, J., Kitchin, R., & Leszczynski, A. (2016). Digital turn, digital geographies? *Progress in Human Geography, 42*(1), 25–43. https://doi.org/10.1177/0309132516664800

Beckert, J. (2016). *Imagined futures: Fictional expectations and capitalist dynamics.* Harvard University Press.

Björkman, L. (2018). The engineer and the plumber: Mediating Mumbai's conflicting infrastructural imaginaries. *International Journal of Urban and Regional Research, 42*(2), 276–294.

Brandt K. (2021). *Our commitment to water stewardship.* Google. https://blog.google/outreach-initiatives/sustainability/replenishing-water/

Carse, A., & Lewis, J. A. (2017). Toward a political ecology of infrastructure stan dards: Or, how to think about ships, waterways, sediment, and communities together. *Environment and Planning A, 49*(1), 9–28.

Chambers, S. (2021, July 7) work on massive water pipeline from north to east begins. *East Anglian Daily Times.* https://www.eadt.co.uk/news/21276642.work-massive-water-pipeline-north-east-begins/

Costain. (2021). *Strategic Pipeline Alliance, digital twin project.* Retrieved April 8, 2025, from https://www.costain.com/insights/2021/strategic-pipeline-alliance-digital-twin-project/

Cousins, J. J. (2019). Malleable infrastructures: Crisis and the engineering of political ecologies in Southern California. *Environment and Planning E: Nature and Space, 3*(3), 927–949. https://doi.org/10.1177/2514848619893208

Coutard, O., Hanley, R. E., & Zimmerman, R. (2005). Network systems revisited: The confounding nature of universal systems. In O. Coutard, R. E. Hanley, & R. Zimmerman (Eds.), *Sustaining urban networks: The social diffusion of large technical systems* (pp. 1–12). Routledge.

Data Centers World Map. (2025). World Map of Data Centers. Retrieved April 8, 2025, from https://map.datacente.rs

Delanty, G. (2021). Futures of sustainability: Perspectives on social imaginaries and social transformation. A comment on frank Adloff and Sighard Neckel's research program. *Social Science Information, 60*(2), 285–294. https://doi.org/10.1177/0539018421999562

Dickel, S. (2021). Der „Technological Fix". Zur Kritik einer kritischen Semantik. In SONA-Netzwerk Soziologie der Nachhaltigkeit (Ed.), *Soziologie der Nachhaltigkeit* (pp. 271–284). Transcript.

Edwards, P., Jackson, S., Bowker, G., & Williams, R. (2009). Introduction: An agenda for infrastructure studies. *Journal of the Association for Information Systems, 10*(5), 364–374.

Ekers, M., & Prudham, S. (2017). The metabolism of socioecological fixes: Capital switching, spatial fixes, and the production of nature. *Annals of the American Association of Geographers, 107*(6), 1370–1388. https://doi.org/10.1080/24694452.2017.1309962

Fouché, R. (2017). Sociotechnological (Re-)configurations. In U. Felt, R. Fouché, C. A. Miller, & L. Smith- Doerr (Eds.), *The handbook of science and technology studies* (4th ed., pp. 495–500). Massachusetts Institute of Technology.

Furlong, K. (2010). Small technologies, big change: Rethinking infrastructure through STS and geography. *Progress in Human Geography, 35*(4), 460–482. https://doi.org/10.1177/0309132510380488

Gregor, G., & Stirland, R. (2019). *BIM4Water case study template. Strategic pipeline Alliance (SPA) pipeline and digital twin—SPA initiation case study (SPA1).* (version 2.2, 19/2/19). BIM4Water. https://cdn.ymaws.com/www.british-water.co.uk/resource/resmgr/bim4water/case_studies/bim4water_case_study_anglian_1.pdf

Gregory G. (2022, February 25). *Anglian Water's strategic pipeline Alliance (SPA) - the use of GIS in the common data environment for the digital twin.* Digital Twin Hub. Retrieved September 9, 2024, from https://digitaltwinhub.co.uk/anglian-waters-strategic-pipeline-alliance-spa-the-use-of-gis-in-the-common-data-environment-for-the-digital-twin/

Guida, S. (2020, August 7). *AI solutions for the Water sector: Interview with prof. Zoran Kapelan.* International Water Association. Retrieved June 10, 2023, from https://iwa-network.org/ai-solutions-for-the-water-sector-interview-with-prof-zoran-kapelan/

Gupta, A. (2015, September 24). *Suspension. The infrastructure toolbox. Society for cultural anthropology.* Retrieved June 9, 2023, from https://culanth.org/fieldsights/suspension

Hajer, M. A., & Pelzer, P. (2018). 2050—An energetic odyssey: Understanding "techniques of Futuring" in the transition towards renewable energy. *Energy Research & Social Science, 44*, 222–231. https://doi.org/10.1016/j.erss.2018.01.013

Harvey, D. (2001). Globalization and the "spatial fix". *Geographische Revue, 3*(2), 23–30.
Hinchliffe, S. (1996). Technology, power, and space-the means and ends of geographies of technology. *Environment and Planning D, 14*, 659–682.
Howe, C., Lockrem, J., Appel, H., Hackett, E., Boyer, D., Hall, R., Schneider-Mayerson, M., Pope, A., Gupta, A., Rodwell, E., Ballestero, A., Durbin, T., el-Dahdah, F., Long, E., & Mody, C. (2015). Paradoxical infrastructures: Ruins, retrofit, and risk. *Science, Technology, & Human Values, 41*(3), 547–565.
Jackson, S., Edwards, P., Bowker, G., & Knobel, C. (2007). Understanding infrastructure: History, heuristics and cyberinfrastructure policy. *First Monday, 12*(6). https://doi.org/10.5210/fm.v12i6.1904
Jasanoff, S. (2015). Future imperfect: Science, technology, and the imaginations of modernity. In S. Jasanoff & S. H. Kim (Eds.), *Dreamscapes of modernity: Sociotechnical imaginaries and the fabrication of power* (pp. 1–33). University of Chicago Press.
Jasanoff, S., & Kim, S. H. (2015). *Dreamscapes of modernity: Sociotechnical imaginaries and the fabrication of power*. University of Chicago Press.
Johnston, S. F. (2018). Alvin Weinberg and the promotion of the technological fix. *Technology and Culture, 59*(3), 620–651.
Kanaris S. (2024). *How Anglian Water's Strategic Pipeline Alliance partners drastically cut cost and carbon*. Retrieved April 8, 2025, from https://www.newcivilengineer.com/in-depth/how-anglian-waters-strategic-pipeline-alliance-partners-drastically-cut-cost-and-carbon-02-05-2024/
Kitchin, R. (2017). The Realtimeness of Smart Cities. *Technoscienzia Italian Journal of Science & Technology Studies, 8*(2), 19–41.
Kitchin, R., & Dodge, M. (2014). *Code/space: Software and everyday life*. MIT Press.
Konrad, K., van Lente, H., Groves, C., & Selin, C. (2017). Performing and governing the future in science and technology. In U. Felt, R. Fouché, C. A. Miller, & L. Smith-Doerr (Eds.), *The handbook of science and technology studies* (4th ed., pp. 465–494). Massachusetts Institute of Technology.
Krznaric, R. (2019, March 19). *Why we need to reinvent democracy for the long-term*. BBC. https://www.bbc.com/future/article/20190318-can-we-reinvent-democracy-for-the-long-term
Kuntsman, A., & Rattle I. (2019). Towards a paradigmatic shift in sustainability studies: A systematic review of peer reviewed literature and future agenda setting to consider environmental (un)sustainability of digital communication. *Environmental Communication, 13*(5), 567–581. https://www.researchgate.net/deref/https://doi.org/10.1080/17524032.2019.1596144?_tp=eyJjb250ZXh0Ijp7ImZpcnN0UGFnZSI6InB1YmxpY2F0aW9uIiwicGFnZSI6InB1YmxpY2F0aW9uIn19

Larkin, B. (2018). Promising forms: The political aesthetics of infrastructure. In N. Anand, A. Gupta, & H. Appel (Eds.), *The promise of infrastructure* (pp. 175–222). Duke University Press.

Lyons, G. (2011). Technology fix versus behaviour change. In M. Grieco & J. Urry (Eds.), *Mobilities: New perspectives on transport and society* (pp. 159–177). Ashgate.

Maciej, G. (2024). Human–place–technology relations in the digital placemaking process. *Geoforum, 149*, 103950. https://doi.org/10.1016/j.geoforum.2024.103950

Mackenzie, A. (1997). The Mortality of the Virtual Real-Time, Archive and Dead-time in Information Networks. *Convergence: the International Journal of Research into New Media Technologies, 3*(2), 59–71.

Mackenzie, A. (2007). Protocols and the Irreducible Traces of Embodiment: The Viterbi Algorithm and the Mosaic of Machine Time. In R. Hassan, & R. Purser (Eds.), *24/7: Time and Temporality in the Network Society.* (pp. 89–107). Stanford University Press.

Mann, G. (2020, June 29). *Anglian Water forms new strategic pipeline alliance.* Smart Water magazine. https://smartwatermagazine.com/blogs/graham-mann/anglian-water-forms-new-strategic-pipeline-alliance

Monserrate, S. G. (2022, Winter). *The cloud is material: On the environmental impacts of computation and data storage.* MIT Case Studies in Social and Ethical Responsibilities of Computing. https://doi.org/10.21428/2c646de5.031d4553

Morozov, E. (2013). *To save everything, Click here. The folly of technological solutions.* PublicAffaris.

Murphy, D. (2012). *The architecture of failure.* Zero Books.

Oomen, J., Hoffman, J., & Hajer, M. A. (2021). Techniques of futuring: On how imagined futures become socially performative. *European Journal of Social Theory*, 1–19. https://doi.org/10.1177/1368431020988826

Pashby, T. (2024). *Anglian Water's 'most important' infrastructure project partly halted until 2027.* Retrieved April 8, 2025, from https://www.newcivilengineer.com/latest/anglian-waters-most-important-infrastructure-project-halted-until-2027-13-11-2024/

Pickren, G. (2018). 'The global assemblage of digital flow': Critical data studies and the infrastructures of computing. *Progress in Human Geography, 42*(2), 225–243. https://doi.org/10.1177/0309132516673241

Picon, A. (2018). Urban infrastructure, imagination and politics: From the networked metropolis to the smart city. *International Journal of Urban and Regional Research, 42*(2), 263–275.

Popartan, L. A., Cortés, À., Garrido-Baserba, M., Verdaguer, M., Poch, M., & Gibert, K. (2022). The digital revolution in the urban Water cycle and its ethical-political implications: A critical perspective. *Applied Sciences, 12*(5), 2511. https://doi.org/10.3390/app12052511

Rosner, L. (2004). *The technological fix: How people use technology to create and solve problems*. Routledge.

Sadowski, J., & Bendor, R. (2019). Selling smartness: Corporate narratives and the Smart City as a sociotechnical imaginary. *Science, Technology & Human Values, 44*(3), 540–563. https://doi.org/10.1177/0162243918806061

Salguero, F. J. (2021, March 5). *What's next in the digital transformation of the water industry?*. Retrieved December 9, 2023, from https://www.idrica.com/blog/digital-transformation-of-the-water-industry/

Sarni, W. (2020). The future of water is digital. *The Solutions Journal, 11*(2). Retrieved September 12, 2025, from https://thesolutionsjournal.com/future-water-digital/

Svarstad, H., Benjaminsen, T. A., & Overå, R. (2018). Power theories in political ecology. *Journal of Political Ecology, 25*(1), 350–363.

Taylor, M. (2022, February 15) *Anglian Water marks halfway point in new Lincoln to Grantham pipeline and submits planning applications for next stage of work*. LincsOnline. https://www.granthamjournal.co.uk/news/construction-of-major-water-pipeline-reaches-halfway-point-9240238/

Turnbull, J., Searle, A., Hartman Davies, O., Dodsworth, J., Chasseray-Peraldi, P., von Essen, E., & Anderson-Elliott, H. (2022). Digital ecologies: Materialities, encounters, governance. *Progress in Environmental Geography, 2*(1–2), 3–32. https://doi.org/10.1177/27539687221145698

Wagner, P. (2016). *Progress: A reconstruction*. Polity.

Walter, C. (2024). Digital technologies for the future of the water sector? Examining the discourse on digital water. *Geoforum, 148*, 103918. https://doi.org/10.1016/j.geoforum.2023.103918

Wiig, A. (2013). Everyday landmarks of networked urbanism: Cellular antenna sites and the infrastructure of Mobile communication in Philadelphia. *Journal of Urban Technology, 20*(3), 21–37. https://doi.org/10.1080/01446193.2013.823051

CHAPTER 6

Towards Inclusionary Future Imaginaries: Extended Reality Technologies (XR) for Marginalized Groups

Jacqueline Kowalski and Tabea Bork-Hüffer

1 Introduction

A plethora of academic, governmental and non-governmental reports have evaluated the impact of digital technologies on social, economic, digital and cultural divides (cf. D4S, 2022; Iddri et al., 2018; WBGU, 2019). These reports consistently highlight that current technological developments are deepening these divides rather than mitigating them. They warn of the dominance of few large Big Tech companies, democracy being undermined and the exacerbation of existing inequalities (Bjola & Papadakis, 2020; van Dijk, 2020; WBGU, 2019). As scholars in digital geography have argued, rather than unfolding as a single global transition, we are witnessing digitalization as "an ongoing series of molecular digital

J. Kowalski (✉)
University of Innsbruck, Innsbruck, Austria
e-mail: jacqueline.kowalski@uibk.ac.at

T. Bork-Hüffer
Heidelberg University, Heidelberg, Germany
e-mail: tabea.bork-hueffer@uni-heidelberg.de

S. Becker, B. Fladvad (eds.), *Contested Imaginaries of Future Technologies*, https://doi.org/10.1007/978-3-032-11497-6_6

revolutions that continue to enact changes in heterogeneous ways across differentiated geographies" (Taffel, 2016, p. 328). The wide-ranging diversity of digital technologies, their uneven accessibility and appropriation, along with overlapping waves of innovation give rise to layered historicities and large socio-spatial differences in the inequities they produce (Bork-Hüffer et al., 2021).

Hence, as digital geography scholarship has argued, what is needed are contextualized and critical analyses of the diverse ways in which digital technologies permeate everyday life across different places and populations (Ash et al., 2019; Osborne & Jones, 2023). In this chapter, we argue that such analyses are necessary not only for understanding the present but also for examining how socio-digital presents are entangled with past discourses and imaginaries of socio-digital futures. Harborth (2022) highlights the need to address challenges accompanying technological developments to propose effective interventions that mitigate their negative effects. Scholars from Critical Disability Studies, similarly, stress the importance of examining "the ways in which different kinds of inequalities and differences are reconfirmed, recalibrated and recreated in this heady mix of technological, globalized, environmental human and non-human entanglements" (Goodley et al., 2021, p. 30). Failure to prioritize accessibility and inclusivity risks creating inaccessible spaces, exclusionary digital citizenship, and new forms of violence towards marginalized groups. It also risks reinforcing dominant norms of "desirable normality" rather than embracing and caring for human diversity (Alper & Goggin, 2017; Goodley et al., 2021; Introna, 2023; Mahlknecht & Bork-Hüffer, 2022).

Furthermore, beyond a better understanding of the effects of current developments, we argue that what is needed is inclusionary anticipatory action. The way we imagine digital futures today significantly influences investments, technology development, appropriation, policies, future everyday practices and livelihoods (Bai et al., 2016; D4S, 2022; Gudowsky et al., 2023; Van Lente et al., 2013; WBGU, 2019). Gudowsky et al. (2023) argue that digital futures are currently shaped predominantly by Big Tech's profit- and growth-oriented strategies, alongside debates centred on technical possibilities. By neglecting the desires and needs of diverse populations, technological advancements risk perpetuating and deepening divides and crises.

Thus, the need for pathways to more inclusive socio-digital futures and the imagination of meaningful alternative futures is urgent. Inclusive, desirable futures must ensure accessibility, non-discrimination and protection, especially for groups such as children, older people, women, migrants, people with disabilities, and non-white and queer individuals. Therefore, this chapter pursues two objectives. Our first objective is to highlight approaches to alternative futuring that can be used to develop different, more inclusive future pathways with diverse population groups. We argue that such alternative futuring could contribute not only to uncovering existing inequalities and power dynamics, but also to challenging patriarchal, racist and ableist structures, and rethinking norms for future technological development. Besides digitization, societal challenges like climate change, war, conflicts and forced migration (Koenitz, 2019), the increasing speed and dynamics of change and uncertainty, and the world's high complexity make it more and more difficult to remake futures in the present (Tutton, 2017).

To address multiple needs and values and to envision inclusive and sustainable socio-digital futures for diverse population groups, we urgently need to imagine futures otherwise. Olufemi's (2021) *Experiments in Imagining Otherwise* explores the transformative power of imaginations through a Black Feminist lens. Her work focuses on feminist imaginations, their connection to futurity and political demands, positioning imaginations as a tool for envisioning alternative futures. She argues that imaginations can embody resistance, foster change and promote revolution, while also giving rise to "politics that express commitment against distress" (Olufemi, 2021). Imaginations allow for the creation of something fundamentally new. However, we must recognize that structural limits often prevent the realization of their full potential. Still, imaginations can manifest in other forms, such as touch, sound and taste. In her review of Olufemi's book, Ashtekar (2022) notes that the "otherwise is not a pre--determined entity, [but a] cluster of open-ended possibilities" highlighting its collective, participatory nature. Eventually, to *imagine otherwise*, we suggest in this chapter, it is necessary to include marginalized groups in co-productive research (methods) and futuring.

As a second objective, we use the example of extended reality (XR) technologies to illustrate the challenges posed by current technological developments and demonstrate how alternative, co-productive XR futuring could foster more inclusive developments. Scholars in computer science, technology assessment, human–computer interaction (HCI) and technology development, as well as businesses, attribute significant potential to XR technologies—such as augmented reality (AR) and virtual reality (VR)—in shaping future publics and, consequently, the futures of humanistic and democratic societies (Dudley et al., 2023; Gudowsky et al., 2023; cf. Kind et al., 2019). Gudowsky et al. (2023, p. 1) note that XR "produces a range of anticipatory imaginations, ranging from hyperbolic visions to fears of their risks, negative effects, and dystopian futures". This highlights the urgent need to engage with the effects of these technologies and reimagine them in more inclusive ways. At the same time, as we will show, XR can assume two distinct roles: first, as a research object in its own right, and second, as a potential co-creative tool for imagining desirable futures—both with a strong focus on the perspectives of underrepresented groups. Still, to pursue both core objectives, in this chapter, we provide an overview of alternative future conceptualizations, drawing from diverse fields of alternative future studies, including perspectives from Critical Black, Feminist, Queer and Critical Disability Studies as well as Crip Theory. Section 2 outlines the growing diversity of these approaches. In Sect. 3 we present a selection of methodologies and debate their potential for co-producing alternative future visions with marginalized groups. Section 4 focuses on the example of XR technology, exploring its current potentials, anticipated developments and projected impacts on marginalized groups. Finally, in Sect. 5 we discuss how such futuring can be used to imagine more inclusive and sustainable digital futures.

2 Conceptions of Alternative Futures: *Imagining Otherwise* as Advancement of Change

Critical Future Studies scholars like Goode and Godhe (2017, p. 110) argue that "utopian and dystopian modes of imagination are vital for reinvigorating a futural public sphere". In the literature, connections between various movements and scholarships engaging with the future are often described only vaguely or omitted entirely. To this end, the authors have developed a comprehensive overview of the field (Fig. 6.1) aimed at shedding light on the intricate and often messy entanglements of scholarly approaches to and concepts of futures. While our overview does not claim to be exhaustive, it highlights approaches that strive to *imagine otherwise*.

The overview in Fig. 6.1 is based on the following logic. First, alternative future studies will be contextualized as a branch of future studies. Rather than focusing on forecasting, these perspectives emphasize foresight, which encompasses probable, plausible, possible and preferable futures, and even go beyond these to include *imagining otherwise*. Second,

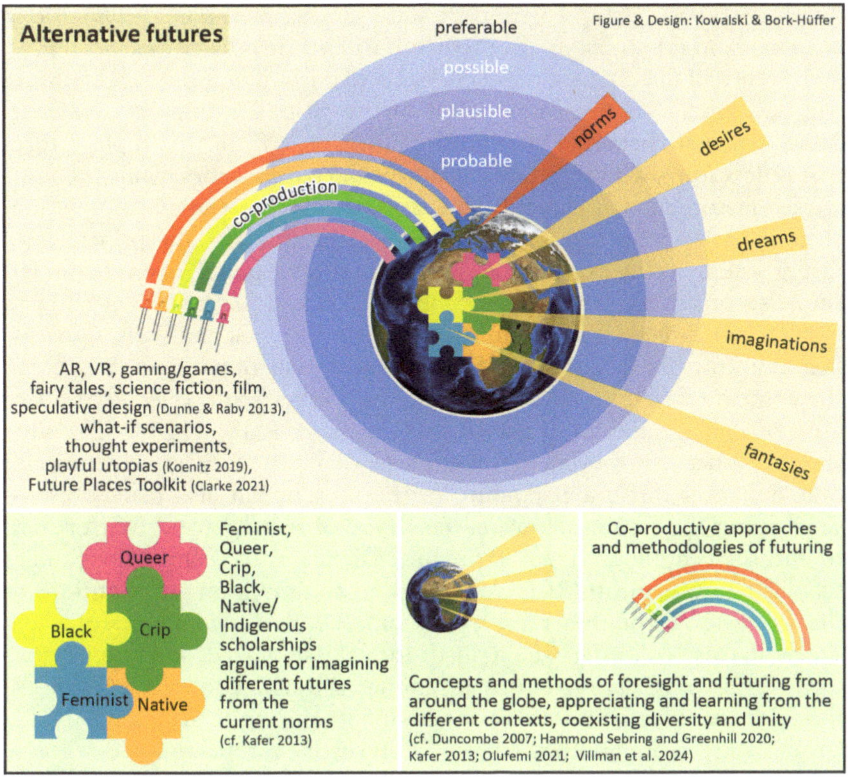

Fig. 6.1 Comprehensive overview of the field of alternative futures. Source: Figure and design by the authors, images by pixabay

the complex, fluid and ever-expanding spectrum of alternative futuring perspectives from around the globe will be briefly sketched, giving special attention to critical scholarship, including Crip Theory and Feminist, Queer, Black and Critical Disability Studies. Third, it will be shown how these perspectives collectively challenge prevailing norms and underscore the urgent need to imagine inclusive, diverse and desirable futures beyond conventional boundaries drawing on concepts such as desires, imaginations, dreams and fantasies. Finally, and addressed in detail in Sect. 3, we argue that knowledge and impact can only be generated collaboratively through co-production approaches with relevant groups (Strnadová et al.,

2022) (see Sect. 3.1). To support this, various methods for *imagining otherwise* and for co-productive research will be introduced (see Sect. 3.2).

In times of uncertainty, rapid change and crisis, it is clear that the future will not simply be an extrapolation of the past (Gümüsay & Reinecke, 2024, p. 2). It becomes crucial, therefore, to envision multiple futures that reflect today's diversity, uncertainties and complexities, while accounting for factors such as climate change and advancing digitalization (Amer et al., 2013). Bengston (2018) identifies the fundamental principles of future studies as the exploration of, among others, plural, open, fuzzy and (non-)surprising futures. While some scholars and think-tanks attempt to predict and forecast a single future or identify trends and weak signals—first indicators for trends in the future—such predictions are inadequate in the context of technological development, as they tend to focus on a singular, dominant and linear trajectory (Dunne & Raby, 2013, p. 2). What is more crucial, however, is the concept of multiple futures, which not only enhances our understanding of the present but also fosters discussions about the futures people either desire or seek to avoid. With regard to future technological development, Science and Technology Studies scholar Sheila Jasanoff (2015, p. 4) has made significant contributions to the discussion through her framework of *sociotechnical imaginaries*, which she defines as "collectively held, institutionally stabilized, and publicly performed visions of desirable futures, animated by shared understandings of forms of social life and social order attainable through, and supportive of, advances in science and technology". Alternative future studies categorize futures according to varying levels of likelihood: probable futures represent what is most likely to occur, excluding extreme but still possible events such as wars, financial crises or climate catastrophes (Dunne & Raby, 2013, p. 3). Plausible futures are the focus of scenario planning and foresight, aiming to explore different ways in which the future might unfold. Beyond this are possible futures which, while scientifically plausible, may be difficult to imagine. These require a coherent sequence of events leading to a new situation, even if entirely fictional (Dunne & Raby, 2013, p. 4). Finally, preferable or desired futures go further still—but it is crucial to ask whose futures are deemed preferable. The desired futures of marginalized groups often diverge from the white, able-bodied, heteronormative vision of the future typically presented by the dominant social majority in the Global North (Dunne & Raby, 2013).

On the one hand, alternative futures can take the form of scenarios, visions or imaginations. *What-if* scenarios open up spaces for discussion and aim to explore different possibilities and directions in which futures might develop (Bowman et al., 2013). This is why they are a popular method for policy and decision-making. Scenarios play a central role, but they are more likely to be used at the possible, plausible or probable level, as many scenarios may not align with the most preferable outcomes (see scenarios in Gudowsky et al., 2023).

On the other hand, alternative futures often have a provocative, fictional nature—"somewhere between reality and the impossible"—and aim to transform reality (Dunne & Raby, 2013, p. 3). To pave the way towards more inclusive socio-digital futures, we must think beyond the plausible and possible, considering the preferable and desirable. Gümüsay and Reinecke (2022, p. 237) advocate for research into desirable futures, calling for the creation of future visions that are theoretically grounded and open up new perspectives for human action in shaping the world. They argue for "future-oriented, imagination-focused and values-based" theories (Gümüsay & Reinecke, 2024, p. 2). As Fig. 6.1 indicates, probable, plausible and/or possible futures may be preferable, but preferable futures might not always be probable, plausible and/or possible. Hence, we will focus more on what might be achieved through imaginations, dreams and desires. We need to ask: How possible is the preferable? What falls within the realm of the probable or plausible when viewed through the lens of current norms? And what could be the possible-desirable if we were *imagining otherwise*? Finally, who is the "change for the better" intended for, given that "better" can hold different meanings for different individuals or groups (Dunne & Raby, 2013, p. 3).

It must also be acknowledged that future studies and foresight are composed of numerous, diverse approaches originating from various contexts and regions around the world. In their anthology *Our World of Future Studies as a Mosaic*, Villman et al. (2024, p. 6) employ the metaphor of a mosaic, describing it as "a complex artistic entity of various pieces connecting to it – here an assembly of chapters forming a unity based on diversity, each adding a unique color to the overall picture of future studies all over the globe". The authors emphasize the rich regional, cultural, historical and contextual diversity within the field and encourage thinking differently by learning from one another (represented by the globe at the centre of Fig. 6.1). Recognizing these diverse perspectives from histories and regions worldwide, this chapter builds on Villman et al.'s mosaic by incorporating critical perspectives and examining the field through the lenses of Crip Theory and Critical Disability, Black, Feminist and Queer Future Studies.

Building upon the mosaic concept in Villman et al.'s (2024) anthology, we adopt the metaphor of a puzzle to describe scholarships that are interlinked. The puzzle can continually be expanded to include additional perspectives that align with similar values, for instance, those advocating for the imaginations of futures that differ from current norms. These scholarships share a common demand for alternative perspectives and approaches to address problems that cannot be resolved within the confines of the current status quo.

Critical Black Future Studies scholars, such as Ouma et al. (2020), question whose futures and interests are being considered and underline the importance of examining transformative visions from underrepresented groups, whose perspectives may challenge or provide alternatives to the global capitalist framework. Similarly, (Critical) Indigenous Future frameworks explore themes of sovereignty and decolonization, drawing connections between contemporary issues and their impacts on Native communities (Lempert, 2014).

Critical Feminist Future Studies scholar Ormerod (2023) highlights the persistence of male-dominated power structures over time and space, which constrain possibilities of *becoming otherwise*. In her book *Feminist, Queer, Crip,* Kafer (2013) brings together these perspectives, urging us to reimagine both future visions and present realities as pathways towards more just, sustainable and accessible ways of being.

Scholars in Crip Theory and Critical Disability Studies, such as Kafer (2013) and Piepzna-Samarasinha (2022), along with those engaging with disabled futures, including Obourn (2020) and Shrodes (2023), advocate for including disabilities as a desirable and integral part of futures imaginations. They argue that ableist futures often exclude disabilities, portraying a future without disability as the more desirable option (Shrodes, 2023, p. 2).

Concepts of futuring such as desires, imaginations, dreams and fantasies seek alternatives to exclusionary ableist, misogynist, binary, heteronormative and white norms. Crip, Feminist, Queer and Black scholars advocate for imagining futures where marginalized identities are embraced as integral and desirable. Desires express a longing for future change, such as social justice, while imaginations, dreams and fantasies are seen as tools for creating new possibilities, perspectives and spaces. Though rooted in the present, these concepts envision alternative futures, illustrated in our figure as “sun beams” extending outward from given reality.

Desires are theorized by Feminist, Queer and Crip Theory scholars as the driving force behind imagining and demanding a different future compared to the present. These are the desires that resist conventional norms, celebrate the diversity of bodies, beings and relationships, and are deeply committed to social justice and transformative change (Hammond Sebring & Greenhill, 2020). According to Gümüsay and Reinecke (2022, p. 238), imaginations involve the capacity of creating mental images or ideas beyond immediate perception or prior experience: “... the irreal, unreal, and surreal. Imagining is making the absent present”. Dunne and Raby (2013, p. 70) explore imaginations as “the ability to literally imagine other worlds and alternatives”, identifying various types of imagination such as social, creative, mathematical, scientific, technological, artistic and sociological. Among other scholars, Gümüsay and Reinecke (2022) emphasize researching the future through imaginations as means to foster societal change. Imaginations remain vital for shaping futures that are not only plausible or probable but also deeply desirable and just.

Another concept explored by alternative future studies scholars is the notion of dreams. As Duncombe (2007) notes, dreams have both positive and negative implications. While they can inspire us to envision a radically different world, they can also fuel consumption and blind us to political or social issues: “Dreams are powerful. They are repositories of our desire. [...] But they also inspire us to imagine that things could be radically different than they are today, and then believe we can progress toward that imaginary world” (Duncombe, 2007, p. 182). Similarly, in her work *Undoing Gender*, Butler (2004, p. 29) uses the term *fantasy* to argue that imaginations foster change: “... fantasy [...] allows us to imagine ourselves and others otherwise”. Like Duncombe, Butler emphasizes that fantasies are not opposed to reality; rather, they expose the limits of reality, expand them and reveal what is possible or not.

Some scholars distance themselves from these four concepts, arguing that they extend far beyond the realm of the possible—too irrational, unrealistic or detached from reality (Dunne & Raby, 2013, p. 4). However, a shift in mindset can emerge through the study of real utopias—utopian ideals that serve as a bridge between dreams and practice, offering guidance for the practical navigation of social change (Wright, 2010). Small-scale real utopias that demonstrate alternative ways of living already exist in the present; by scaling them up or envisioning yet-to-exist futures with prefigurative potential, these future visions can then be *backcast* into socio-political practices to shape pathways towards broader societal change (Gümüsay & Reinecke, 2022, p. 239). Collectives or communities have "the power to imagine", which is what can become a framework of *socio-technical imaginaries* by the social construction of collective ideas, values and desires (Jasanoff, 2015). In the next section, we will discuss how these concepts can produce new visions and imaginations with marginalized groups.

3 Co-Productive Methodologies for Inclusive Futuring

By exploring a selection of alternative future perspectives—imaginary, speculative, playful, co-created, co-designed, community-led or participatory approaches—we aim to investigate whether these creative methods of participatory futuring can enhance capacities to *imagine otherwise* (Olufemi, 2021) and co-create alternative, "more socially constructive [and inclusive] imaginaries" (Dunne & Raby, 2013, p. 6). By uncovering and enabling imaginations of possible alternative futures people can be included who might be less represented by society or conventional approaches (Cork et al., 2023).

3.1 Building the Future We Want Together

For building the future we want together, it is crucial to consider diverse perspectives of marginalized groups when imagining the future. This can only fully be completed by the means of co-productive research. Although the terms come with slight differences regarding their field of application and implementation, in this chapter, we use co-production, co-design and co-creation simultaneously as their aim is similar: *Doing Research Inclusively* (Strnadová et al., 2022).

To implement multiple perspectives in research, we suggest pursuing a dialogical, co-productive form of research and innovation (Curran et al., 2021). To achieve real and sustainable impact, it is crucial to create knowledge together with marginalized groups and create solutions that are co-led, co-developed and co-implemented (Strnadová et al., 2022). According to Zamenopoulos and Alexiou (2018, p. 5), co-design is a "commitment to creating research practices that enable diverse experiences of life and diverse knowledge traditions to be voiced and heard". Co-production fosters inclusion, questions power relations and predominant knowledge systems, and advocates for creating new and just knowledge (Vincent, 2022).

Therefore, Strnadová et al. (2022) suggest that participants take the role of co-researchers: this is what the correspondent *co-* in co-production (or co-design) stands for. It implies that the participants are informed throughout the whole research process, take part as equal members of the research team, and have the possibility to actively shape all matters of the research (Curran et al., 2021; Fudge Schormans et al., 2019).

3.2 Methodologies for Inclusionary Imaginaries

This part of the chapter shows various tools and methodological strategies that make alternative futures and *imagining otherwise* amendable to empirical research with marginalized groups. Diverse scholars have been experimenting with what-if scenarios, thought experiments, utopias, sketching, speculations, games, gaming, science fiction and design about possible or desirable (alternative) futures, e.g., in *Speculative Everything* (Dunne & Raby, 2013), *Participatory Utopian Sketching* (Törnroth et al., 2022) or *Playful Utopias* (Koenitz, 2019). All of these approaches contribute to expanding future imaginaries and developing practices of socially just future-making.

Different genres are being consulted as tools for speculating with and imagining desired futures of marginalized groups: science fiction, for example, has long been "engag[ing] critically with disability and neurodivergence [...] including when mainstream literature ignored disability" (Piepzna-Samarasinha, 2022, p. 26, in epublication). Many science fiction worlds already include disabled main characters, represent the quality of disabled geniuses, and transcend the idea of non-existing disabilities or disabilities as illness (Piepzna-Samarasinha, 2022). Films are being inquired by Critical Disability and Gender Studies scholars, e.g., Obourn (2020) or Hammond Sebring and Greenhill (2020), to analyse desired (disabled) futures. Furthermore, literature and fairy tales can be a medium for dreams, desires and imaginations: Hammond Sebring and Greenhill (2020, p. 259) give the example that fairy tales can be such spaces where imaginations can grow and be tried out, where creative rethinking can take place, where "impossible dreams in current sociopolitical contexts [can be] imagined and explored".

Playful and creative methods are highly recommended because they allow space for experimentation and failure (Koenitz, 2019). Arts-based methods, meanwhile, offer expressive forms where words fall short—especially for those who use alternative forms of articulation or who prefer not to speak about sensitive topics (Kearns et al., 2021, p. 113). Games and gaming environments enable us to explore and simulate (future) situations, providing safe spaces to test strategies without *real world* risks and consequences. This makes them particularly valuable for addressing both current and future challenges (Koenitz, 2019, p. 253). In *Playful Utopias*, for example, Koenitz (2019) suggests "sandboxes for the future"—interactive digital narratives such as video games or AR/VR experiences—that playfully support the simulation of (utopian) future scenarios. Since failure is possible—and even encouraged in this game-based approach—it fosters imaginations and promotes the development of positive visions that can shape future practices and inspire a future worth striving for.

According to Dunne and Raby (2013) in *Speculative Everything*, design serves as a tool for speculation—useful for proposing, recommending and sketching what could be possible. They argue that utopias, speculation, social dreaming and experimentation create a space in which ideas and preferable futures can be imaginatively co-created. Such approaches may "allow us to develop alternative social imaginaries that open new perspectives on the challenges facing us" (Dunne & Raby, 2013, p. 189).

Other methods similarly combine collaborative, utopian and sketching-based approaches, such as in *Participatory Utopian Sketching* by Törnroth et al. (2022, p. 1), which suggests that citizen engagement can be enhanced through this methodological framework. XR also falls within this spectrum of methodologies aimed at fostering inclusionary imaginaries. XR will be further discussed in the following section, where its application in *imagining otherwise* is explored.

4 (Future) Extended Reality (XR) Technologies and the Inclusion and Exclusion of Marginalized Groups

This section has two purposes. First, it provides an overview of current XR technologies, assessing the potential and challenges these technologies pose for including or excluding marginalized groups. Second, it introduces alternative futuring approaches that leverage XR technologies to envision more inclusive futures. This highlights XR's dual role: both as a technology shaping future developments and as a tool for fostering more inclusive futuring processes.

4.1 *Developments of Extended Reality (XR) Technologies*

Current and Proclaimed Future Uses of Extended Reality (XR) Technologies

XR technologies have become increasingly affordable and functional over the past two decades, leading to their growing adoption. However, despite their anticipated proliferation and the risks XR poses for excluding marginalized groups (Fox & Thornton, 2022), research on creating inclusive XR experiences—whether it is in AR or VR—remains limited (Creed et al., 2023a; Dudley et al., 2023). The European Disability Forum (EDF, 2018) warns that without proactive inclusivity efforts, the growth of XR technologies will exacerbate existing inequalities.

Universal Design (UD) has been promoted as a standard for accessibility in technology development, aiming to create products and environments usable by all people, regardless of abilities or demographics (Convention on the Rights of Persons with Disabilities, 2006; Steinfeld & Maisel, 2012). Core UD principles include user-awareness, customizability and multimodal solutions, ensuring adaptability to diverse user needs (CEUD, Center for Excellence in Universal Design, 2023; Creed et al., 2023a, 2023b; Dudley et al., 2023). Adaptability, personalization, customizable user experiences and multimodality are all crucial in designing suitable solutions accessible to and addressing requirements for diverse population groups (Creed et al., 2023a, 2023b; Dudley et al., 2023). Yet, despite HCI's frequent claims of being UD-driven, many developments fail to address the barriers posed by exclusive spatial, social, economic and political environments.

Critical scholars highlight that patriarchal, misogynist, racist and ableist biases are embedded in data and AI technologies used in XR (Charitsis & Lehtiniemi, 2023; Nakamura, 2020; Shew, 2020). AI-powered XR solutions rely on large datasets that are heavily biased, with the voices of marginalized groups significantly underrepresented (Kamikubo et al., 2022). For example, an OECD study found that only 7% of AI solutions for the labour market tailored to people with disabilities were based on inclusive data initiatives (Touzet, 2023, p. 21). Additionally, XR developers often lack awareness of diverse user needs, further excluding marginalized groups (Dudley et al., 2023; Touzet, 2023). Testing frequently relies on convenience samples, excluding non-male, non-white, non-able-bodied and older individuals. As a result, biased designs limit the self-representation, participation and co-creation potential of marginalized populations in socio-digital futures. XR technologies are complex, demanding knowledge and resources that marginalized groups often lack, including physical and financial access, infrastructure and training (van Dijk, 2020; Kleine & Poveda, 2017; Macdonald & Clayton, 2013). These inequalities hinder participation in VR workspaces, social and leisure activities, and AR content in public spaces. Often, XR technologies facilitate superficial "alibi participation" rather than genuine inclusion (cf. Cardullo & Kitchin, 2019). Furthermore, algorithmic classifications privilege overrepresented groups while neglecting non-male, non-white and non-able-bodied populations, limiting their opportunities for participation (Cinnamon, 2017; Nakamura, 2020).

Emerging XR technologies also pose broader risks, such as enhanced surveillance, data exploitation and biopolitical control. Scholars warn that surveillance capitalism and Big Tech dominance may exacerbate de-democratization and disproportionately harm marginalized groups (Zuboff, 2018). Additionally, AI increasingly replaces human decision-making, eroding autonomy and oversight while enabling misuse, misinformation and manipulation (Del Casino et al., 2020; Harborth, 2022; Kind et al., 2019; Lynch, 2020; Zuboff, 2018).

Building on the general developments in XR and AI outlined above, we now focus on specific advancements in AR and VR. This will help illustrate current challenges, potentials and the prospects of emerging technologies that have not yet reached the consumer market.

Current and Proclaimed Developments in Virtual Reality (VR) Technologies

Virtual reality (VR) immerses users in simulated environments, primarily accessed through head-mounted devices (Dudley et al., 2023). The technology is noted for providing a "radically different viewing experience" compared to other digital technologies, as evidenced by users'emotional reactions, including fear, surprise and delight (Nakamura, 2020, p. 50). The most widespread and lucrative applications of the medium are video games, alongside pornography (Nakamura, 2020). Yet, initially developed for home use, consumer VR is now increasingly adopted in workplaces, educational institutions, and for additional social and leisure activities, especially with the rise of the Metaverse (Gerling & Spiel, 2021). A pivotal moment in VR's evolution was Facebook's 2014 acquisition of Oculus VR, merging "visually immersive media with socially addictive networked media" (Nakamura, 2020, p. 47).

Critical perspectives from cultural studies, sociology and media studies challenge claims of VR's inclusiveness and accessibility. Gerling and Spiel (2021, p. 1) describe VR as a "body-centric" and "inherently ableist technology" that assumes a "corporeal standard", non-disabled human body, failing to accommodate disabled people. They argue that the complex material setup of VR devices often excludes individuals with physical disabilities, as navigation and interaction rely heavily on full-body involvement (e.g., head, neck, spine and limbs) and fine motor skills like pointing and pressing buttons. This design not only excludes people with physical disabilities but can also interfere with assistive devices (e.g., hearing aids, wheelchairs) and cause discomfort or injury (Gerling & Spiel, 2021).

Further criticism highlights the HCI community's portrayal of VR as an "ultimate empathy engine" (Milk, 2015), enabling designers, families, friends or target user groups to virtually experience the perspectives of others (Cotton, 2021; Jarvis, 2019; Raz, 2022). Nakamura (2020, p. 48) argues that framing VR as an empathy machine bridging differences is part of Big Tech's effort to rebrand VR as a solution to criticisms of its role in exacerbating class inequality, violating user privacy and amplifying far-right fascism, racism and sexism. The author criticizes *VR for good* initiatives, suggesting they allow white producers and audiences to claim empathy with marginalized, racialized and gendered bodies while the industry simultaneously perpetuates violence, infringes privacy, and profits from monetizing these stories (Nakamura, 2020). Furthermore, the dominant video games and pornography "offer common gendered fantasies of empowerment that rely upon mastery and subjugation of virtual non-male, non-white bodies and space, of toxic embodiment" (Nakamura, 2020, p. 52). What is needed instead is a VR design that embraces bodily diversity, challenges established standards and invests in individualized design solutions (Gerling & Spiel, 2021).

Current and Proclaimed Developments in Augmented Reality (AR) Technologies

Augmented reality (AR) refers to "the computationally mediated perception [...] of (possibly but not necessarily) location-based content through (mostly mobile) end devices" in entangled socio-material-digital spaces (Gudowsky et al., 2023, p. 2). AR is used in leisure activities like gaming, sports, arts and navigation, as well as in political activism (Gudowsky et al., 2023; Harborth, 2022; WBGU, 2019).

Currently, AR primarily operates on handheld devices like smartphones, tablets and wearables such as smartwatches. Its use in public space has increased, especially for advertisements on billboards and public screens (Azuma, 2019; Nijholt, 2021). Emerging AR technologies, such as optical see-through devices and mobile glasses, have had limited consumer success, with adoption hindered by concerns over usefulness, privacy and security (Kernaghan, 2022; Rauschnabel et al., 2016; Rauschnabel & Ro, 2016). These devices are mainly used in cycling and automotive head-up displays. Scholars believe a groundbreaking "killer application" could expand AR use, and predict that, due to its integration into daily life, AR may surpass VR in the future (Azuma, 2019; Kind et al., 2019). Future AR technologies may include implants, larger field-of-view displays, and deeper integration with the Internet of Things, enabling more immersive experiences (Azuma, 2019; Nijholt, 2021). AR's potential could extend beyond visual experiences, incorporating auditory, tactile, olfactory and gustatory dimensions (Nijholt, 2021).

AR technologies pose risks related to privacy, data protection, safety and security, and currently do not meet privacy regulations in public spaces (Harborth, 2022; Nijholt, 2021). These technologies collect vast amounts of data—often without the knowledge of bystanders or users—such as visual data, emotional states and personality traits (Nijholt, 2021; WBGU, 2019). Technical limitations affect all users but may particularly challenge certain groups. Handheld devices, for instance, can tire users and have a limited field of vision, restricting use for people with limited fine motor skills or without limbs (Azuma, 2019). AR applications in public spaces can also pose safety risks, as seen with the Pokémon Go phenomenon, where distracted users caused traffic accidents, among other things (Harborth, 2022; Nijholt, 2021). The growing use of AR in marketing has led to the commercialization of public spaces, raising concerns about privacy violations through face recognition and Big Data (Rauschnabel et al., 2022). Additionally, overstimulating advertisements in public spaces can disturb people, cause stress and diminish positive health effects, e.g., of local green environments such as parks. The detrimental effects will likely be felt more strongly by certain groups, for example, individuals with autism.

Section 4.1 highlighted that XR developments are primarily driven by technical advancements rather than societal needs, let alone those of marginalized groups. We argue that what is needed are inclusionary imaginaries of the futures aspired to by diverse populations, such as disabled people. Technology should then be developed to support achieving these futures. Scholars in alternative future studies have begun employing XR itself as a tool for futuring. We will introduce these approaches next.

4.2 *Applied Extended Reality (XR) Technologies for* **Imagining Otherwise**

The following section presents selected examples of how XR is successfully applied in collaboration with marginalized groups and through co-design processes. As this is still a relatively new and experimental field, the number of existing studies remains limited—hence, we present both types of applications together in this subsection. Overall, VR appears to be more commonly used in these contexts than AR. This is somewhat surprising, given AR's greater potential for seamless integration into everyday lives.

Numerous studies have explored the use of (social) VR by marginalized and underrepresented communities, such as older people, to connect and receive support from others with similar experiences (Jones & Osborne, 2022). Other examples show how VR has been tested for co-designing objects, products (Mei et al., 2021) and even public spaces (Matthys et al., 2023). By bringing these approaches together, we argue that VR can serve as a method for co-designing inclusive future spaces with marginalized groups.

For example, the application *School days* was developed, tested and co-designed by older people. This social VR platform provides space for social communication and encourages interaction by reminiscing about the past. Using a participatory action research approach, all participants were involved in every step of the development and research process (Baker et al., 2021, p. 5). Additionally, immersive co-design tools, like the app *VRCake*, which uses real-time, realistic 3D visualizations, enable co-design and communication, especially for product development and design. It supports co-designing, testing products and exploring their usability, creating space for prototyping ideas and decision-making, particularly when users struggle to describe concepts or visualizations (Mei et al., 2021).

Matthys et al. (2023) demonstrate the benefits of using VR, gamification and 3D interactive tools for engaging citizens in co-designing public spaces. Public spaces are still being developed primarily in 2D environments by designers, and even when citizens are involved, 3D tools or VR environments are not typically used. Incorporating XR and 3D interactive tools into all phases of public space design can transform the process, highlighting the need for broader awareness and promotion to enhance design quality and inform spatial policy. Although the study broadly views "citizens" as participants in public spaces co-design, they are especially seen as "the future users of the public space" (Matthys et al., 2023, p. 2).

The examples presented not only show objects or products that can be co-designed in VR, but also (digital and public) spaces. Marginalized groups can be a key target audience, as VR facilitates description, testing and decision-making. However, using VR may have undesirable side effects, such as nausea and VR motion sickness (Osborne & Jones, 2023), which can exclude affected individuals from VR experiences.

Finally, we introduce Clarke's *Future Places Toolkit*, which builds upon the methodologies from the theatric guided tour *Billenium* by the performance group Uninvited Guests and Duncan Speakman (Clarke, 2021, p. 206). While *Billenium* allows participants to experience a city's potential future locations of utopian and dystopian science fiction narratives, the *Future Places Toolkit* adopts a co-productive AR approach. This method enables individuals and their communities to collaboratively imagine, create and visualize the future of their local places. Drawing on practice-as-research, creative collaboration and knowledge exchange research, Clarke (2021) integrates performance studies and digital placemaking in his work. He investigates whether science fiction storytelling, AR and respective interactive technologies can effectively inspire communities to imagine desirable inclusive futures for their neighbourhoods. By blending AR with science fiction elements, the *Future Places Toolkit* has proven particularly engaging, especially for younger generations. The overarching aim is to empower communities to co-design performances and technological tools that foster engagement. This includes promoting the involvement of marginalized groups and highlighting the full diversity of urban populations through digital placemaking.

5 Conclusion

Harborth (2022, p. 2) emphasizes that it is "imperative for us researchers to investigate [...] technologies as early as possible in order to ensure that they do not harm our societal and democratic developments". In this chapter, we have argued that it is crucial to explore the visions and purposes of diverse population groups for these technologies and to ensure their development aligns with these desires. This process should be carried out in a participatory and co-creative way.

Technological advances, particularly XR and AI, have the potential to create inclusive and sustainable tools by fostering inclusive exchanges between diverse individuals and their environments (OECD, 2022). Yet, as we have exemplified with reference to the XR discourse, technology development and HCI focus on technical specifics rather than addressing accessibility, social, economic and political divides and broader consequences.

Simultaneously, we have noted that XR technologies have proven to be a valuable method for imagining desirable futures. This means that XR technologies can play the role of providing opportunities for immersion into alternative futures spaces. *Imagining otherwise* is the key for immersion into desired futures while at the same time still being located in the present. While providing unique opportunities for immersion in the future, especially VR can also come with disadvantages, particularly for marginalized groups. We therefore propose applying AR, among others, as an alternative co-productive method for inclusionary imaginaries. In this way, VR's disadvantages can be reduced, in such a way as to enable older people, women and other marginalized groups to be more likely to participate, and those with VR nausea will not be excluded. Challenges when using XR as methods for research are especially of an ethical nature. Approaches must be applied that are in line with an ethics of care, are responsive, are inclusive of different groups' requirements, and at the same time include policy-makers, technology developers and stakeholders in addition to the target populations to ensure implementation. XR can be applied for imaginary futuring, but only when appropriate and desirable by the groups concerned.

Overall, we argue, research and development should prioritize the visions and needs of diverse population groups through co-productive processes, ensuring technology is inclusive, accessible and sustainable. This needs to happen before the technology is designed—reversing the current approach taken by Big Tech companies. In any case those approaches need to be adapted to the local socio-material-digital contexts, respecting local discourses and ways of using technologies and potentially the choice to refrain from using technology in the process for imagination.

To this end, we have outlined alternative futures approaches that are critical, imagination-focused and values-based, encouraging the questioning of current technology discourses and norms. Alternative futuring encourages *imagining otherwise* and seeks contribution to the creation of desirable socio-digital futures. Concepts such as desires, future imaginations, dreams and fantasies can be drawn on in this process.

The chapter also emphasizes the importance not only of imagining socio-digital futures, but also of becoming more aware of preferable futures and finding strategies to implement these imaginaries in the present. Referring to what Gümüsay and Reinecke (2022, p. 239) propose, desired futures can be first visualized to then backcast these imaginaries into the present to foster action. Furthermore, both Kafer (2013) and Obourn (2020) highlight the importance of addressing histories of oppression, bodyminds and intersecting identities to create futures that consider and learn from positive and negative realities. Similarly, Olufemi (2021) emphasizes the multidirectional nature of the future, urging us to consider intersections between past, present and future. Kafer (2013) expands upon the idea and urges us to "begin to anticipate presents and to imagine futures that include all of us". Intersectionality is crucial in this context, as demonstrated by the overlap of identities such as disabled and queer (Shrodes, 2023) or disabled and people of colour (Piepzna-Samarasinha, 2022), especially in addressing racism, (cis)sexism and ableism. These intersections are essential for envisioning truly diverse and inclusive futures. We must note that while we draw on Black, Indigenous, Queer and Critical Disabilities Studies' perspectives, as temporarily able-bodied, white women, we can only represent them in a limited way.

As Gümüsay and Reinecke (2022) also argued, imagination will help to anticipate *what-if* pathways. It allows researchers to explore consequences, guiding decisions towards more desirable developments. Regarding technologies like XR or AI, this means foreshadowing their future developments even before their widespread adoption to "identify the differences between paths towards an AI utopia from an AI dystopia and help mobilize the socio-political resources for creating the former" (Gümüsay & Reinecke, 2022, p. 240).

In the process of alternative futuring, we will always need to ask: Who will benefit from preferred futures? Is everyone benefiting or, if some groups are being included in depicting desirable futures in technology development, will it automatically exclude others? We argue that to ensure more just and inclusive futures, it is crucial to increase the representation of marginalized groups, who are often overlooked or underrepresented in mainstream discourses and decision-making processes. However, this focus must not be at the expense of the needs of the majority to ensure that no group feels excluded. Here, the challenge lies in balancing these competing demands to create a more equitable environment. At present, this ideal remains far from being realized.

Acknowledgements This work was supported by the Austrian Academy of Sciences (grant number: GDNG_2018-019_DigitAS) and the Austrian Science Fund.

References

Alper, M., & Goggin, G. (2017). Digital technology and rights in the lives of children with disabilities. *New Media & Society, 19*(5), 726–740. https://doi.org/10.1177/1461444816686323

Amer, M., Daim, T. U., & Jetter, A. (2013). A review of scenario planning. *Futures, 46*, 23–40. https://doi.org/10.1016/j.futures.2012.10.003

Ash, J., Kitchin, R., & Leszczynski, A. (2019). Introducing digital geographies. In J. Ash, R. Kitchin, & A. Leszczynski (Eds.), *Digital geographies* (pp. 1–10. (pre-print version))). SAGE.

Ashtekar, A. (2022, July 15). Book review: Experiments in imagining otherwise by Lola Olufemi. *LSE Review of Books*. https://blogs.lse.ac.uk/lsereviewofbooks/2022/07/15/book-review-experiments-in-imagining-otherwise-by-lola-olufemi/

Azuma, R. T. (2019). The road to ubiquitous consumer augmented reality systems. *Human Behavior and Emerging Technologies, 1*(1), 26–32. https://doi.org/10.1002/hbe2.113

Bai, X., Van Der Leeuw, S., O'Brien, K., Berkhout, F., Biermann, F., Brondizio, E. S., Cudennec, C., Dearing, J., Duraiappah, A., Glaser, M., Revkin, A., Steffen, W., & Syvitski, J. (2016). Plausible and desirable futures in the Anthropocene: A new research agenda. *Global Environmental Change, 39*, 351–362. https://doi.org/10.1016/j.gloenvcha.2015.09.017

Baker, S., Kelly, R. M., Waycott, J., Carrasco, R., Bell, R., Joukhadar, Z., Hoang, T., Ozanne, E., & Vetere, F. (2021). School's Back: Scaffolding reminiscence in social virtual reality with older adults. *Proceedings of the ACM on Human-Computer Interaction, 4*(CSCW3), 1–25. https://doi.org/10.1145/3434176

Bengston, D. N. (2018). Principles for thinking about the future and foresight education. *World Futures Review, 10*(3), 193–202. https://doi.org/10.1177/1946756718777252

Bjola, C., & Papadakis, K. (2020). Digital propaganda, counterpublics and the disruption of the public sphere: The Finnish approach to building digital resilience. *Cambridge Review of International Affairs, 33*(5), 638–666. https://doi.org/10.1080/09557571.2019.1704221

Bork-Hüffer, T., Füller, H., & Straube, T. (2021). Einleitung: Digitale Geographien als forschende Praxis. In T. Bork-Hüffer, H. Füller, & T. Straube (Eds.), *Handbuch Digitale Geographien—Welt, Wissen, Werkzeuge* (pp. 9–24). Brill Schöningh (UTB).

Bowman, G., MacKay, R. B., Masrani, S., & McKiernan, P. (2013). Storytelling and the scenario process. *Technological Forecasting and Social Change, 80*(4), 735–748. https://doi.org/10.1016/j.techfore.2012.04.009

Butler, J. (2004). *Undoing gender*. Routledge.

Cardullo, P., & Kitchin, R. (2019). Being a 'citizen' in the smart city: Up and down the scaffold of smart citizen participation in Dublin, Ireland. *GeoJournal, 84*(1), 1–13. https://doi.org/10.1007/s10708-018-9845-8

CEUD, Center for Excellence in Universal Design. (2023). *About universal design*. Centre for Excellence in Universal Design. https://universaldesign.ie/

Charitsis, V., & Lehtiniemi, T. (2023). Data ableism: Ability expectations and marginalization in automated societies. *Television & New Media, 24*(1), 3–18. https://doi.org/10.1177/15274764221077660

Cinnamon, J. (2017). Social injustice in surveillance capitalism. *Surveillance & Society, 15*, 609–625.

Clarke, P. (2021). Future places toolkit: Engaging communities through augmented reality and performance. *Research for All, 5*(2), 205–226. https://doi.org/10.14324/RFA.05.2.03

Convention on the Rights of Persons with Disabilities. (2006). https://www.ohchr.org/sites/default/files/Ch_IV_15.pdf

Cork, S., Alexandra, C., Alvarez-Romero, J. G., Bennett, E. M., Berbés-Blázquez, M., Bohensky, E., Bok, B., Costanza, R., Hashimoto, S., Hill, R., Inayatullah, S., Kok, K., Kuiper, J. J., Moglia, M., Pereira, L., Peterson, G., Weeks, R., & Wyborn, C. (2023). Exploring alternative futures in the Anthropocene. *Annual Review of Environment and Resources, 48*(1), 25–54. https://doi.org/10.1146/annurev-environ-112321-095011

Cotton, M. (2021). *Virtual reality, Empathy and Ethics*. Springer International Publishing. https://doi.org/10.1007/978-3-030-72907-3

Creed, C., Al-Kalbani, M., Theil, A., Sarcar, S., & Williams, I. (2023a). Inclusive AR/VR: Accessibility barriers for immersive technologies. *Universal Access in the Information Society*. https://doi.org/10.1007/s10209-023-00969-0

Creed, C., Al-Kalbani, M., Theil, A., Sarcar, S., & Williams, I. (2023b). Inclusive augmented and virtual reality: A research agenda. *International Journal of Human-Computer Interaction*, (20), 1. https://doi.org/10.1080/10447318.2023.2247614

Curran, T., Jones, M., Ferguson, S., Reed, M., Lawrence, A., Cull, N., & Stabb, M. (2021). Disabled young people's hopes and dreams in a rapidly changing society: A co-production peer research study. *Disability & Society, 36*(4), 561–578. https://doi.org/10.1080/09687599.2020.1755234

D4S, D. for S. (2022). *Digital reset. Redirecting technologies for the deep sustainability transformation.* TU Berlin. https://doi.org/10.14279/depositonce-16187.2

Del Casino, V. J., House-Peters, L., Crampton, J. W., & Gerhardt, H. (2020). The social life of robots: The politics of algorithms, governance, and sovereignty. *Antipode, 52*(3), 605–618. https://doi.org/10.1111/anti.12616

Dudley, J., Yin, L., Garaj, V., & Kristensson, P. O. (2023). Inclusive immersion: A review of efforts to improve accessibility in virtual reality, augmented reality and the metaverse. *Virtual Reality, 27*(4), 2989–3020. https://doi.org/10.1007/s10055-023-00850-8

Duncombe, S. (2007). *Dream: Re-imagining progressive politics in an age of fantasy.* New Press; Distributed by W.W. Norton.

Dunne, A., & Raby, F. (2013). *Speculative everything: Design, fiction, and social dreaming.* MIT Press.

EDF. (2018). *Plug and Pray? A disability perspective on artificial intelligence, automated decision-making and emerging technologies.* https://www.edf-feph.org/content/uploads/2020/12/edf-emerging-tech-report-accessible.pdf

Fox, D., & Thornton, I. G. (2022). *The IEEE global initiative on ethics of extended reality (XR) report: Extended reality (XR) ethics and diversity, inclusion, and accessibility.*

Fudge Schormans, A., Wilton, R., & Marquis, N. (2019). Building collaboration in the co-production of knowledge with people with intellectual disabilities about their everyday use of city space. *Area, 51*(3), 415–422. https://doi.org/10.1111/area.12492

Gerling, K., Spiel, K. (2021). A critical examination of virtual reality Technology in the Context of the minority body. In *Proceedings of the 2021 CHI conference on human factors in computing systems* (pp. 1–14). https://doi.org/10.1145/3411764.3445196

Goode, L., & Godhe, M. (2017). Beyond capitalist realism—Why we need critical future studies. *Culture Unbound, 9*(1), 108–129. https://doi.org/10.3384/cu.2000.1525.1790615

Goodley, D., Lawthom, R., Liddiard, K., & Runswick-Cole, K. (2021). Key concerns for critical disability studies. *International Journal of Disability and Social Justice, 1*(1), 27–49. https://doi.org/10.13169/intljofdissocjus.1.1.0027

Gudowsky, N., Kowalski, J., & Bork-Hüffer, T. (2023). Augmented futures? Scenarios and implications of augmented reality use in public spaces. *Futures, 151*, 103193. https://doi.org/10.1016/j.futures.2023.103193

Gümüsay, A. A., & Reinecke, J. (2022). Researching for desirable futures: From real utopias to imagining alternatives. *Journal of Management Studies, 59*(1), 236–242. https://doi.org/10.1111/joms.12709

Gümüsay, A. A., & Reinecke, J. (2024). Imagining desirable futures: A call for prospective theorizing with speculative rigour. *Organization Theory, 5*(1), 26317877241235939. https://doi.org/10.1177/26317877241235939

Hammond Sebring, J., & Greenhill, P. (2020). The body binary: Compulsory able-bodiedness and desirably disabled futures in Disney's the little mermaid and the little mermaid II: Return to the sea. *Marvels & Tales, 34*(2), 256. https://doi.org/10.13110/marvelstales.34.2.0256

Harborth, D. (2022). Human autonomy in the era of augmented reality—A roadmap for future work. *Information, 13*(6). https://doi.org/10.3390/info13060289

Iddri, FING, WWF France, GreenIT.fr. (2018). White paper: Digital technology and environment. *Using the digital transition to accelerate the ecological transition.* https://www.iddri.org/en/publications-and-events/report/white-paper-digital-economy-and-environment

Introna, A. (2023). Pandemic lived experience, Crip utopias, and Dismodernist revolutions: For a more-than-social model of disability. *Social Inclusion, 11*(1), 82–91.

Jarvis, L. (2019). *Immersive embodiment: Theatres of mislocalized sensation.* Palgrave Macmillan.

Jasanoff, S. (2015). Future imperfect: Science, technology, and the imaginations of modernity. In S. Jasanoff & S.-H. Kim (Eds.), *dreamscapes of modernity: Sociotechnical imaginaries and the fabrication of power.* University of Chicago Press. https://doi.org/10.7208/chicago/9780226276663.001.0001

Jones, P., & Osborne, T. (2022). FOUR: Working with social VR. In *virtual reality methods: A guide for researchers in the social sciences and humanities.* Policy Press. https://doi.org/10.47674/9781447360773

Kafer, A. (2013). *Feminist, queer, crip.* Indiana University Press.

Kamikubo, R., Wang, L., Marte, C., Mahmood, A., & Kacorri, H. (2022). Data representativeness in accessibility datasets: A meta-analysis. In *Proceedings of the 24th international ACM SIGACCESS conference on computers and accessibility* (pp. 1–15). https://doi.org/10.1145/3517428.3544826

Kearns, R., Eggleton, K., Van Der Plas, A., & Coleman, T. (2021). Drawing and graffiti-based approaches. In N. Von Benzon, M. Holton, C. Wilkinson, S. Wilkinson (Eds), *Creative methods for human geographers* (pp. 113–126). SAGE Publications Ltd. https://doi.org/10.4135/9781529739152.n9

Kernaghan, S. (2022). *Google glass: An evaluation of social acceptance.* Thesis, University of Kent [Dataset]. https://www.researchgate.net/publication/305340049_Google_Glass_An_Evaluation_of_Social_Acceptance

Kind, S., Ferdinand, J.-P., Jetzke, T., Richter, S., & Weide, S. (2019). *Virtual und augmented reality: Status quo, Herausforderungen und zukünftige Entwicklungen. TA-Vorstudie.* Büro für Technikfolgen-Abschätzung beim Deutschen Bundestag (TAB). https://doi.org/10.5445/IR/1000131346

Kleine, D., & Poveda, S. (2017). Digital divide. In D. Richardson, N. Castree, M. F. Goodchild, A. Kobayashi, W. Liu, R. A. Marston (Eds.), *The international encyclopedia of geography* (p. digital version paging: 1–5). Wiley.

Koenitz, H. (2019). Playful utopias. Sandboxes for the future. In B. Beil, G. S. Freyermuth, & H. C. Schmidt (Eds.), *Playing Utopia* (pp. 253–266). transcript Verlag. https://doi.org/10.1515/9783839450505-009

Lempert, W. (2014). Decolonizing encounters of the third Kind: Alternative Futuring in native science fiction film. *Visual Anthropology Review, 30*(2), 164–176. https://doi.org/10.1111/var.12046

Lynch, C. R. (2020). Contesting digital futures: Urban politics, alternative economies, and the movement for technological sovereignty in Barcelona. *Antipode, 52*(3), 660–680. https://doi.org/10.1111/anti.12522

Macdonald, S. J., & Clayton, J. (2013). Back to the future, disability and the digital divide. *Disability & Society, 28*(5), 702–718. https://doi.org/10.1080/09687599.2012.732538

Mahlknecht, B., & Bork-Hüffer, T. (2022). She felt incredibly ashamed': Gendered (cyber-)bullying and the hypersexualized female body. *Gender, Place and Culture*, 1–23. https://doi.org/10.1080/0966369X.2022.2115981

Matthys, M., De Cock, L., Mertens, L., Boussauw, K., De Maeyer, P., & Van De Weghe, N. (2023). Rethinking the public space design process using extended reality as a game changer for 3D co-design. *Applied Sciences, 13*(14), 8392. https://doi.org/10.3390/app13148392

Mei, Y., Li, J., De Ridder, H., & Cesar, P. (2021). CakeVR: A social virtual reality (VR) tool for co-designing cakes. In *Proceedings of the 2021 CHI conference on human factors in computing systems* (pp. 1–14). https://doi.org/10.1145/3411764.3445503

Milk, C. (2015). *How virtual reality can create the ultimate empathy machine.* https://www.ted.com/talks/chris_milk_how_virtual_reality_can_create_the_ultimate_empathy_machine/transcript

Nakamura, L. (2020). Feeling good about feeling bad: Virtuous virtual reality and the automation of racial empathy. *Journal of Visual Culture, 19*(1), 47–64. https://doi.org/10.1177/1470412920906259

Nijholt, A. (2021). Experiencing social augmented reality in public spaces. In *Adjunct proceedings of the 2021 ACM international joint conference on pervasive and ubiquitous computing and proceedings of the 2021 ACM international symposium on wearable computers* (pp. 570–574). https://doi.org/10.1145/3460418.3480157

Obourn, M. W. (2020). *Disabled futures: A framework for radical inclusion.* Temple University Press.

OECD. (2022). *Disability, Work and Inclusion: Mainstreaming in All Policies and Practices.* OECD Publishing. https://doi.org/10.1787/1eaa5e9c-en

Olufemi, L. (2021). *Experiments in imagining otherwise.* Hajar Press.

Ormerod, E. (2023). Level with us, regional development is still 'man shaped': Feminism, futurity and leadership. *Regional Studies, 57*(9), 1893–1902. https://doi.org/10.1080/00343404.2022.2153114

Osborne, T., & Jones, P. (2023). *Introduction to a research agenda for digital geographies.* Edwar Elgar.

Ouma, S., Hughes, A., Murphy, J. T., & Opondo, M. (2020). Envisioning African futures: Perspectives from economic geography. *Geoforum, 115*, 146–147. https://doi.org/10.1016/j.geoforum.2019.05.030

Piepzna-Samarasinha, L. L. (2022). *The future is disabled: Prophecies, love notes, and mourning songs.* Arsenal Pulp Press.

Rauschnabel, P. A., Babin, B. J., Tom Dieck, M. C., Krey, N., & Jung, T. (2022). What is augmented reality marketing? Its definition, complexity, and future. *Journal of Business Research, 142*, 1140–1150. https://doi.org/10.1016/j.jbusres.2021.12.084

Rauschnabel, P. A., Hein, D. W. E., He, J., Ro, Y. K., Rawashdeh, S., & Krulikowski, B. (2016). Fashion or technology? A Fashnology perspective on the perception and adoption of augmented reality smart glasses. *I-Com, 15*(2), 179–194. https://doi.org/10.1515/icom-2016-0021

Rauschnabel, P. A., & Ro, Y. K. (2016). Augmented reality smart glasses: An investigation of technology acceptance drivers. *International Journal of Technology Marketing, 11*(2), 123. https://doi.org/10.1504/IJTMKT.2016.075690

Raz, G. (2022). Rage against the empathy machine revisited: The ethics of empathy-related affordances of virtual reality. *Convergence, 28*(5), 1457–1475. https://doi.org/10.1177/13548565221086406

Shew, A. (2020). Ableism, Technoableism, and Future AI. *IEEE Technology and Society Magazine, 39*(1), 40–85. https://doi.org/10.1109/MTS.2020.2967492

Shrodes, A. (2023). "The word 'getting over' is really weird": Storying disability in desired futures. *Curriculum Inquiry*, 1–20. https://doi.org/10.1080/03626784.2023.2206932

Steinfeld, E., & Maisel, J. (2012). *Universal design: Creating inclusive environments.* John Wiley & Sons, Inc.

Strnadová, I., Dowse, L., & Garcia-Lee, B. (2022). *Doing research inclusively: Co-Production in Action.* https://apo.org.au/sites/default/files/resource-files/2022-05/apo-nid318294.pdf

Taffel, S. (2016). Perspectives on the postdigital: Beyond rhetorics of progress and novelty. *Convergence (London, England), 22*(3), 324–338. https://doi.org/10.1177/1354856514567827

Törnroth, S., Day, J., Fürst, M. F., & Mander, S. (2022). Participatory utopian sketching: A methodological framework for collaborative citizen (re)imagination of urban spatial futures. *Futures, 139*, 102938. https://doi.org/10.1016/j.futures.2022.102938

Touzet, C. (2023). *Using AI to support people with disability in the labour market: Opportunities and challenges.* OECD artificial intelligence papers 7; OECD artificial intelligence papers, Vol. 7. OECD Publishing. https://doi.org/10.1787/008b32b7-en.

Tutton, R. (2017). Wicked futures: Meaning, matter and the sociology of the future. *The Sociological Review, 65*(3), 478–492. https://doi.org/10.1111/1467-954X.12443

van Dijk, J. (2020). *The digital divide.* Polity.

Van Lente, H., Spitters, C., & Peine, A. (2013). Comparing technological hype cycles: Towards a theory. *Technological Forecasting and Social Change, 80*(8), 1615–1628. https://doi.org/10.1016/j.techfore.2012.12.004

Villman, T., Heinonen, S., & Pouru-Mikkola, L. (2024). *Our world as future studies as a mosaic.* The Finnish Society for Futures Studies.

Vincent, K. (2022). Development geography I: Co-production. *Progress in Human Geography, 46*(3), 890–897. https://doi.org/10.1177/03091325221079054

WBGU. (2019). *A European way to our common digital future.* Policy paper 11. WBGU. https://www.wbgu.de/fileadmin/user_upload/wbgu/publikationen/politikpapiere/pp11_2019/wbgu_pp11_en_navi.pdf

Wright, E. O. (2010). *Envisioning real utopias.* Verso.

Zamenopoulos, T., & Alexiou, K. (2018). *Co-design as collaborative research.* Connected communities foundation series.

Zuboff, S. (2018). Der dressierte Mensch. Die Tyrannei des Überwachungskapitalismus. *Blätter für deutsche und internationale Politik, 2018*(11), 101–111.

PART III

Engineering the Planetary

CHAPTER 7

Tinkering With the Planet: The Contested Imaginaries of a Digital Twin Earth

Delf Rothe

1 Introduction

> What we need is to open space all over Europe – in large and small countries, throughout the entire EU. We need advanced computing and clever ways of analyzing data. We need more capacities to process images: quantum computing is a key way; [and also] the science of the Anthropocene: it requires a new approach including integrating EO with IT systems. (Manuel Heitor, Minister of Science, Technology and Higher Education, Portugal at the EU Space Week 2020, Field notes, December 7, 2020)

The ability to see into the future and anticipate potential harms and threats has a particularly strong appeal for political actors. The European Union is no exception in this regard. The various experts who gathered online for the European Space Week 2020 convention co-hosted by the European Space Agency (ESA) and the European Commission (EC) were well aware of this. At the European Space Week and a series of related

D. Rothe (✉)
Institute for Peace Research and Security Policy at the University of Hamburg, Hamburg, Germany
e-mail: rothe@ifsh.de

S. Becker, B. Fladvad (eds.), *Contested Imaginaries of Future Technologies*, https://doi.org/10.1007/978-3-032-11497-6_7

meetings, such as the ESA's Phi Week 2020, or the EU' *Big Data from Space Conference* 2021, they discussed how to advance a new technological initiative: the vision of a digital twin Earth (DTE).[1] The DTE envisions exploiting the vast amounts of data provided by the European Earth observation program Copernicus—one of the two flagship programs of the EU space policy, along with the satellite navigation program Galileo.[2] In March 2022, the European Commission announced the launch of Destination Earth (DestinE) in partnership with the ESA, the European Center for Medium-Range Weather Forecasts (ECMWF), and the European Organisation for the Exploitation of Meteorological Satellites (EUMETSAT).[3] As a first step, the EU provided €150 million for developing two thematic digital twins on extreme weather and climate adaptation until 2024 (European Commission, 2022).

The vision of DestinE and related initiatives is bold. By combining Copernicus Earth Observation (EO) data with advanced computer modeling, AI, and machine learning, it aims to create a detailed digital replica of our planet. The planned digital twins would not only include the geophysical Earth system, but also social systems at scales ranging from the local to the planetary (expert interview #9, September 2, 2021).[4] This would allow for the development of future scenarios to test, for example, the impact of major natural disasters and climatic events on societies or (vice-versa) the effects of certain policy measures on physical systems.

Those who dig deeper and take a closer look at the projects, technologies, and infrastructures pursued therein, however, are quickly disappointed. Instead of an integrated, holistic virtual globe, one will find a plethora of small-scale models, tools, platforms, and maps being developed under the umbrella of the DTE. At the EU level there is the hope that in the end, all these fragmented "pieces will come together" (expert

[1] Actors in the European space sector use different labels to describe the idea of building a digital data double of the Earth (expert interview #1, August 25, 2021). For the sake of simplicity, I use *digital twin Earth* (DTE) as an umbrella term.

[2] EO refers to the "gathering of information about planet Earth's physical, chemical, and biological systems via remote sensing technologies, usually involving satellites carrying imaging devices." EU Science Hub (2023). Earth Observation. Joint Research Center.

[3] In addition, the ESA pursues its own R&D program under the label of "Digital Twin Earth." While DestinE and *Digital Twin Earth* are two separate initiatives, they are closely linked in terms of aims, involved actors, and underlying infrastructures.

[4] A full list of interviews can be found in the Appendix.

interview #6, August 25, 2021). This stark contrast between vision and reality raises the question of why the DTE concept has recently "received this increased attention at the institutional level with initiatives such as Destination Earth" (expert interview #14, September 23, 2021). This question arises above all because the vision of a digital twin of our planet is not new. As early as the 1990s, then-Vice President Al Gore had launched a similar initiative in the United States (see below).

In this contribution,[5] I mobilize the concept of sociotechnical imaginaries to explore these questions and study how and why the DTE has recently become a centering device or attractor in the complex and vast European space ecosystem. As I argue below, the DTE is neither a concrete technology nor a coherent policy program. Rather, it combines a range of different technologies with ideas of desirable futures for the EU. In this respect, the vagueness of the vision is not a weakness but an asset because it enables actors from very different policy fields and scientific disciplines to relate to the DTE vision (Rothe, 2024). Crucially for the volume at hand, the DTE's future imaginary has several important spatial dimensions. The discourse around the DTE not only relates to the collective self-identity of the Union in a future characterized by risks and uncertainties but also simultaneously negotiates Europe as a spatial construct.

I trace the spatial dimension of the DTE imaginary along three axes. The first dimension is what I call *transversal assembling*. It refers to the ability of the DTE imaginary to forge new associations between heretofore unrelated actors. As I show below, the result is a transnational, transversal actor-network that supports the DTE across established geographic borders and disciplinary boundaries. These transversal lines of flight are disentangled again by a second spatial dimension of the DTE imaginary

[5] This chapter is an outcome of a larger research project on the intersection of knowledge production, digital technologies, and security governance in the Anthropocene from 2018 to 2021. To be able to study the networks, practices, and infrastructures I relied on participant observation of major events in the European space field (see Appendix). This ethnographic field study was supported by 22 semi-structured interviews with experts from different parts of the complex European space ecosystem (see Appendix). In addition, the study of policy documents and reports allowed me to trace the evolution of the DTE vision over time. Finally, I studied the dominant imaginaries and related forms of visuality behind the DTE vision, through a (visual) discourse analysis of official homepages, image films, and other online resources.

that could be described as *spatial realignment*. Here, the vision of a DTE is placed in relation to existing, dominant spatial concepts—for example, the EU as an area of freedom, security, and justice vs. an unsafe discursive outside. The third form of space discussed in the contribution describes the *spatial construction of epistemic objects* brought about and addressed by the DTE. As I will show through a discussion of the DTE4Security platform, the DTE would bring about a new governance object—a scalable virtual planet as the object of experimentation and intervention.

By revealing these spatial dimensions of the DTE imaginary, I advance the evolving literature on the intersections of sociotechnical imaginaries and the production and contestation of space (Becker and Fladvad, this volume). Furthermore, I contribute to debates on the role of sociotechnical imaginaries in European integration and identity formation (e.g., Baur, 2024; Klimburg-Witjes, 2024). Finally, the chapter speaks to recent debates on imaginaries and security technologies (Csernatoni & Martins, 2024; Evans et al., 2021). As I show below, the imaginaries driving the development of the DTE are also security imaginaries. The desirable futures for Europe imagined here are not based on positive visions but are rather defined negatively as the ability to foresee and avert potential dangers. Perceptions of growing uncertainty and insecurity, thus, become a driver of technological innovation here.

The chapter proceeds as follows. In the next section, I provide a more detailed description of the sociotechnical imaginaries informing the DTE and its development in the European space sector. Section 3 traces the emergence of a transnational expert network around the vision of a digital Earth. Sections 4 and 5 explore how this vision was adopted by European experts and decision-makers and, in this process, was redirected toward dominant discourses, self-identities, and demands of the Commission and other EU actors. The final section concludes by answering the outlined research question and identifying several avenues for further research.

2 Digital Twin Earth as a Sociotechnical Imaginary

The basic rationale of the DTE vision is to combine large amounts of Earth observation data produced by the satellite missions of EU Copernicus with advanced computer models to generate "an interactive model of the Earth that can facilitate the monitoring and understanding of the planet itself" (expert interview #14, September 23, 2021). This digital replica is envisaged as a "virtual globe constructed of massive, multiresolution, multitemporal, multitype Earth observation data and socio-economic data combined with relevant analysis algorithms and models" (Liu et al., 2020, p. 3). The resulting DTE, it is hoped, would not only provide an accurate picture of past and present states of the Earth system but would also allow for the prediction of future changes (see Fig. 7.1). For this, a comprehensive infrastructure, or ecosystem of diverse digital technologies, would be required: from big data to AI and machine learning, to cloud platforms, to supercomputing. According to the DTE vision, this platform will enable the development of anticipatory scenarios of future environmental changes and resulting risks, such as disasters, migration, or conflicts (European Commission, 2022). What would happen if China unilaterally conducted a large-scale climate engineering program? Or what would happen if a major hurricane hit Manhattan, already struggling with sea-level rise, in 2067? According to proponents, these and similar *what-if* scenarios could be simulated with the DTE, enabling prediction and experimenting with the planet in a *safe* virtual environment.

The European DTE initiative is an almost ideal example of the notion of sociotechnical imaginaries by Jasanoff and Kim (2015, p. 4; Becker and

Fig. 7.1 A summary of the DTE vision. Source: European Space Agency, 2022

Fladvad in this volume). It illustrates how technological development is co-produced with socially shared ideas about desirable futures. In the present, this imaginary already becomes manifest in prototypes, models, presentations, videos, and many other visual artifacts. A good example is the official image film of the DestinE program by the European Commission (DigitalEU, 2023). The film begins with a view of the Earth from space, overlaid with geometric drawings and numerical data. The words "Imagine the world in 2050" are displayed to the sound of a positive, melodious piano tune. The following scene fades to a night vision satellite view of Europe and the Mediterranean region to visually support the next text line: "And Europe on that map."

The future to be imagined, according to the movie's narrative, is one of Europe as a "greener, more resilient and healthy continent for current and future generations." This is aesthetically supported by a collage of video loops of wind turbines and green forests in the sunlight as symbols of sustainability, technical progress, and intact nature. This future Europe would be "equipped with a better understanding of how the climate will evolve and how to best tackle environmental changes." This would not only be vital to protect European citizens from environmental harm but also enable the EU to become an international vanguard of environmental protection and build "climate resilience for the whole world" (0:30 min). The subsequent scene then resolves this arch of tension and introduces "Destination Earth," which "could be the key to that [imaginary future] (0:36 min)." The program is visually represented by a simulated Earth as seen from space, surrounded by several data layers that give the image a futuristic look.

The following scenes explain the program and the technologies involved, such as Copernicus satellites as "our eyes in the sky." What is interesting here is the particular combination of videos. These show an Earth observation satellite in space, an aerial view of a hurricane with its famous *eye*, a porthole-like window of a space station, and a woman looking at several monitors with data visualizations. Together, these visual metaphors create an image of Europe as a collective body and present the DTE as a prosthetic extension of that organism. This imaginary ties into the established metaphors of the *body politic*, but is also coherent with popular depictions of the Digital Earth "as a digital nervous system for the globe, actively informing users about events happening on or near the Earth's surface by connecting to sensor networks and situation-aware systems" (Liu et al., 2020, p. 12). The film also refutes the impression that the DTE is a technocratic instrument and emphasizes, for example, that the tool gives citizens the opportunity "to critically assess policies and measures that affect them."

The next scenes show a whole series of video shots that represent the various threats posed by the anthropogenic environmental crisis: a person walking over dry, cracked earth, collapsing glaciers, false-color satellite images of a tropical storm, and large-scale forest fires. The reference object of these threats is identified in the following scene with a large text line reading: "*Human lives* can be saved in case of natural disasters and the socio-economic impact reduced" (1:20 min, emphasis added). The film concludes with the core governmental promise of the DTE vision, i.e., with Destination Earth we can analyze the past, monitor the present, and predict the future (see Fig. 7.2).

At a textual level, the image film presents the imaginary of the DTE in a straightforward manner: this is a future in which the EU continues to thrive despite the unfolding planetary crisis thanks to digital transformation and tools like the DTE. At the aesthetic and affective level, however, the image film is more ambiguous. For example, it combines images of disasters and images of ecological destruction with cheerful and uplifting classical music. Or it shows collages from different visual genres, or ways

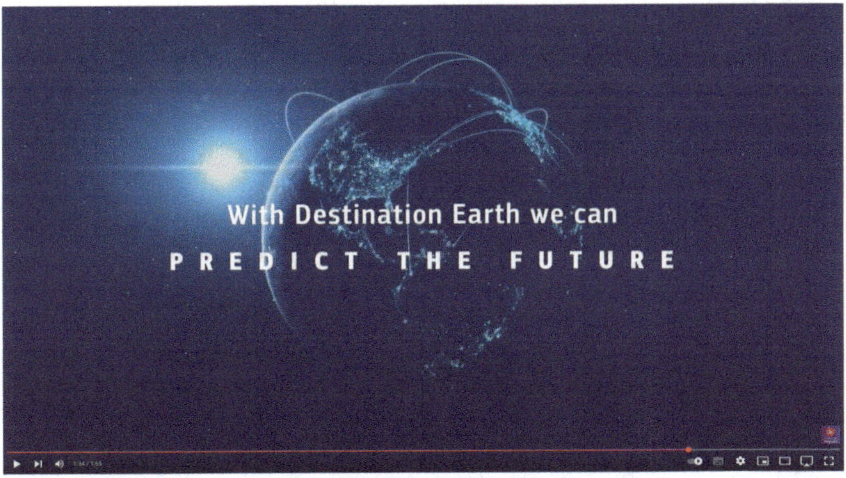

Fig. 7.2 Film still from the official DestinE image film. Source: https://www.youtube.com/watch?v=FKVHZlGqEyw

of seeing the global environmental crisis: images of pristine nature, alongside images of technical control, alongside symbols of catastrophic change.

One way of making sense of the aesthetic and affective qualities of the film is through the Kantian notion of the sublime (Austin & Leander, 2023). For Immanuel Kant, the latter is an aesthetic experience resulting from an encounter with objects or phenomena that are beyond human comprehension. The encounter with the unimaginable is an affective experience that is both awe-inspiring and frightening but also ennobling (Davies, 2015). On the one hand, the sublime experience is terrifying because the human subject is confronted with the very limits of knowledge and understanding. On the other, this experience is pleasurable because it raises hopes in the possibility of overcoming and transcending these epistemic limits. Jonathan Austin and Anna Leander show how in contemporary societies aesthetic design is used to "simultaneously locate sublime imaginaries of insecurity in our midst whilst also allowing us to live-with, accept, and forget their presence" (2023, 730). This perfectly describes the representation of the global ecological crisis in the DTE image film, which is presented both as an existential global threat and at the same time as an opportunity to overcome existing epistemic limits (with the help of the DTE).

The aesthetic protocol actualized by the video is what Austin and Leander (2023, 754) call "juxtapositional enrolling." The latter refers to aesthetic experiences that, on the one hand, continuously remind the viewing subject of the existence of threats like climate change. On the other hand, the aesthetics of juxtapositional enrollment promise that normal life can go on (at least for some), thereby normalizing the catastrophe and inscribing it in our everyday lives. The imagined future of the official DestinE image film is thus one of omnipresent crisis, in which the global environmental crisis and its implications for Europe have become a fact. Yet, through the development of new epistemic infrastructures, such as the DTE, the EU and its citizens are enabled to cope with such omnipresent risks.

As this short discussion has shown, the DTE is, on the one hand, a paradigmatic example of the notion of sociotechnical imaginaries. On the other hand, it allows us to advance and elaborate on the initial concept as proposed by Jasanoff and Kim (2015). While the latter originally examined these co-production processes primarily at the national level (consider the co-production of the French nuclear program with the self-image and future vision of the European major power), it was subsequently broadened to account for transnational spaces and collective identities as well. In the words of Olbrich and Witjes (2016, p. 117): "... the concept is compatible with various units of analysis beyond the nation-state but can also address common visions and narratives of how our techno-political world should be socially ordered as articulated by expert groups, NGOs, companies, or foundations." This applies in particular to the case of the European Union, where technical harmonization and progress have long been seen as drivers of political integration (Klimburg-Witjes, 2024, p. 832). A second difference concerns the observation that in the case of the DTE, emerging technologies are not only associated with imaginaries of desirable futures (Martins & Mawdsley, 2021). Rather, the future image is negatively defined here as the absence of a whole range of risks and harms that are currently discussed under the label of polycrisis. Finally, and most importantly for this volume, the DTE project is coproduced with several competing spatial constructs. The question of which of these spatialities will prevail and dominate the public and political discourse around the DTE will also shape the further development and implementation of the initiative.

To unpack this spatial dimension of the DTE imaginary, I briefly summarize how this vision managed to assemble an expanding transnational network of heterogeneous experts, before showing how it was then recently realigned with European political goals, discourses, and institutions.

3 Transversal Assembling: The Topology of the DTE Network

Since it was first formulated in the 1990s, the vision of a digital Earth has attracted the attention of a wide range of different actors. These actors come from different geographical regions, epistemic fields, and political camps. In the STS literature, such artefacts or phenomena that manage to bring together experts from different fields have been famously described as *boundary objects* (Star & Griesemer, 1989). In a recent article, I suggested the notion of *visual objects* to highlight the importance of visuality in the crafting of new associations through the DTE (Rothe, 2024). Here, I would like to focus less on the visual practices and ways of seeing through the DTE and more on the spatiality of the associations enabled by the DTE and the elements assembled therein. This space is topological rather than topographic. I am here following Collier's (2009, p. 80) analytics of political spaces as *topologies of power*, where he refers to "topology as a branch of mathematics concerned [...] with how spaces are organized, with the connectivity properties that arise from certain arrangements of elements, and with their transformations." This analysis shows how the DTE idea generates proximity between experts across geographic and ideological distances, and how it organizes an emerging and constantly evolving actor-network that transcends established geographic boundaries and spheres of political authority—a process that can be described as transversal assembling.

As already mentioned in the introduction, the idea behind the DTE and related European initiatives is nothing new. Quite the contrary: as an interviewee stressed, "it has been around for decades" (expert interview #5, August 23, 2021). It was first mentioned, at least so the story goes, in the book *Earth in the Balance* published by former US Vice President Al Gore (1992). However, it was only in 1998, through a speech by Gore at the opening of the California Science Center, that this vision became popular with the broader public (Liu et al., 2020, p. 2). In the aftermath of the speech, the Clinton administration founded a new Digital Earth office at NASA, which developed a series of prototypes but was scrapped by the newly elected Bush administration soon thereafter in 2001 (Parks, 2002, p. 280). After the cancelation of the NASA initiative, a top-down government-sponsored generation of the DTE seemed increasingly unlikely (Goodchild et al., 2012, p. 11092). However, the vision of a digital twin of Earth was out in the world, sparking the interest of other experts beyond the United States and beyond the public domain.

In the private sector, Gore's vision sparked the development of commercial *geobrowsers*. Keyhole's Earth Viewer in 2001 "demonstrated the technical feasibility of providing a global view of the world using imagery on desktop computers" (Craglia et al., 2008, p. 149). Three years later, Google acquired Keyhole as the basis for its powerful Google Earth platform released in 2004. As Goodchild et al. (2012, p. 11088) remark, "... with the 2005 launch of the Google Earth service, a fine-resolution, digital replica of the planet, or at least of its surface, was within reach of anyone with a broadband Internet connection." Similar geobrowsers were developed by Microsoft (Atlas 2000) or ESRI (ArcGIS Explorer) facilitated by the increasing opening and commercialization of satellite Earth observation data (Craglia et al., 2008, p. 150).

In parallel to these commercial projects, the vision of a DTE was further advanced by a growing transnational network of experts from various scientific disciplines such as Earth System Science, climate science, and the geospatial community. Various national governments have supported the development of this transnational network of experts over time. After the United States dropped NASA's digital Earth initiative, the Chinese government took an interest in the vision and promoted international cooperation on the concept through the Chinese Academy of Sciences and its Institute for Remote Sensing Applications (Foresman, 2008, p. 5). In contrast to other geospatial (surveillance) technologies, however, the focus has always been on international scientific cooperation. This was evident, for example, in its commitment to the founding of the International Society for Digital Earth (ISDE) in 2006 (Liu et al., 2020). The ISDE is an international non-profit organization that promotes the DTE idea through bi-annual international symposia and the publication of the *International Journal of Digital Earth* (Foresman, 2008, pp. 8–9). A further step in the institutionalization of this transnational community happened in 2009, when the ISDE joined the Group on Earth Observations (GEO)—an intergovernmental organization dedicated to the global integration of national Earth observation systems (Liu et al., 2020, p. 6). Several other international organizations also took an interest in the DTE idea. For example, Foresman (2008, p. 10) notes that "beginning in 2000, the United Nations Environment Programme (UNEP) adopted the Digital Earth architecture, as expressed through the Digital Earth Reference Model (or DERM) for the design of UNEP's data and information resources reorganisation." According to Liu et al. (2020), this level of interest is no coincidence, as the vision aligns with the rationale of many international organizations to promote international cooperation through knowledge sharing and technological collaboration.

In addition to China, the government of New Zealand has also committed itself to the further development of the DTE vision. In 2006, the Digital Earth Summit on Sustainability took place in Auckland. The then Prime Minister Helen Clark underlined the importance of the initiative for the government and its national orientation toward sustainable development by participating in the summit (Foresman, 2008, p. 9). However, as in the case of China, New Zealand has never translated the vision of a DTE into concrete infrastructures or policy programs at the national level.

This brief overview shows how the idea of a digital representation of Earth sparks tremendous resonance and thus became the common reference point of a transnational network of diverse actors. One important reason for this is the openness and fluidity of the DTE imaginary. The technologies presented and discussed at DTE-related events and panels ranged from classical analyses of satellite data through time-series or change detection to cloud platforms to various data analytics applications, machine vision, and natural language processing algorithms, to computer modeling and even quantum computing (field notes October 2, 2020; December 10, 2020; May 18–20, 2021). To draw all these things together—to paraphrase Latour (1986)—the DTE is not only technically but also thematically open and promises future insights that could be used in many different policy fields. This openness makes it attractive for actors from heterogeneous contexts— from security and foreign policy to climate governance (expert interview #9, September 2, 2021). The referent object of the DTE imaginary, thus, seems to continuously *mutate* and cannot be pinned down to a concrete set of political demands or rationales. I hold that that it is exactly this semantic and technical openness that makes the DTE an attractive common point of reference for so many actors from the geosciences to the security community. The imaginary becomes a projection for hopes in emerging technologies such as AI and their promised political merits—such as the ability to predict complex risks and provide comprehensive future scenarios.

The ambiguity and openness of the imaginary are more important than questions of feasibility for the popularity of the DTE vision. Many experts I have spoken to are well aware that the promise of a synoptic view of the future will probably never be fulfilled. As one researcher involved in the initiative told me, "I can describe these ideas, but I have no idea how to implement them [laughs]" (expert interview #8, September 2, 2021). In fact, the applications and tools presented at the different expert sessions I observed were much less spectacular than the DTE vision. This sentiment was also shared by some of my interviewees, who argued that DTE might simply be a new buzzword for already existing approaches like machine learning or data analytics (expert interview #17, September 24, 2021). However, the fact that this promise of all-encompassing vision and knowledge will never be fulfilled does not diminish the attraction of the DTE. Quite the contrary: it guarantees the "continuation of the structure of wanting" on the side of the experts (Knorr Cetina, 1997, p. 13). Predicting the future may not be possible yet, but it could very well become possible with the next technological breakthrough (be it AI, cloud infrastructures, or even quantum computing).

Although this network repeatedly manifests itself in temporary spatial densifications (e.g., NASA, Chinese Academy of Sciences), the vision was never implemented in concrete policy programs or infrastructures before the recent European initiatives. What seemed to be lacking was sufficient financial and political support to build the massive infrastructures required for the realization of the vision (expert interview #5, August 23, 2021). Technical developments are one factor here; for example, Al Gore's vision of a virtual globe was influenced by advances in graphics card technology and the associated possibilities for computer animation in the 1990s (Goodchild et al., 2012, p. 11092). In the 2010s, new possibilities for generating, storing, and analyzing geospatial big data gave new impetus to the idea of a DTE (Foresman, 2008, p. 11). Similarly, recent advances in computing power, cloud infrastructures, and AI models have certainly helped to raise the popularity of the DTE idea. But "computers don't drive politics" (ibid., p. 14), and technologies are not developed in a vacuum, but against the backdrop of concrete social and political discourses. Hence, the most important factor for the lack of institutional support for the DTE in the past was its (missing) spatial anchoring. The future it imagined was a cosmopolitan one, where a range of planetary, or at least transboundary, problems would be addressed through international cooperation and knowledge exchange. This fits in with dominant imaginaries of the mobilizing effects of global ICT infrastructures that would turn the world into a global village and enable the emergence of a global civil society. The political reality, however, was that neither within the system of the United Nations nor beyond was the necessary governance structure in place to implement the DTE vision in practice. In the words of one of my interviewees:

> In the end, important is: how can these ideas feed into something that is actually actionable, that has funding and partners and a commitment to the agenda, you know, apart from ideas and concepts that people propose at various places. So, I think Destination Earth is probably the first really comprehensive, funded action. (Expert interview #6, August 25, 2021)

The cosmopolitan nature of the DTE imaginary explains part of its appeal: Through a process I have described as transversal assembling, it became the common reference point of a global expert network. At the same time, this vision lacked a communitarian grounding where it could create the necessary momentum by anchoring it in collectively shared ideas of desirable futures for a given community.

4 Spatial Realignment: The DTE as a Nodal Point in European Space Policy

This brings us to a second spatial dimension of the DTE imaginary, which I call spatial realignment. It refers to discourses and practices that reconnect the DTE to already established, dominant spatial concepts and identities. It is this alignment process that creates the necessary gravity for its implementation. This realization is important for understanding why the DTE has become a central project of EU space policy. Here, the DestinE/DTE concept is co-produced with particular self-understandings and visions of the EU as well as hegemonic (security) discourses—or better: desirable futures of Europe in the world.

4.1 *The Fragmented Landscape of European Space Policy*

To understand this point, it is necessary to briefly consider the history of European space and technology policy, which is driven by competing actor communities and policy visions (Bowen, 2010). In Brussels, the dominant discourse frames space as a field of scientific, technical, and economic cooperation with anticipated spill-over effects on other sectors, including common security and defense policy, digitalization, and the common market (Klimburg-Witjes, 2021, p. 529). However, in reality, the landscape of European space policy is rather fragmented, with overlapping and competing spheres of authority between actors including the ESA, the Commission, and individual member states (Hörber, 2016b, p. 3). Member states pursue political and economic interests through national space programs, for example, in the area of satellite reconnaissance for national defense. However, space and satellite infrastructures have historically been very capital-intensive (this is changing due to the development of microsatellites and other technological advances) and require a great deal of specialized knowledge. Hence, against the backdrop of economic and geopolitical competition with the United States and the Soviet Union, the European Space Agency (ESA) was established in 1975 to pool European capabilities in the space sector (Hörber, 2016a, p. 15). It is not part of the EU institutions, but an independent organization whose underlying rationales and political ideals often differ from those of Brussels (Klimburg-Witjes, 2021, p. 526). Two features stood out: the intergovernmental character of the organization, in which the ideas of major space nations such as France and the United Kingdom set the direction, and the civilian character of all

ESA activities. In line with this discourse, technical cooperation in space was seen as a means of further promoting and consolidating peace between formerly hostile European nations (Bowen, 2010, p. 2).

Given its civilian and intergovernmental nature, ESA's position differed considerably from that of the European Commission, which from the beginning interpreted space policy as a possible driver of European (security) integration (Klimburg-Witjes, 2021, p. 529). The Commission developed an interest in space policy in the 1990s, when the US decision to open and commercialize its national satellite program sparked the desire of the European space community to establish a genuine European space program (Davis Cross, 2020, p. 217). According to Klimburg-Witjes (2021, p. 533), for many in Brussels the experience of the Balkan wars, when Europeans were denied access to American satellite intelligence, served as a wake-up call: "... *space for security* had emerged as a powerful paradigm in EU space policymaking." In this political environment, the foundation of the European satellite navigation project Galileo and the EO program Copernicus was laid (Brachet & Deloffre, 2006). Adopting the Lisbon Treaty in 2009 provided the basis for the continued integration of satellite Earth Observation and its application to the EU's Common Security and Defence Policy (Klimburg-Witjes, 2021, p. 527). Further steps toward an integrated space policy followed: the publication of the Space Strategy for Europe in 2016, the creation of a Directorate-General for Defence Industry and Space (DG DEFIS), as well as the new EU Agency for the Space Programme (EUSPA) in 2021.

Despite these integration steps, the landscape of European space policy remains fragmented—embedded in overlapping and competing national, supranational, and intergovernmental structures. The competing political projects are informed by disparate political discourses and associated spatial imaginaries, such as geopolitical competition, economic growth, competitiveness, (broadening of) security, and scientific collaboration (Hörber, 2016b). Accordingly, there are conflicts over the fundamental orientation of European space policy: between civilian applications and dual-use, commercialization and public interests, and open data and security requirements. Finally, there are also competing notions of Europe undergirding these discourses: Europe as a community of peaceful nation-states (the ESA's mandate), or as an integrated geopolitical actor operating in an increasingly uncertain environment (EC). In line with the idea of co-production, these political discourses and ideas have also influenced the technical development of infrastructures, for example, in the field of Earth observation (Rothe, 2017).

4.2 *The Unifying Imaginary of the DTE*

This brief overview of the fragmented field of European space policy helps us understand why the imaginary of the DTE would create such resonance among various actors in this sector. The imaginary served as a common reference point or attractor that would bring together various actors from ESA as well as EU agencies, from defense, science, and industry, and—at least partly—pacify the competing discourses and visions informing these actors. As one interviewee involved in the development of the program put it: "Users, researchers, academia, external action service, the Commission, the industry … that's where we would like to go: Everything interconnected" (expert interview #14, September 23, 2021). This imaginary portrays the EU as planetary steward, but also as a powerful geopolitical player. The source of this power is knowledge, information, and reliable predictions about planetary processes, their interactions, and security-related effects. This went along with a broadening of the understanding of security, reoriented toward a series of transnational threats in a planetary crisis. Through this (dis-)association with military defense, the differentiation between civilian and security applications in EO became less important. DTE finally brings about a new object of knowledge and governance (or rather, envisions doing so): a virtual, scalable replica of planet Earth that would become the subject of both experimentation and intervention.

First, the digital twin imaginary manages to reconcile the civilian-, science- and environmentally oriented elements of the European space ecosystem with security- and defense-centered ones. In this imaginary, the EU would exert power internationally, not merely through coercion and military strength but through technological leadership, knowledge sharing, and persuasion. The DTE rearticulates the established discourse of Europe as a civil power in a twofold sense. First, by linking it to more recent debates on the EU's *digital sovereignty.* Digital sovereignty is understood here as "Europe's ability to act independently in the digital world" (Madiega, 2020), which would require, among other things, "offensive tools to foster digital innovation" (ibid.). The DTE is envisioned as precisely such a tool, which promotes the development of European supercomputing and satellite EO infrastructures and also links the two thematically (field notes, 28 September 2020). For example, at the ESA Phi Week 2020, the then Deputy Director General at the European Commission Directorate-General for Defence Industry and

Space (DG DEFIS) stressed the need for initiatives like the DTE by claiming "Europe is lagging behind on many, many technologies; so, you need disruptive technologies [...]. We need Europe to remain in the race, and remain innovative" (field notes, 28 September 2020).

Second, the DTE imaginary linked technical innovation to the emerging discourse on the Anthropocene as an unfolding planetary crisis (Peoples & Stevens, 2020, p. 298; Rothe, 2020, pp. 194–196). The term Anthropocene, first coined in 2000 by Nobel Prize winner Paul Crutzen, expresses the idea that the Earth has entered a new geological epoch characterized by the impact of humans on planet Earth. This idea is largely influenced by the findings of Earth system research, which describes the planet as an interplay of interconnected Earth systems. In this discourse, the man-made imbalance of these systems and their knock-on effects are accompanied by an increase in transnational and cross-border security risks. The vision of a DTE takes up this problematization and presents the EU as a stable container (cf. Drulák, 2006) in an environment characterized by increasing uncertainty, complexity, and instability (field notes, 28 September 2020; field notes 18 May 2021). Against this background, the DTE appears as a tool to make complex risks for Europe both predictable and manageable, to promote the digital sovereignty of the Union, and to produce knowledge for international cooperation partners, thereby expanding Europe's position as a civilian power.

All of these capabilities are linked to hegemonic "ways of seeing" (Berger, 1973) that the DTE is intended to enable. Lisa Parks (2002, p. 284) already detailed these ways of seeing in her article on the Digital Earth vision put forward by Gore and NASA in 1998:

> What is being articulated here, then, is a kind of neo-imperialism in which the distinctions between outer, global, and cyberspaces are collapsed in a way that encourages the user to image herself as occupying all of these spaces at once (much like the US government or a high tech firm).

According to her, even the ability to imagine such a capacity of a completely transparent, scalable virtual Earth is an expression of an "immense visual capital of the US" (ibid.). The DTE vision includes an attempt to build a similar *visual capital* for the EU, through the use of Copernicus satellite services and advanced computer modeling, for example by the ECMWF (field notes, 28 September 2020; field notes, 21 March 2021).

Aesthetically, this promise is constructed by the combination of two visual technologies: first, the *planetary gaze* of satellite EO, which is associated with objectivity, power, and overcoming human boundaries by technical means; and second, technologies of (big) data visualization (Davies, 2015; McCosker & Wilken, 2014). The planetary gaze—the view of planet Earth from space— is often associated with scientific neutrality and authority. It performs a "god trick," as Donna Haraway (Haraway, 1988) has prominently argued, "... the claim of a *view from nowhere* that relies on the fantasy of gaining a distance on the world in order to achieve a neutral, dispassionate knowledge of it" (Daggett, 2019, p. 41). The planetary gaze, accordingly, is characteristic of a scientific worldview that revolves around the idea of technical mastery and control of the Earth. The DTE radicalizes the "god trick" performed by conventional satellite and space imagery. Not only does it promise an undistorted view of the entire planet, but furthermore the ability to look into the future and to zoom in and out of the digital globe (Schneider & Walsh, 2019, p. 2).

Big data visuality, on the other hand, does not carry the claim of authenticity and undistorted representation of the satellite image. Instead, the authority of such visualizations stems from the ability to present vast, almost unimaginable amounts of data in a single image (McCosker & Wilken, 2014, p. 156). Here, the viewing subject is confronted with beautiful visualizations of enormous amounts of data—and, as Davies (Davies, 2015: n.p.) notes, "... the sheer quantitative magnitude is as disturbing as exciting." According to current estimates, about 12 petabytes of data are produced by the program every day (DG DEFIS, 2024). Data visualizations are not only visually appealing; they furthermore carry the promise of overcoming existing limits to knowledge by revealing hidden patterns and detecting overlooked anomalies or dangerous trends.

5 Spatial Governance: The Planet as Object of Knowledge and Intervention

The geopolitical vision of the DTE described in the previous section is informed by a redefinition of security in planetary terms (Peoples & Stevens, 2020). This discourse revolves around two referent objects in need of protection: the fragile Earth system, jeopardized by human impact, and the EU, which is seen as acting in an ever more complex and uncertain environment. Crucially, these security imaginaries are co-produced with technological projects such as the DTE and become inscribed into technical decisions and developments within the program.

A good example to illustrate this shift in European security discourses and its co-production with the DTE is the *Digital Twin Earth for Security* (DTE4Security) project pursued by the Research, Technology Development, and Innovation Unit of the European Union Satellite Centre (SatCen) based in Madrid (field notes, October 2, 2020). SatCen is an agency of the Council of the EU providing traditional geospatial intelligence to a narrow set of users within the CFSP/CSDP (expert interview #14, September 23, 2021). This focus on traditional security threats also produces specific technical requirements, as a SatCen expert explained in a talk at the *Big Data from Space* conference:

> When we talk about security in the geospatial intelligence domain, we are used to one specific situation; so, we are tasked with something to be analyzed and we are in a specific situation with regard to time and location; and then we use [high-resolution] satellite imagery to see what is going on there. (Field notes, May 20, 2021)

With its DTE4Security project, however, SatCen is leaving its established narrow focus on defense and intelligence behind and instead pursuing what they call a *new security* agenda. New security here refers to a number of emerging, globally interconnected security threats, including climate change, migration, and pandemics.

The *new security* agenda, meanwhile, requires methods and approaches to knowledge production that differ from SatCen's established procedures. High-resolution images of single locations are of little use for monitoring complex and interconnected "security threats" such as pandemics, or migration. Furthermore, one cannot rely on observation to grasp how these problems might unfold in the future: "We will have environmental states that we have never observed before, you know, so we can't train any artificial intelligence with that data because it doesn't exist yet. So, this can only be done by simulation models" (expert interview #6, August 25, 2021). Hence, new sources of data (e.g., meteorological) and new technologies (such as AI) are required: "We need a global model, we need a model that is an integrated model of the Earth focused on security that helps us understand what is going on" (field notes, May 20, 2021). With the help of the DTE platform, according to this vision, one will be able to "move from a local to a global scale and to add to the traditional mono-dimensional security scenarios, multidimensional, interconnected ones" (expert interview #14, September 23, 2021). To build these interconnected models SatCen seeks to build on three pillars: (1) new additional and interoperable data sources; (2) technologies such as new sensors or cloud technologies, to collect, distribute, and harmonize the data; and (3) new (AI) models to analyze the data (field notes, October 2, 2020). To integrate the three pillars, SatCen is establishing what it calls a "GEOspatial Data Management Platform" (GEO-DAMP).

Crucially, the DTE4Security model implies an inversion of the process of knowledge production. Within a traditional model of military security, SatCen would start from a concrete request to gather information about a concrete localized situation: "We are delivering products to people, which are in the field, very quickly and on a 24/7 basis. We have a reactive interface with Brussels. We have a reactive interface with the industry" (expert interview #14, September 23, 2021). In the DTE model, on the contrary, the security problem to be addressed emerges out of the models, out of the data itself. As a result, the "production and consumption of knowledge and governance are not separated anymore" (Olbrich & Witjes, 2016, p. 117). Rather than addressing a clearly delineated object, these governance mechanisms start out with a loose understanding of possible problems—such as the notion of "new security" in the DTE4Security platform. "And then", one interviewee explained to me, "you can start playing scenarios. You know, *what happens if* [...]. And you can start playing these scenarios and at least tracing the implications of the kind of response you could possibly envisage" (expert interview #9, September 2, 2021).

This fusion of knowledge production and governance, illustrated by the DTE4Security project, also affects the spatial dimension of the DTE imaginary. It promises to enable seamless vision and cut through scales to identify and trace problems that are interconnected and hard to pin down. Through creative and playful application of what-if scenarios, these entangled problems would iteratively condense into clearer governance objects. The DTE is thus equally a technology of governance and the construction of space.

6 Conclusion

In this chapter, I have explored the sociotechnical imaginary of a digital twin Earth (DTE) that has recently become popular as a major tool for complex Earth observation and modeling. The DTE combines large amounts of satellite data with advanced computer models and AI with the aim of building a digital replica of the planet to monitor present and predict future developments on Earth. Understanding the DTE as a sociotechnical imaginary, as I have shown in this chapter, allows us to understand why this vision, which had been around for decades, has gained traction within the EU in recent years. This perspective highlights how the development of European space and supercomputing infrastructures (as the required technologies behind the DTE) was co-produced with discourses of European digital sovereignty and a redirection of security toward complex planetary threats. The vision, in this reading, is closely linked to a self-image of the EU as a global, civilian power that would tackle the challenges of the Anthropocene through innovation, knowledge sharing, and international cooperation.

At the same time, I have shown how the example of the DTE allows for the advancement of the conception of sociotechnical imaginaries, in particular by shedding light on its inherent spatial dimensions. The notion of *transversal assembling* was proposed to capture the ability of the DTE imaginary to forge new actor-networks across geographic and disciplinary boundaries. The dimension of *spatial realignment* described how the DTE imaginary becomes bound to existing, dominant spatial concepts and constructs—including regional constructions of the EU as an area of freedom, security, and justice. Finally, I have discussed how the DTE brings about and enables intervention in epistemic objects at various spatial scales. In this sense, the DTE is itself an "environing" (Wickberg & Gärdebo, 2020) or space-making technology whose objects—the Earth system, the EU's dangerous neighborhood, etc.—do not precede their mediation but are brought about through these technology-enabled ways of seeing.

Additional research is required to further scrutinize the politics of the DTE and related sociotechnical imaginaries. This scholarship could involve genealogical research on the emergence of the DTE vision. Equally pertinent would be comparative studies further scrutinizing the differences between competing projects of planetary visualization and experimentation by other commercial and (geo)political actors. Finally, additional research on forms of counter-imaginaries and critical forms of geovisualization would be desirable.

Acknowledgments This work was funded by the Deutsche Forschungsgemeinschaft (DFG, German Research Foundation), under Grant Number: 335616337, and under Germany's Excellence Strategy – EXC 2037 "CLICCS – Climate, Climatic Change, and Society" – Project Number: 390683824, contribution to the Center for Earth System Research and Sustainability (CEN) of the University of Hamburg.

Appendix

(a) *List of interviews*

1. Senior satellite imagery analyst, April 4, 2018, Oakland, CA.
2. NGO representative, CEO, April 1, 2019, Washington, DC.
3. NGO representative, GIS specialist, Mai 3, 2019, online.
4. NGO representative, Director, April 14, 2019.
5. EU official, DG DEFIS, August 23, 2021, online.
6. ECWMF official, August 25, 2021, online.
7. Geospatial analytics provider, August 27, 2021, online.
8. NGO representative, Head Geospatial Team, September 2, 2021, online.
9. EU Official, DG CONNECT, September 2, 2021, online.
10. German Coordinator of Copernicus security services, September 6, 2021, online. (old #8)
11. NGO representative, Deputy Director, September 9, 2021, online.
12. Geospatial expert at the German Federal Agency for Cartography and Geodesy, September 10, 2021, online.
13. Researcher, geospatial information services, September 22, 2022, online.
14. EU SatCen representative, Research, Technology Development and Innovation unit, September 23, 2021, online.
15. EU SatCen representative, Copernicus unit, September 23, 2021, online.
16. Technology expert at GIZ (Deutsche Gesellschaft für Internationale Zusammenarbeit), September 30, 2021, online.
17. Satellite expert at German Aerospace Center (DLR), September 24, 2021, online.
18. Expert on digital surveillance at German Federal Maritime and Hydrographic Agency, September 30, 2021, online.

19. Geospatial technology expert at the Federal Office for Civil Protection and Disaster Assistance, Germany, September 30, 2021.
20. Senior project officer at European Maritime Safety Organisation, October 20, 2021, online.
21. Researcher at University of Athens, December 16, 2021, online.
22. Member of Satellite intelligence service, German Aerospace Center (DLR), December 17, 2021, online.

(b) *List of observed events*

1. National Forum on Copernicus and Earth Observation 2018, German Federal Government, November 27–29, Berlin.
2. European Space Week 2019, hosted by the European Commission, December 3–5, Helsinki.
3. ESA Phi-Week 2020, European Space Agency, September 28–October 2, online.
4. European Space Week 2020, hosted by the European Commission, December 7–11, online.
5. German Forum on Copernicus and Earth Observation 2021, German Federal Government, March 21–23, online.
6. 9. Launch event of the European Commission Knowledge Center on Earth Observation, April 20, 2021, online.
7. Big Data from Space 2021, conference by the European Space Agency, the European Union Satellite Centre, and the European Commission, May 18–20, online.

References

Austin, J. L., & Leander, A. (2023). *The state of the sublime: Aesthetic protocols and global security. Millennium: Journal of International Studies, 50*(3), 730–759.

Baur, A. (2024). European dreams of the cloud: Imagining innovation and political control. *Geopolitics, 29*(3), 796–820.

Berger, J. (1973). *Ways of seeing*. Penguin Books.

Bowen, B. E. (2010). Outer space, and security as integration in Europe. *E-International Relations*.

Brachet, G., & Deloffre, B. (2006). Space for defence: A European vision. *Space Policy, 22*, 92–99.

Collier, S. J. (2009). Topologies of power Foucault's analysis of political government beyond 'governmentality'. *Theory, Culture & Society, 26*(6), 78–108.
Craglia, M., Goodchild, M. F., Annoni, A., Camara, G., Gould, M. F., Kuhn, W., Mark, D., Masser, I., Maguire, D., & Liang, S. (2008). Next-generation digital earth - a position paper from the Vespucci initiative for the advancement of geographic information science. *International Journal of Spatial Data Infrastructures Research, 3*, 146–167.
Csernatoni, R., & Martins, B. O. (2024). Disruptive Technologies for Security and Defence: Temporality, Performativity and Imagination. *Geopolitics, 29*(3), 849–872.
Daggett, C. (2019). World-viewing as world-making: Feminist Technoscience, international relations, and the aesthetics of the Anthropocene. In J. P. Singh, M. Carr, & R. Marlin-Bennett (Eds.), *Science, technology, and art in international relations* (pp. 40–49). Routledge.
Davies, W. (2015). *The data sublime.* The New Inquiry.
Davis Cross, M. K. (2020). The European space and intelligence networks. *Journal of Transatlantic Studies, 18*(2), 209–230.
DG DEFIS, (2024). Directorate General Defence Industry and Space. Copernicus. https://defence-industry-space.ec.europa.eu/eu-space-policy/copernicus_en (last accessed August 10, 2024).
DigitalEU (2023). Destination Earth – new digital twin of the Earth will help tackle climate change and protect nature, available at https://www.youtube.com/watch?v=FKVHZlGqEyw (last accessed January 20, 2026).
Drulák, P. (2006). Motion, container and equilibrium: Metaphors in the discourse about European integration. *European Journal of International Relations, 12*(4), 499–531.
ECMWF (2024). European Centre for Medium-Range Weather Forecasts. Destination Earth. https://www.ecmwf.int/en/about/what-we-do/environmental-services-and-future-vision/destination-earth (last accessed April 11, 2024).
EU Science Hub. (2023). Earth observation. Joint Research Center. https://joint-research-centre.ec.europa.eu/jrc-science-and-knowledge-activities/earth-observation_en (last accessed April 11, 2024).
European Commission. (2022). *Destination earth—New digital twin of the earth will help tackle climate change and protect nature.* https://ec.europa.eu/commission/presscorner/detail/en/ip_22_1977 (last accessed March 02, 2026).
Evans, S. W., Leese, M., & Rychnovská, D. (2021). Science, technology, security: Towards critical collaboration. *Social Studies of Science, 51*(2), 189–213.
Foresman, T. W. (2008). Evolution and implementation of the digital earth vision, technology and society. *International Journal of Digital Earth, 1*(1), 4–16.

Goodchild, M. F., Guo, H., Annoni, A., Bian, L., De Bie, K., Campbell, F., Craglia, M., Ehlers, M., Van Genderen, J., Jackson, D., Lewis, A. J., Pesaresi, M., Remetey-Fülöpp, G., Simpson, R., Skidmore, A., Wang, C., & Woodgate, P. (2012). Next-generation digital earth. *Proceedings of the National Academy of Sciences, 109*(28), 11088–11094.

Gore, A. (1992). *Earth in the balance: Ecology and the human Spirit*. Houghton Mifflin.

Haraway, D. (1988). Situated knowledges: The science question in feminism and the privilege of partial perspective. *Feminist Studies, 14*(3), 575–599.

Hörber, T. (2016a). Chaos or consolidation? Post-war space policy in Europe. In T. Hörber & P. Stephenson (Eds.), *European space policy European integration and the final frontier* (pp. 15–30). Routledge.

Hörber, T. (2016b). Introduction: Towards a European space policy? In T. Hörber & P. Stephenson (Eds.), *European space policy European integration and the final frontier* (pp. 1–14). Routledge.

Jasanoff, S., & Kim, S.-H. (2015). *Dreamscapes of modernity: Sociotechnical imaginaries and the fabrication of power*. University of Chicago Press.

Klimburg-Witjes, N. (2021). Shifting articulations of space and security: Boundary work in European space policy making. *European Security, 30*(4), 526–546.

Klimburg-Witjes, N. (2024). A rocket to protect? Sociotechnical imaginaries of strategic autonomy in controversies about the European rocket program. *Geopolitics, 29*(3), 821–848.

Knorr Cetina, K. (1997). Sociality with objects: Social relations in postsocial knowledge societies. *Theory, Culture & Society, 14*(4), 1–30.

Latour, B. (1986). Visualisation and cognition: Drawing things together. In H. Kuklick (Ed.), *Knowledge and society studies in the sociology of culture past and present* (pp. 1–44). Jai Press.

Liu, Z., Foresman, T., van Genderen, J., & Wang, L. (2020). Understanding digital earth. In H. Guo, M. F. Goodchild, & A. Annoni (Eds.), *Manual of digital earth* (pp. 1–21). Springer Singapore.

Madiega, T. (2020). *Digital sovereignty for Europe*, EPRS Ideas Paper. European Parliamentary Research Service.

Martins, B. O., & Mawdsley, J. (2021). Sociotechnical imaginaries of EU Defence: The past and the future in the European Defence fund. *JCMS: Journal of Common Market Studies, 59*, 1458.

McCosker, A., & Wilken, R. (2014). Rethinking 'big data'as visual knowledge: The sublime and the diagrammatic in data visualisation. *Visual Studies, 29*(2), 155–164.

Olbrich, P., & Witjes, N. (2016). Sociotechnical imaginaries of big data: Commercial satellite imagery and its promise of speed and transparency. In A. Bunnik, A. Cawley, M. Mulqueen, & A. Zwitter (Eds.), *Big data challenges: Society, security, innovation and ethics* (pp. 115–126). Palgrave Macmillan.

Parks, L. (2002). Satellite and cyber Visualities: Analyzing digital earth. In N. Mirzoeff (Ed.), *The visual culture reader* (pp. 279–290). Routledge.
Peoples, C., & Stevens, T. (2020). At the outer limits of the international: Orbital infrastructures and the technopolitics of planetary (in)security. *European Journal of International Security, 5*(3), 294–314.
Rothe, D. (2017). Seeing like a satellite: Remote sensing and the ontological politics of environmental security. *Security Dialogue, 48*(4), 334–353.
Rothe, D. (2020). Europas Blick auf die Erde. EU Copernicus und die visuelle Versicherheitlichung von Umwelt. In G. Schlag & A. Heck (Eds.), *Visualität und Weltpolitik: Praktiken des Zeigens und Sehens in den Internationalen Beziehungen* (pp. 181–214). Springer Fachmedien Wiesbaden.
Rothe, D. (2024). When the world is an object: On the governmental promise of a digital twin earth. *International Political Sociology, 18*(3), olae022.
Schneider, B., & Walsh, L. (2019). The politics of zoom: Problems with downscaling climate visualizations. *Geo: Geography and Environment, 6*(1), 1–11.
Star, S. L., & Griesemer, J. R. (1989). Institutional ecology, `translations' and boundary objects: Amateurs and professionals in Berkeley's Museum of Vertebrate Zoology, 1907–39. *Social Studies of Science, 19*(3), 387–420.
Wickberg, A., & Gärdebo, J. (2020). Where humans and the planetary conflate—An introduction to environing media. *Humanities, 9*(3), 65.

CHAPTER 8

Geoengineering in Germany and South Africa: Between Normalization and Emancipative Catastrophism

Iris Hilbrich

1 Introduction

From today's perspective, 2006 marked a radical discursive shift in debates on climate and sustainability: in a widely acclaimed essay at the time, Nobel Prize Laureate in chemistry Paul Crutzen referred to the need for massive technological interventions in the Earth system, so-called geoengineering, as a consequence of "gross political failures" to reduce emissions (Crutzen, 2006, p. 211). Although the debates about technological climate and weather manipulation date back to the post-World War II era or even beyond (Keith, 2000; Oomen & Meiske, 2021), Crutzen's initiative put the notion of a "climate management" on the international scientific and political agenda (cf. Blackstock & Low, 2018). What is considered a commonplace today was a scandal at the time. Crutzen's essay was often seen as breaking a taboo, as many scientists were reluctant to discuss the topic publicly—out of concern that geoengineering could be

I. Hilbrich (✉)
Austrian Institute of Technology, Vienna, Austria
e-mail: iris.hilbrich@ait.ac.at

S. Becker, B. Fladvad (eds.), *Contested Imaginaries of Future Technologies*, https://doi.org/10.1007/978-3-032-11497-6_8

misunderstood as an alternative to climate protection and undermine global sustainability goals (Boettcher & Schäfer, 2017). Since 2009 however, geoengineering is being defined by the Royal Society as "deliberate large-scale manipulation of the planetary environment to counteract anthropogenic climate change" (Shepherd, 2009, p. 1). While the initial debates discussed the various technologies as distant and quasi-dystopian emergency measures, a strong qualitative change in the discourse can be observed (cf. Anshelm & Hansson, 2014). There is now consensus in mainstream climate politics and the majority of natural science discourse that the discussion about technological interventions in the global climate is no longer guided by the question of *if* the interventions will take place, but rather *how* they will be implemented (Wagner, 2021).

The starting point for the analysis in this chapter is an appeal by scientists from the Global South published in *Nature* in April 2018, in which they point to hegemonic inequalities within academic research on geoengineering. The core of their argument is that research into technological intervention options is being carried out without sufficient participation from the Global South, even though the regions in question are already severely affected by the consequences of climate change today:

> Developing countries have most to gain or lose. [...] But most solar-geoengineering research is being done in the well-heeled universities of Europe and North America. Unless that changes, voices from the global north will set the policy agenda and decide which research projects should be accelerated or shut down. [...] Developing countries must be in a position to make up their own minds. Local scientists, in collaboration with others, need to conduct research that is sensitive to regional concerns and conditions. (Rahman et al., 2018, p. 23 f.)

In order to make their voices heard, scientists from the Global South have joined the DEGREES Initiative.[1] Since 2010, the non-profit organization—formerly known as the SRM Governance Initiative (SRMGI)—has been funding research projects on solar geoengineering explicitly in countries of the Global South, including Argentina, Bangladesh, Benin, Indonesia, Iran, Côte d'Ivoire, Jamaica and South Africa. In addition to

[1] https://www.degrees.ngo/, last accessed: 18.07.2024. Self-description of the NGO: "The use or rejection of SRM could be one of the biggest decisions humanity has faced, and this matters most to climate-vulnerable regions".

funding individual, region-specific research, networking workshops are also held at regular intervals.

Controversial discussions about large-scale technological interventions into the Earth system to battle climate change condense fundamental questions about sustainable development, intergenerational equity and regional justice. However, most of these technologies only exist as blueprints to future technological innovation. Moreover, the discursive construction of technological responses to climate change differs fundamentally when adopting a spatial perspective. Vulnerable countries in the Global South are exposed to different threats than comparatively stronger industrialized nations and are particularly compromised when their voices are being excluded from the discourse. Therefore, this contribution argues that an analysis of technological innovation sensitive to spatial difference and neocolonial continuities is paramount for technology assessment and global governance strategies for high-risk technologies.

The empirical analysis of the debates on geoengineering presented in this chapter is based on field research with South African and German scientists working on different geoengineering technologies, conducted between 2019 and 2023. South Africa was chosen as the country of comparative investigation in the tradition of Science Technology Studies (STS), since climate scientists emphasize the particular vulnerability of South Africa, whose semi-arid climate is extremely influenced and endangered by climate variability (Vogel & Swilling, 2018). South Africa's cultivation system is based on rain-fed agriculture, which means it uses water almost exclusively from rainfall without artificial irrigation. Thus, livelihoods are more at risk from the ongoing climate crisis than in other regions of the world due to changing precipitation patterns (Orimoloye et al., 2021). In principle, countries in the Global South are more vulnerable to climatic changes than economically stronger industrialized nations like Germany due to a lack of infrastructure and adaptation options, among other things, in case certain geoengineering technologies were to be implemented. At the same time, the production of knowledge on geoengineering is "heavily dominated by the major research institutions in North America and Europe" (Biermann & Möller, 2019, p. 153). Hence, there is a risk that the greater vulnerability of the Global South will not be adequately represented in the discourse. The regions of the Global South are particularly at risk if their knowledge is excluded from the discourse (Ayalew & Gasc, 2018; Suarez et al., 2018). Geoengineering technologies, especially those related to the manipulation of solar radiation, have global dimensions. The consequences and potential risks would not be limited to the locations of the application, but could also have effects on the global climate, some of which could hardly be anticipated.

Furthermore, in line with the work of STS, major technological changes cannot simply be regarded as the introduction of a new tool into an existing society (Latour & Venn, 2002). Technologies intervene in a society by fundamentally changing the practices and organization of social relationships and social order (Nordmann, 2014). Framed this way, geoengineering appears as an object that not only functions as a potential response to climate change, but also produces its own worlds (Szerszynski, 2010, 2017). Moreover, Sheila Jasanoff (2015)—who initially introduced the concept of sociotechnical imaginaries —defines these as collective visions of a desirable future that emerge from and shape the complex interplay of science, technology and social values. In the context of geoengineering, this framework can shed light on how different actors, institutions and communities envision the role of geoengineering technologies in tackling climate change. Which options are being discussed in response to climate change, to what extent and at what level—global, national or regional—also provides information about deep social negotiation processes of what constitutes a *good life* in the Anthropocene.

After an introduction to the objectives and critique of different categories of geoengineering technologies, this chapter first classifies different discourse positions and underlying sociotechnical imaginaries associated with these high-risk technologies, focusing on solar geoengineering, marine and terrestrial carbon dioxide removal, and the question of whether and how perceptions of the technologies differ in the Global North and South. Based on an extensive document analysis and interviews with experts, four ideal-typical argumentation patterns in the debate on geoengineering were identified, which point to different perceptions of the technologies in South Africa and Germany.

In a second part, the divergent "matters of concern" (Latour, 2004) of geoengineering scientists from the Global North and South are discussed in detail in order to supplement the social science debates on climate technologies. The comparative empirical approach enables the identification of relevant discursive frameworks that provide information about the sociocultural premises of technological innovation processes. The analysis therefore concentrates on the question of why certain technologies are politically and scientifically preferred and, furthermore, how the opportunities for participation in the discourse are structured, particularly with regard to the Global South.

2 Geoengineering: Insights Into a Dynamic and Polarized Controversy

The proposed geoengineering technologies vary greatly. They range from natural forms of reforestation to science fiction-like ideas of mirrors in space or the simulation of volcanic eruptions. However, the technologies are basically divided into two groups.

Carbon dioxide removal technologies (CDR) involve the capture and partial storage of CO_2 using either targeted nature-based approaches like afforestation or technical equipment like direct air capture (DAC). If the captured carbon dioxide is not only stored (so-called carbon capture and storage, CCS) but used in other chemical processes such as fuel production or construction, this is known as Carbon Capture and Utilization (CCU). Marine forms of geoengineering, on the other hand, are designed to stimulate algae growth to sequester and bind CO2 in biomass. If these algae die and sink to the seabed, carbon will be removed from the atmospheric cycle. Discussions on CDR are embedded in the climate policy debates on so-called negative emissions, which are based on the assumption that the reduction in CO_2 concentrations required to meet the Paris climate goals can only be achieved through targeted measures (Tavoni & Socolow, 2013).

On the other hand, research is being carried out into technologies to reduce solar radiation, known as *solar radiation management* (SRM) (Crutzen, 2006; Blackstock & Low, 2018). Proposals for SRM include, for example, mirrors in space, brightening ocean clouds, introducing particles into the stratosphere, and increasing the reflectivity of crops. Especially the introduction of aerosols into the stratosphere (stratospheric aerosol injection, SAI) is the subject of intense and controversial debate, as this could represent a rapid and "cost-effective" crisis intervention in the event of extreme temperature rises (Bellamy et al., 2012). However, SRM technologies are still subject to heated criticism, as they are expected to have highly variable regional impacts, including many undesired (and even unanticipated) side effects. For example, the spatial distribution of precipitation and temperatures, including the monsoon, could change (Niemeier, 2018). Further concern refers to the so-called termination shock. As solar geoengineering only addresses the symptoms but not the causes of climate change, there is a huge risk of an uncontrolled, abrupt rise in temperature if far-reaching social transformation processes are not carried out simultaneously (Keith, 2013). These approaches are therefore discussed only as emergency measures against the threat of catastrophic climate consequences.

Within just six years, the Intergovernmental Panel on Climate Change (IPCC) report changed its perception of geoengineering from a marginal topic involving technologies "that remain largely speculative and unproven and carry the risk of unknown side effects" (IPCC, 2007), to treating it as a "viable option" (IPCC, 2013). Since 2013, all three IPCC working groups have been working on technology assessment of CDR technologies. In the latest IPCC reports from 2022 and 2023, there is no scenario to limit global warming to less than 1.5 degrees without carbon dioxide removal, especially relying on bioenergy production with carbon capture and storage (BECCS). Thus, political and scientific experts agree that the Paris climate goals can only be met if the respective CDR technologies are developed at the required speed and scale.

In Germany, discussions about the use of geoengineering technologies have gained traction since 2019 (Haikola et al., 2019; Linzenich et al., 2019). At the end of February 2024, then German Minister of Economic Affairs, Robert Habeck, announced a re-evaluation of the German CO2 Storage Act, stating: "Without CCS, we cannot possibly achieve the climate targets" (German Federal Ministry for Economic Affairs and Climate Protection, 2024a, own translation).

Simultaneously, the Africa Carbon Markets Initiative (ACMI), launched at the 27th World Climate Summit in Egypt in 2022, emphasizes the role of voluntary carbon markets for the energy transition in Africa (Osinbajo et al., 2022). In addition to the areas of forestry and land use, agriculture, blue carbon, renewable energy, household appliances, transport, livestock, waste management and industrial gases, the strategic plan also refers to the monetary potential of "Engineered Carbon Dioxide Removal" (ibid., p. 16 f.).

The rapidly changing perception of the technologies points to far-reaching processes which can provide information about possible future social trajectories in the Anthropocene. As illustrated below, criticism of geoengineering focuses primarily on SRM technologies, whereas the risks and as yet unknown side effects of CDR technologies are often underestimated. This can have a significant impact on the ecological future, especially when looking at countries in the Global South.

3 Sociotechnical Imaginaries and the Global South

The search for suitable adaptation options and solutions to the ongoing ecological crises is a global issue. However, the urgency of this search is perceived very differently from region to region: while Sub-Saharan Africa has been identified as the most vulnerable region in terms of the effects of climate change and the lack of adaptation options (Kotir, 2011), Germany is considered to be more resilient. For example, the food supply in Germany is still considered secure despite prospects of floods and periods of drought. A key question for the future is therefore: How can humanity respond effectively and cohesively to climate change if the problems/impacts vary greatly from region to region?

Just as sustainability is fundamentally oriented towards the future, technologies and innovations always refer to a specific form of the future—in the case of the proponents of geoengineering, to a technologically shapeable future that sees the solution to the climate problem in the establishment of new technologies by relying on the power of innovation (Keith, 2000; Asafu-Adjaye et al., 2015). Opponents perceive the more extreme measures as a dystopian future that leaves the control of the global climate to a small technocratic elite and imagines the onset of geopolitical hegemonic struggles and even global war scenarios (Klein, 2015). Moreover, most of the technologies under discussion have not materialized yet and currently only exist as models (Rothe, 2020). Experiments with different futures of the Earth system can be carried out in computer laboratories (ibid.). The debate about geoengineering must therefore be seen as a negotiation of speculative futures that can provide information about social developments in the present.

Social imaginations are of central importance here: social visions are co-produced with and projected onto technologies; they shape and are shaped by their development and implementation. According to Sheila Jasanoff, collective sociotechnical imaginaries are embedded as social practices in "assemblages of materiality, meaning and morality" (Jasanoff, 2015, p. 5). The resulting technologies are thus experienced as embedded in worlds and patterns of social relations, which in turn unfold socially as the technology unfolds. Different sociotechnical imaginaries can also coexist dialectically and are always subject to the possibility of exclusion within hegemonic orders (ibid.). Jasanoff's (2004, 2015) comparative research points to power dynamics which determine whose ideas about the future are considered legitimate and highlights the role of institutional structures that favour certain forms of knowledge. Drawing on the distinctive properties of sociotechnical imaginaries in contrast to discourses and narratives, Smith and Tidwell (2016) emphasize the central meaning of state power (Jasanoff & Kim, 2009, p. 123, cited after Smith and Tidwell, 2016): "These exercises of power, such as through the selection of policy priorities, fund allocation, and infrastructure investment, draw attention to the performative nature of sociotechnical imaginaries" (ibid., p. 330). In light of the fierce competition about research funding, tracing the allocation of resources plays a crucial role and sheds light on the underlying imaginaries of the responsible actors. As the following empirical analysis of the debate on geoengineering technologies will highlight, in Germany the focus both politically and scientifically lies mainly on carbon capture and storage technologies (Hilbrich & Adloff, 2021), while SRM plays a much greater role in South Africa through the promotion of funding bodies like the DEGREES Initiative.

4 Typologizing the Debate on High-Risk Technologies

As a theoretical and analytical concept sociotechnical imaginaries "straddle the line between structure and agency". A special emphasis is placed on comparative case studies highlighting "the commonalities and differences in the cultural resources and practices brought to bear on the production and stabilization of sociotechnical imaginaries in different settings".[2] To access this complex interplay methodologically, STS embraces the tool kit of interpretative social research (Law 2016). Hence, in the tradition of the sociotechnical imaginaries framework, the qualitative, comparative analysis of geoengineering technologies in different geographical settings presented here is based on an extensive document analysis (media publications, newsletters, conference papers, open letters, policy papers), ethnographic field research in Germany and South Africa, and the collection of guided expert interviews with scientists involved in research on SRM, CDR or both technology strands (see Table 8.1).

Based on the empirical material, four ideal-typical positions of the discourse on geoengineering have been reconstructed (see Fig. 8.1). These

[2] Cited from: https://sts.hks.harvard.edu/research/platforms/imaginaries/ii.methods/methodological-pointers/, last accessed 01.02.2025.

Table 8.1 Overview of empirical data gathering, 2019–2023. Source: Own compilation

Document analysis	*Ethnographic fieldwork*	*Semi-structured expert interviews*
Policy papers (e.g. IPCC) **Media** publications (newspaper articles, online videos, TV) **Expert** discussions (newsletters, conference papers) **Science policy** and funding frameworks (e.g. HORIZON)	**Panel discussions** **Fairs** (Carbon Capture and Storage Fair, Bremen) **Museums** (Natural History Museum, Berlin; The Future Museum, Nuremberg) **Workshop** on Geoengineering and the Global South, Istanbul **Lab work** with geologists at University of Hamburg **Ethnographic fieldwork South Africa:** three-month stay at Climate System Analysis Group, University of Cape Town	**N = 25** (15 m, 10 w, age 23–65) 15 South Africa, 10 Germany (T = 45–150 minutes) Countries of origin/residence of interviewees: USA, Germany, Botswana, Benin, Brazil, Nigeria, South Africa, Zimbabwe, UK

do not only refer to different patterns of argumentation, but also vary in terms of their acceptance in scientific and public discourse.[3]

Inevitability of CDR (position 1): In the case of the first position, carbon dioxide removal technologies are seen as an unavoidable strategy to address the climate crisis and achieve the 1.5-degree climate target.

Non-use of SRM (position 2): The second line of argument sees solar radiation management as incalculable hubris. It calls for an international agreement on the non-use of these technological interventions, whereby a certain degree of research should generally be permitted.

Unfeasibility of CDR (position 3): The third position unites critical voices from civil society and academia. Experts point to the risks associated with CDR technologies and express their concern or even fear that it is too late to achieve climate policy goals through the use of CDR technologies.

[3] See Pfaller et al. (2018) for an intriguing examination of different types of discourse positions in the context of ethically complex and controversial biomedical discussions.

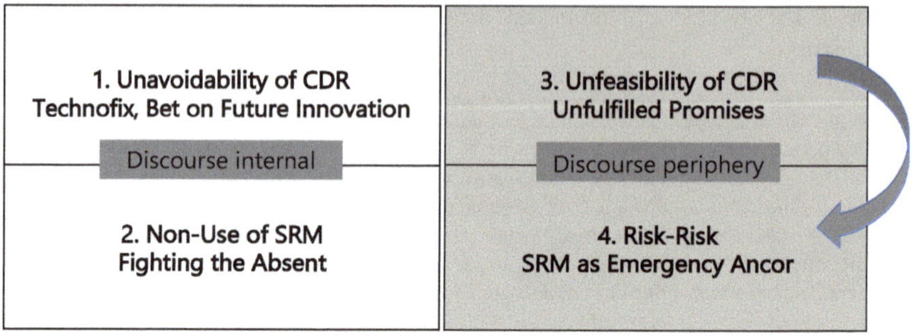

Fig. 8.1 Typology of discourse positions on geoengineering: conflicts and reactions. Source: Own compliation. Discourse internal positions (left) reflect mainstream climate politics, while peripheral positions (right) derived from interviews with climate scientists reveal contradictory perceptions in regard to feasibility and deployment of geoengineering technologies

Risk-risk: SRM as an emergency anchor (position 4): The fourth discourse position opposes the tabooing of SRM and advocates for the use of solar radiation management in the event of a climate emergency. According to this line of argumentation, the effects and risks of increasing global warming must be weighed against the potential risks of SRM.

Positions 1 and 2 can be described as discourse-internal argumentation patterns, as they align with the official political and policy interpretations. As described earlier, the position of an unavoidability of carbon dioxide removal has manifested both nationally (German Carbon Management Strategy) and internationally (IPCC, 2022, 2023). The first position goes hand in hand with the demand for the non-use of SRM (Biermann et al., 2022). Critics point to the incalculable and unanticipated risks of a possible manipulation of solar radiation. As a result, the implementation of these measures should be categorically rejected.

The more marginal, discourse-peripheral positions[4] emerged during the empirical field research. Position 3, which was primarily discussed

[4] From the perspective of communication and discourse theory, the question of who is recognized as a speaker in a situation and in what form is the result of communicative negotiation processes that are never free of power dynamics (cf. Link, 2008). Whoever holds the prerogative of interpretation in a discourse thus decides on the legitimacy or illegitimacy of speaker positions (ibid.). Marginalizations or exclusions are by no means to be understood as the result of binary processes. There is no one morally right or wrong position. Rather, the strategies of exclusion function gradually; the further they move away from the center of the

within the expert interviews, points to the potential unfeasibility of CDR. Many of the interviewees—both in Germany and South Africa—including, interestingly, those who were researching CDR themselves, shared their assessment or even fear that it may be too late to reduce global CO2 concentrations with these technologies. They refer to the possibility of a general failure of CDR strategies, including doubts about necessary scaling and technical feasibility. This stands in strong contradiction to position 1, which frames negative emissions technologies such as CDR as a core component of climate policy solutions.

The fourth discourse position sees SRM as an emergency anchor and conflicts with the second position, which is based on the non-utilization of SRM. This discursive framing also entails the possibility of technological failure and must be seen as a consequence of the third position, the unfeasibility of CDR. Both South African and German scientists, some of whom have been working on SRM technologies since the very beginning, embedded these extreme interventions within a risk-risk paradigm. In the event of a failure of carbon dioxide removal strategies and the associated unregulated global warming, SRM could represent a necessary lifeline for limiting extreme temperature increases. Accordingly, these voices call for a symmetrical technology assessment without excluding SRM from the assessment ex ante while perceiving the possibility of unchecked climate change as an existential risk. After a brief explanation of the discursive separation of CDR and SRM technologies (Sect. 4.1), the specifics and contextualization of the four different discourse positions are discussed in detail below (Sects. 4.2, 4.3, and 4.4).

4.1 Discursive Separation of Carbon Dioxide Removal and Solar Radiation Management

In political and academic publications on geoengineering, a discursive separation of the two technology strands CDR and SRM is evident. This separation, however, can be considered a recent development. While the Royal Society's ground-breaking report (Shepherd, 2009) referred to the differences between the technologies, both approaches were nevertheless subsumed under the collective term "geoengineering". During my interviews, each scientist was asked about their attitude towards both the

"sayable," the higher the probability of crossing the line and being considered irrelevant or wrong and thus excluded from the discourse (Herzog, 2013).

concept and the term geoengineering. Particularly those researchers who focused on CDR technologies pointed to the differences and a necessary distinction from solar radiation management. CDR should be separated from the broader concept of geoengineering, as the idea and the term are historically taboo. Ms Schwartz, a German specialist in solar radiation management who was involved in the first ever publications on SRM with Paul Crutzen, speaks about another aspect that illustrates the divergent academic and social perceptions of the different approaches. On the one hand, she emphasizes the differences between the technologies; on the other hand, she is fundamentally offended by the CDR community's tendency to differentiate between supposedly *good* and *bad* approaches: "What the others would like to have so that they can set themselves apart a bit: They're the bad guys and we're the good guys, because we're taking the CO2 out again". According to Ms Schwartz, the discursive separation results in a devaluation of SRM technologies. This corresponds to the internal discourse argument that CDR addresses the fundamental problem of climate change, while SRM only serves as an additional emergency measure to "buy" time for necessary transformation efforts (Boettcher & Schäfer, 2017; Neuber & Ott, 2020).

The discursive separation of CDR and SRM shows how a particular socio-technical order is stabilizing socially and politically. Science and Technology Studies (STS), and above all Sheila Jasanoff (2004) with her idiom "co-production", remind us how closely interwoven the cultural and the material are. The normative foundations of technology development cannot be separated from its design and implementation, as these are always subject to a process of co-production. Based on the empirical insights into the discourse on geoengineering, particularly with regard to the Global South, it is argued that not all actors share the assessment or necessity of a discursive separation. Rather, from the perspective of some researchers, CDR and SRM represent mutually constitutive socio-material practices. This position is located on the periphery of the discourse.

4.2 From Taboo to Normalization: The Inevitability of Carbon Dioxide Removal

The position of the *inevitability of CDR* illustrates the rapid dynamics of the discourse. As mentioned earlier, geoengineering in the form of CDR has only been officially discussed in the IPCC report since 2013 and is now inevitably included in all scenarios (IPCC, 2022, 2023). The discursive power of the IPCC report has a noticeable impact on scientific research into climate technologies. Mr Miller, a 56-year-old climate modeller and CDR specialist in Germany who has been involved in the geoengineering discussions since the beginning, summarizes the evolution of the debate from recent years as follows:

> I mean, the whole notion of geoengineering or climate engineering was toxic to a lot of scientists for a while. Many people wouldn't touch the subject. Didn't want to be involved with it. (...) I guess until recently now that sort of the IPCC has given it's okay and said, okay, we need CO2 removal.

Mr Miller describes a turning point in the development of the discourse on geoengineering. A taboo subject, which no one in the research community wanted to seriously address and which was even "toxic", became a recognized research topic thanks to the IPCC's "okay". It is only through the external attribution by the IPCC that carbon dioxide removal is discursively validated as a mitigation strategy. This shows a rapid discursive shift from taboo to normalization.

These accelerated developments can also be observed in Germany. While conservative and neoliberal political actors have long expressed their support for technological solutions in the form of CDR (Hilbrich & Adloff, 2021), the German carbon management strategy is now also supported by a radical change of course by the Green Party (Tagesschau, 2023). Then German Minister of Economic Affairs, Robert Habeck, a member of the Green Party, traditionally considered as rather sceptical about technological solutionism, announced in a press release dated 26 February 2024:

> We are taking a pragmatic and responsible decision today: CCS and CCU should be made possible in Germany. Otherwise it will be impossible to achieve the climate targets. The technology is also important for the competitiveness of Germany as an industrial location. Not doing so would put us at a competitive disadvantage and cost us dearly. (Federal Ministry for Economic Affairs and Climate Protection, 2024a, own translation)

These statements can be interpreted as a reaction to failed climate policy and the unforeseen acceleration of climate change. These discursive shifts also show how rapidly a socio-material practice is stabilizing sociopolitically as a future modality of action. Although none of the technologies in question yet exist on a large scale, political decision-makers are placing a bet on future innovations. The former Minister of Economic Affairs also established a link between the necessary use of negative emission technologies and economic competitiveness. A political rejection of the use of CDR therefore seems impossible from an economic perspective: "…abandoning it would cost us dearly".

The normalization of CDR represents a techno-optimistic, eco-modernist scenario, which locates the solution to climate change within the application of various "techno-fixes" (see, among others, Sand et al., 2023). At the same time, this position implies the infrastructural closure of a future (Bowker, 1995) that would be based on a radical transformation of society and its economic structures without technological intervention in the climate.

Another much-discussed position within the discourse is the call for the non-use of solar radiation management. These technologies are the subject of the most controversial debate—both scientifically and in civil society—although they have not yet been (politically) discussed as seriously viable options in the fight against climate change (IPCC, 2022, 2023).

4.3 Non-Use of SRM: Fighting Against the Absent

Numerous arguments against solar radiation management can be found both in political documents and media articles as well as in the differentiated academic publications, which illustrate the clear discursive rejection of these approaches (Hamilton, 2014; Klein, 2015; Stilgoe, 2016; Preston, 2013; Gardiner, 2013). The reports of the Intergovernmental Panel on Climate Change are in favour of carbon dioxide removal, but reject solar geoengineering due to the unpredictable side effects (IPCC, 2013, 2022, 2023). Furthermore, in 2022, more than 60 high-ranking climate scientists and governance experts launched a global initiative calling for an international agreement on the non-use of solar geoengineering (Non-Use Agreement) (Biermann et al., 2022).[5] Their aim is to ban SRM experiments and deployments, but still allow a certain amount of research (ibid.).

The enormous conflict potential of approaches to the manipulation of solar radiation is causing even specialized researchers to turn away from the topic. This is exemplified by a statement from Ms Wimmer, a German

[5] https://www.solargeoeng.org/, last accessed: 18.07.2024.

climate physicist and Earth system modelling specialist who researched SRM as part of her doctorate. She explains her decision to refrain from this research altogether:

> The potential for conflict is so great that I don't think it's a good idea. [....] So why should I do research on something that I don't think we should use? [....] So I think there is a certain arrogance of humanity behind saying that we are manipulating the climate here and can control it.

In the further course of her career, Ms Wimmer decided to only conduct research on CDR technologies. Based on her research findings, she refused to be part of the SRM research community. She sees SRM as Promethean hubris, as "a certain arrogance of humanity" that believes it can control this degree of intervention into the Earth system.

Although debates on the injection of particles into the stratosphere to reduce global temperatures are led much more openly today than at the beginning of Crutzen's intervention, the potential implementation of these approaches is not politically indicated (IPCC, 2022, 2023).[6] Rather, the strong rejection hints at the socio-political negotiation of more or less ecological imaginations of the future.

More recent approaches in Science and Technology Studies assume that it is not technophobic tendencies within a society that lead to resistance to certain technologies— see, for example, genetically modified seeds or criticism of embryo research—but that fundamental social negotiation processes are manifested precisely in resistance to what is absent (Felt, 2015): "The (non) development of specific technoscientific projects, on the one hand, and imagined preferred ways of living, value structures, and social order, on the other, are mutually constitutive" (ibid., p. 104).

Currently there is a unique opportunity to observe and evaluate these climate technology developments, as they mainly exist as blueprints that are currently being defined and contested. As long as socio-technical ideas have not yet stabilized, science and society have an equally important role to play in shaping their future development (Jasanoff & Kim, 2009). Apart

[6] The Climate Overshoot Commission, which emerged from the Paris Peace Forum, is currently calling for a global moratorium on SRM—both experiments and potential use should be strictly regulated politically (Climate Overshoot Commission, 2023). At the same time, the expansion of governance strategies and a research focus on the Global South are being discussed.

from the criticism of SRM and the hopes associated with CDR described above, there have been many critical voices, primarily from civil society, pointing to the risks associated with CDR. However, as will be discussed below, the empirical interviews with CDR experts reveal a further discursive framing that points to a fundamental failure of negative emissions strategies.

4.4 *The Unfeasibility of CDR: Unfulfilled Expectations*

Environmental associations and civil society actors have long pointed out the risks associated with CDR (Schneider & Ribeiro, 2021). The current legislative amendments proposed by the Ministry of Economic Affairs are fuelling the debate in Germany (BUND, 2024).[7] Underground carbon capture and storage (CCS) technologies have been criticized for high costs, lack of scalability and undermining radical transformation efforts (see, among others, Gunderson et al., 2019; Hamilton, 2014). Without a complete conversion to renewable energies, the use of carbon capture technologies would actually increase the demand for fossil resources, as the huge plants require an enormous amount of energy (Buck, 2019). Moreover, the effects would only be visible decades later. There may also be unintended side effects, as with marine geoengineering proposals. For example, the targeted increase in algae growth could contribute to ocean acidification (Schneider, 2020).

An international consortium of renowned scientists recently carried out the first comprehensive assessment of CDR technologies. In the report *The State of Carbon Dioxide Removal* from February 2023, the experts point to glaring dissonances between political expectations of innovation and actual comprehensible technology development. The so-called CDR gap elucidates that the political commitment to CDR is not in line with the actual progress made in technology development and that, further, rapid investment is needed to achieve anywhere near the required scaling of these technologies (Smith et al., 2023).

[7] Among other things, the German carbon management strategy provides for ratification of the amendment to the London Protocol to enable CO_2 exports for offshore storage. The focus is increasingly on the exploration of offshore storage capacities. There are still no intentions to store CO_2 on land (see Federal Ministry for Economic Affairs and Climate Protection, 2024b).

On the one hand, the divergences in terms of scalability stand in contrast to the political expectations of innovation. On the other hand, critical voices point to the possibility of a general failure of negative emission strategies. Mr Bader, an expert on marine CDR from Germany, refers to aspects of the temporality of innovation processes and expresses fundamental doubts about the method of marine carbon dioxide removal:

> If I have to make an assessment on this, I'm not sure humanity would want what we're doing. For that, we have to have sensible, well-founded research. By the time we have that available, it will be too late. Maybe we should have started sensibly ten or twenty years ago.

For Mr Bader, a moral conflict becomes apparent. His statement that he is "not sure humanity would want what we're doing" implies deep ambivalences that reach far beyond rational criticism of technology. He holds fundamental doubts about such major interventions into the Earth system, such as the potential fertilization of the world's oceans, which is the focus of his doctoral thesis. These profound concerns refer to the potential unfeasibility of CDR and thus stand in stark contrast to petro-capitalist framings of carbon dioxide removal as a "solution" to the climate crisis.

The work of the sociologist Jens Beckert helps to provide some guidance here: His analysis points to the constitutive links between technological innovation, imaginations and the role of capitalist structures. Particularly in the initial phases of the innovation processes, actors' fictional expectations are decisive for investments in future technologies (Beckert, 2016). According to Beckert, "...[c]ompetition in capitalist economies [...] is in no small measure a struggle over imaginaries of future technologies" (2016, p. 169). In line with this discourse position, the political hopes associated with CDR are fictitious expectations of an imagined future based on the fulfilment of future technological promises. So far, these concerns have not been translated into political action. However, the results illustrate the dynamic and highly controversial discussions in parts of academia and civil society. CDR technologies therefore carry their own potential risks and pitfalls.

4.5 *Risk-Risk: SRM as Emergency Anchor*

The fourth position, which also has a peripheral discursive status, sees solar radiation management as an "emergency anchor" in the event of unregulated global warming. This is exemplified by the statements of aforementioned climate modeller Ms Schwartz. She challenges the basic idea of solar geoengineering. At the same time, however, she points to a potential failure of climate policies and the slow pace of social change. She is shocked by the lack of transformation efforts, as she says: "We didn't imagine that we would be sitting in 2022 and nothing would happen".

In her view, the risks of geoengineering must be weighed against the risks of unchecked warming due to the serious political omissions. However, she argues that only radical social transformation including massive emissions reductions can provide a viable solution to the climate crisis:

> We all keep emphasizing that no form of geoengineering is viable without drastic emissions reductions; the risk of the weather and climate completely blowing up in our faces if we stop this would simply be enormous.

A rather (techno-)pessimistic scenario and the anticipation of technological failure are manifested here. This is an interesting complementary dimension of the discourse in which solar geoengineering is primarily portrayed as Promethean hubris by social scientists and civil society (Klein, 2015; Hamilton, 2014; Surprise, 2020). However, a closer look at Ms Schwartz's argument reveals a sociotechnical imaginary of deep despair and techno-pessimism rather than a desire for control over nature.

These ambivalences should not be discursively superimposed, but rather recognized as part of a differentiated analysis of geoengineering. The experts themselves refer to the unknown risks and see solar geoengineering only as a "Plan B", which is, however, linked to the fear that solar geoengineering may be necessary in response to the aforementioned climate policy failures (Keith, 2013; Wagner, 2021). Gernot Wagner, one of the founders of the Harvard Solar Radiation Management Program, describes solar geoengineering as a "gamble" with an uncertain outcome (2021).

Moreover, looking at the discursive framings of geoengineering researchers from the Global South opens up yet another layer of complexity. The comparative case study provided insights into the way in which the scientists' contexts shape their perception of the technologies. The positions in Germany and South Africa diverge strongly in the perception of climate-induced risks and dangers.

While most African researchers expressed their desire for a differentiated and unbiased assessment of solar geoengineering, in Germany the call for a discursive separation of CDR and SRM prevailed. The following section argues that the concerns and worries of experts on the African continent can be interpreted as a reaction to colonial legacies and discourses on climate justice. Framed in this way, the analysis of geoengineering discourses in the Global North and South enables a far-reaching understanding of global dynamics and historical contingencies.

5 Reactive Geoengineering: Colonial Legacies

Although the DEGREES Initiative explicitly aims at countering hegemonic epistemological inequalities by funding SRM research in the Global South, it is faced with criticism by both activists and members of the academic community. One of the earliest and harshest critics of the initiative, the Geoengineering Monitor activist group, accuses the DEGREES fund of "Global South washing".[8] They criticize the sponsors of the initiative as tech-oligarchs from the Global North with potential business interests in the technology. For example, a large part of the initiative is funded by the Open Philanthropy foundation, which owns and operates platforms such as Facebook, Instagram and WhatsApp. Moreover, former funders of the initiative include the Carbon War Room, owned by UK billionaire and owner of the second biggest UK airline Richard Branson.[9] This criticism aims to reflect the continued influence of petro-capitalist investors from the Global North on research funding in the Global South. This again shows the complexity of the discourse, as there are also voices from the Global South arguing for the need to conduct more region-sensitive research on solar radiation management in the Global South.

Taking up these claims, in February 2023, 110 climate scientists published a letter in response to the non-use agreement's call for solar geoengineering. The experts, primarily from the Global South, actively advocated for more region-specific analyses to contribute to both a better

[8] https://www.geoengineeringmonitor.org/the-degrees-initiative, last accessed 08.04.2025.

[9] https://www.virgin.com/branson-family/richard-branson-blog/story-carbon-war-room, last accessed 08.04.2025.

understanding and the minimization of potential risks of SRM approaches. Although the Climate Intervention Research Letter does not advocate the implementation of SRM, its appeal is aimed at a holistic view of geoengineering with regard to a potentially necessary application. The urgency of an international technology assessment and the governance of SRM technologies is emphasized, among other things with regard to unintended effects of ecologically oriented policies (Climate Intervention Research Letter, 2023).

Both public letters deal with the challenges and hegemonies of political control of high-risk technologies, but come to divergent conclusions. The Non-Use Agreement emphasizes that fair governance and scientific analysis are simply impossible, which is why geoengineering should not be implemented at all:

> Science networks are dominated by a few industrialized countries, with less economically powerful countries having little or no direct control over them. Technocratic governance based on expert commissions cannot adjudicate complex global conflicts over values, risk allocation and differences in risk acceptance that arise within the context of solar geoengineering. (Biermann et al., 2022, p. n.p.)

While the Climate Intervention Research Letter's appeal also reflects inequalities, it does not advocate for a fundamental ban of SRM. The academics call for more research and strongly ask for the participation of countries in the Global South. This is in line with the statements of a climate modeller and SRM specialist from South Africa, Mr Wright:

> Africa, for instance, it's one of the MOST vulnerable regions to climate change impact. And (…) it's very important for researchers from the South to be able to design their own research when it comes to solar geoengineering and to be able to use those research findings to inform the people living in those regions, but also policy-makers and decision-makers related to what solar geoengineering is, how it could influence their region, et cetera, so that we, too, could have a voice when there is need to discuss the issue.

Mr Wright refers to epistemological inequalities and also calls for more region-specific SRM research for the Global South. In order to have a "voice" in a potential discussion on the implementation of SRM technologies and to make appropriate political decisions, it is important to have a sufficiently differentiated body of knowledge. He also emphasizes the importance of promoting differentiated knowledge production processes in the Global South. It is *very important that researchers from the South are able to develop their own research on solar geoengineering*.

As Biermann and Möller point out, the discussions surrounding geoengineering are largely shaped "by experts from just a small set of countries in the Global North" (2019, p. 151). According to current calculations and modelling, the potential benefits of SRM would be very unevenly distributed. Precipitation levels in particular could vary drastically from region to region (Ricke et al., 2023). What benefits Southern Africa, for example, could have devastating effects on rainfall in Central Africa (Pinto et al., 2020). As a counterpoint to a potential non-use agreement, Ms Smith, an environmental biologist and SRM expert from Nigeria, expresses her fear that only solar geoengineering is a way out of the climate crisis:

> In terms of climate change, the input of Africa is very little in terms of their emission but we are bearing the brunt of climate change. (...) if we inject aerosols, inject several things to the atmosphere it's going to reduce global warming. So it looks like a new messiah, like since man cannot really reduce (...) anthropogenic climate change.

Ms Smith refers to discussions of the polluter pays principle. She addresses the historically unequal distribution of climate-related risks and those responsible for them. While Western societies are significantly responsible for the increase in global emissions, it is primarily poorer societies in the Global South that are already affected by the consequences of global warming. From their perspective, SRM acts as a "new messiah" for people on the African continent. Technological interventions are the only option for Africa in response to worsening climatic conditions. She creates the image of technology as salvation, which is linked to a deterministic doubt about change and social transformation. In her view, there is no hope for fundamental global transformation. Geoengineering is framed as an empowering strategy to counter historical injustices.

Mr Katz, an internationally recognized expert in risk assessment from the University of Cape Town, who has been involved in evaluations of climate-induced impacts on the African continent for decades, establishes a constitutive link between failing climate policies using CDR approaches and the reactive use of solar radiation management:

> It's either carbon dioxide removal to kind of minimize overshoot and then, get back down below two degrees or, if that fails, then solar radiation management and other approaches. […] I think it's sort of misleading that suddenly it looks like there is a solution out there. Something that we've already done. Well, number one is carbon dioxide removal, that actually is not proven yet that it can actually work at the kind of scales that are needed. […] It's quite a dangerous approach to take to base your solutions on as yet unproven, unscaled technologies.

Mr Katz's scepticism is in line with the critical discourse on the unfeasibility of CDR described above, but with a different impetus. As in the case of Ms Smith, a socio-political failure is anticipated and expanded to include the possibility of technological failure. This perspective illustrates the multi-layered levels of discourse in the debate when looking at voices from the Global South.

The effects of historical contingencies in the discourse on geoengineering also become apparent with regard to the opportunities for researchers from the Global South to participate in international research networks.

6 Diverging "Matters of Concern": Continuity Versus Transformation

While debates about CO_2 storage are mainly being promoted on national levels, discussions about a global CO_2 budget and (supposed) CO_2 offsetting[10] are often linked to land use claims in the Global South (Lyons & Westoby, 2014). One reason is that there is simply not enough land available in Europe for reforestation measures or bioenergy production required for carbon capture and storage (BECCS). Accordingly, discussions on justice aspects in carbon dioxide removal strategies are negotiated differently depending on the respective location.

As an example, Mr Gatsby, a biodiversity and climate modelling expert who conducts research on both CDR and SRM approaches at the University of Cape Town, reports strong dissonance in the context of a European research collaboration on CDR. Alongside 17 stakeholders

[10] A scandal involving forged climate certificates in China is currently being investigated in Germany. As the responsible authority, the Federal Environment Agency had approved climate projects in China that apparently only existed on paper (see https://www.bundestag.de/dokumente/textarchiv/2024/kw24-de-aktuelle-stunde-klima-1008086, last accessed: 18.07.2024).

from Europe, he was the only researcher from the Global South to be involved:

> ALL of them from Europe. (...). I mean, I came here frustrated because I just saw it was no much discussion about just like cutting some privileges. (...) There was no discussion about how the Global North should just decrease their energy demand. (...) You talk about at first AFFORESTATION and BECCS which would be done mostly in low-income countries. Because this, for the Global South for those countries would be a sacrifice. If you have to replace a food crop by a biofuel crop. (...) So, and I guess if this will be used to inform policy in the future, which I believe it will, these might be used by the Global North. So okay, 'this is what we need to do' and they'll try maybe to persuade the Global South; this is what you guys need to do. We can't plant here. We need to do afforestation where you are. We can't do it here. It could just perpetuate colonialism in climate science.

This case illustrates the divergent "matters of concern" (Latour, 2004) of scientists, depending on their location. Compared to his European colleagues, the researcher from South Africa argues more strongly in favour of placing carbon dioxide removal technologies in the broader context of (climate) justice. While Mr Gatsby emphasizes the need for a fundamental transformation of energy policies, for example a reduction in energy demand and the dismantling of privileges of the Global North, his European colleagues used the narrative of CDR as a *techno-fix* to maintain the energy policy status quo.

This perspective entails a common criticism within the CDR discourse, which is mainly expressed by voices from the Global South. CDR approaches are associated with fears of neocolonial land grabbing, whereby economically stronger nations purchase land in the Global South on favourable terms (Lyons & Westoby, 2014). This could potentially exacerbate the struggle for food sovereignty in many countries of the Global South, which are already suffering from climate-related crop losses (Hunsberger et al., 2015). This could violate the principles of local climate justice (Batres et al., 2021). In addition, actors from the Global North hold discourse sovereignty over discussions on carbon dioxide removal (Sovacool, 2023) to such an extent that actors from the Global South could ultimately be persuaded to accept an unfavourable situation. Consequently, hegemonic relations could manifest and reproduce in political actions and structures, which would then lead to the maintenance of a *colonialism of climate science.*

Jasanoff's concept of sociotechnical imaginaries emphasizes that science and technology are deeply embedded in the societies that create and utilize them. In the case of geoengineering, while the technologies themselves appear to address the universal climate crisis, the research and discourse surrounding them are shaped by particular cultural values, historical narratives and political interests, revealing the complex interdependencies of a globalized and hegemonic world. While answers to possible climate adaptation and mitigation measures undoubtedly need to be found quickly, the conclusion argues that debates on geoengineering require a high degree of tolerance for ambiguity, as well as thorough, multidimensional assessments in order to evaluate the impact of each technology according to its complexity.

7 Geoengineering in a Global Risk Society: Do We Need More Tolerance for Ambiguity?

In his book The Principle of Responsibility, first published in 1979, German-American philosopher Hans Jonas develops an ethics dedicated to the new civilizational challenges of a high-tech age. The problems addressed by Jonas could hardly be more topical. He argued against naïve faith in technology and referred to the intrinsic rights of nature. Against the backdrop of the Cold War and the debate about nuclear energy, he actively spoke out against research into high-risk technologies in order to prevent the implementation of incalculable technologies. Although Jonas' analysis is impressively far-sighted, the uncomfortable question remains as to whether rapidly advancing climate change could significantly alter the discourse on high-risk technologies. Paul Crutzen would probably have replied to Hans Jonas that the ongoing ecological crises are forcing us to adopt a global perspective.

The climate emergency presents all societies around the globe with a multitude of challenges. However, the possibility of participating in these social debates is shaped by hegemonic discourse structures, depending on the position from which the actors speak. In the context of a "sociology of absences", Portuguese sociologist Boaventura de Sousa Santos describes the invisibility of certain forms of knowledge with the term "epistemicide" (Santos, 2015, 2016). Accordingly, the dominance of Western knowledge is the result of postcolonial practices of domination, which go hand in hand with the marginalization of knowledge from the Global South. As

Sheila Jasanoff shows with the concept of sociotechnical imaginaries, certain visions of alternative social orders are always subject to the potential danger of exclusion if they do not correspond to the hegemonic orders of a discourse (Jasanoff, 2015).

One could fundamentally question whether an inherently pathological discourse can and should be diversified. The imagination of a world in which the climate crisis has progressed to such an extent that humanity is prepared to darken the sun and use technologies with unknown risks is, to a certain extent, a pathological idea whose fundamental advocacy lacks any rationality. However, the rapid developments—in terms of climate, sociopolitics and technology—indicate that the debates surrounding geoengineering will play a central role in shaping more or less ecological futures in the coming decades.

Many of the social science framings of geoengineering, such as the Non-Use Agreement initiated by a social scientist (Biermann et al., 2022), serve to evaluate and normatively classify the phenomenon. The highly polarized discourse sometimes leaves little room for ambivalence. However, deliberation on such far-reaching and contingent phenomena as geoengineering requires a high degree of tolerance for ambiguity. Hence, the perspective chosen here does not aim at a value-based impact assessment, but rather a reconstruction of existing strands of discourse from two distinct geographical settings. In this sense, both carbon dioxide removal and solar radiation management can be framed as ecomodernist narratives, both of which stem from a petro-capitalist logic and are mutually dependent.

In light of the rapid socio-political changes, in one of his last essays with the provocative title "How Climate Change Might Save the World", Ulrich Beck (2014) asked the seemingly disturbing question "What is climate change good for?" Instead of a one-sided focus on the threats posed by climate change, he argues for a cosmopolitan turn towards an "emancipatory catastrophism" (Beck, 2015). According to Beck, the side effects of the climate crisis could create normative horizons that make previously repressed and hidden inequalities visible, so that the past can be "reproblematized through the imagination of a threatening future" (Beck, 2015, p. 83). For him, risk is not synonymous with catastrophe, but rather "the anticipation of future catastrophe in the present, as a horizon of the present future" (Beck, 2014, p. 170). From that angle, the climate crisis in general and the discussions about geoengineering in particular could make historical and spatial inequalities visible and shed light on hegemonic perceptions of risk, colonial continuities and paternalism (also in science). While the focus in Europe rests on maintaining the energy policy status quo, the desire for differentiated research into high-risk technologies, as expressed by the South African researchers, implies the anticipation of an escalation of the climate problem. However, the accelerating climate catastrophes in Europe could significantly modify this divergence in the nearer future. In their *Oxford Open Climate Change* editorial, Wieners et al. (2023) call for balanced research on solar radiation management. Countering the oftentimes polarized discussions of geoengineering, they conclude that a rejection of research into SRM could be in itself undemocratic due to the unjust allocation of resources. In their eyes, "…[t]ransparent research, outreach and capacity building, especially in vulnerable developing countries, can empower citizens and underrepresented regions to take part in the debate and pre-empt rogue actors from monopolizing SRM knowledge" (Wieners et al., 2023, p. 2). Thus, in a worst-case scenario, the progression of climate change will encourage talks about the introduction of solar geoengineering. In a best-case scenario, discussions about geoengineering act as an impetus for far-reaching global debates about responsibility and justice in a rapidly changing world.

Acknowledgement Firstly, I would like to express my deep gratitude to all the interview participants for devoting their time and expertise. Their knowledge forms the basis of this study. Special thanks go to the African Climate and Development Initiative at the University of Cape Town and the Humanities Centre for Advanced Studies "Futures of Sustainability" at the University of Hamburg, without whom this research would not have been possible. My gratitude also goes to the editors and reviewers for their constructive feedback and support.

References

Anshelm, J., & Hansson, A. (2014). The last chance to save the planet? An analysis of the geoengineering advocacy discourse in the public debate. *Environmental Humanities, 5*(1), 101–123.

Asafu-Adjaye, J., Blomqvist, L., Brand, S., Brook, B., Defries, R., Ellis, E., Foreman, C., Keith, D., Lewis, M., Lynas, M., Nordhaus, T., Pielke, R., Jr., Pritzker, R., Roy, J., Sagoff, M., Shellenberger, M., Stone, R., & Teague, P. (2015). *An ecomodernist manifesto.* Breakthrough Institute.

Ayalew, M. M., & Gasc, F. (2018). Managing climate risks in Africa. The role of geoengineering. In J. J. Blackstock & S. Low (Eds.), *Geoengineering our climate? Ethics, politics, and governance* (pp. 175–178). Routledge.

Batres, M., Wang, F. M., Buck, H., Kapila, R., Kosar, U., Licker, R., Nagabhushan, D., Rekhelman, E., & Suarez, V. (2021). Environmental and climate justice and technological carbon removal. *The Electricity Journal, 34*(7), 107002.

Beck, U. (2014). How climate change might save the world. *Development and Society, 43*(2), 169–183.

Beck, U. (2015). Emancipatory catastrophism: What does it mean to climate change and risk society? *Current Sociology, 63*(1), 75–88.

Beckert, J. (2016). *Imagined futures. Fictional expectations and capitalist dynamics.* Harvard University Press.

Bellamy, R., Chilvers, J., Vaughan, N. E., & Lenton, T. M. (2012). A review of climate geoengineering appraisals. *Wiley Interdisciplinary Reviews: Climate Change, 3*(6), 597–615.

Biermann, F., & Möller, I. (2019). Rich man's solution? Climate engineering discourses and the marginalization of the global south. *International Environmental Agreements: Politics, Law and Economics, 19*, 151–167.

Biermann, F., Oomen, J., Gupta, A., Ali, S. H., Conca, K., Hajer, M. A., Kashwan, P., Kotzé, L. J., Leach, M., Messner, D., Okereke, C., Persson, Å., Potočnik, J., Schlosberg, D., Scobie, M., & VanDeveer, S. D. (2022). Solar geoengineering: The case for an international non-use agreement. *Wiley Interdisciplinary Reviews: Climate Change, 13*(3), e754.

Blackstock, J. J., & Low, S. (Eds.). (2018). *Geoengineering our climate? Ethics, politics, and governance.* Routledge.

Boettcher, M., & Schäfer, S. (2017). Reflecting upon 10 years of geoengineering research: Introduction to the Crutzen + 10 special issue. *Earth's Future, 5*(3), 266–277.

Bowker, G. C. (1995). Second nature once removed: Time, space and representations. *Time and Society, 4*(1), 47–66.

Buck, H. J. (2019). *After geoengineering. Climate tragedy, repair, and restoration.* Verso Books.

BUND. (2024). CCS: Breites Umweltbündnis warnt vor gefährlichem Irrweg. *BUND, Pressemitteilung.* Retrieved July 17, 2024, from https://www.bund.net/service/presse/pressemitteilungen/detail/news/ccs-breites-umweltbuendnis-warnt-vor-gefaehrlichem-irrweg/.

Bundesministerium für Wirtschaft und Klimaschutz. [German Federal Ministry for Economic Affairs and Climate Action]. (2024a). Habeck will den Einsatz von CCS ermöglichen: Ohne CCS können wir unmöglich die Klimaziele erreichen. *Bundesministerium für Wirtschaft und Klimaschutz, Pressemitteilung.* Retrieved July 17, 2024, from https://www.bmwk.de/Redaktion/DE/Pressemitteilungen/2024/02/20240226-habeck-will-den-einsatz-von-ccs-ermoeglichen.html

Bundesministerium für Wirtschaft und Klimaschutz. [German Federal Ministry for Economic Affairs and Climate Action]. (2024b). Eckpunkte der

Bundesregierung für eine Carbon Management-Strategie. Retrieved July 17, 2024, from https://www.bundeswirtschaftsministerium.de/Redaktion/DE/Downloads/E/240226-eckpunkte-cms.pdf?__blob=publicationFile&v=6.

Climate Intervention Research Letter. (2023). An open letter regarding research on reflecting sunlight to reduce the risks of climate change. *Climate Intervention Research Letter*. Retrieved July 17, 2024, from https://climate-intervention-research-letter.org/.

Climate Overshoot Commission. (2023). Reducing the risks of climate overshoot. *Climate Overshoot Commission*. Retrieved July 17, 2024, from https://www.overshootcommission.org/report.

Crutzen, P. J. (2006). Albedo enhancement by stratospheric sulfur injections: A contribution to resolve a policy dilemma? *Climatic Change, 77*, 211–220.

Felt, U. (2015). Keeping technologies out: Sociotechnical imaginaries and the formation of Austria's technopolitical identity. In S. Jasanoff & S.-H. Kim (Eds.), *Dreamscapes of Modernity. sociotechnical imaginaries and the fabrication of power* (pp. 103–125). University of Chicago Press.

Gardiner, S. (2013). "The desperation argument for geoengineering", *PS. Political Science and Politics, 46*(1), 28–33.

Gunderson, R., Stuart, D., & Petersen, B. (2019). The political economy of geoengineering as Plan B: Technological rationality, moral hazard, and new technology. *New Political Economy, 24*(5), 696–715.

Haikola, S., Hansson, A., & Anshelm, J. (2019). From polarization to reluctant acceptance – Bioenergy with Carbon capture and storage (BECCS) and the post-normalization of the climate debate. *Journal of Integrative Environmental Sciences, 16*(1), 45–69.

Hamilton, C. (2014). *Earthmasters. The dawn of the age of climate engineering*. Yale University Press.

Herzog, B. (2013). Ausschluss im (?) Diskurs. Diskursive Exklusion und die neuere soziologische Diskursforschung. *FQS, 14*(2), 19.

Hilbrich, I., & Adloff, F. (2021, November). Heil oder Hybris. Wäre Geoengineering ein realistischer Weg, um die Erderwärmung zu drosseln? *taz am Wochenende, 13* (14), 15.

Hunsberger, C., Corbera, E., Borras, S. M., Jr., de la Rosa, R., Eang, V., Franco, J. C., Herre, R., Kham, S. S., Park, C., Pred, D., Sokheng, H., Spoor, M., Thein, S., Thu, K., Thuon, R., Vaddhanaphuti, C., Woods, K., & Work, C. (2015). Land-based climate change mitigation, land grabbing and conflict: Understanding intersections and linkages, exploring actions for change. *MOSAIC Working Paper Series, 1*, 1–26.

IPCC. (2007). Climate change 2007. Synthesis report. In R. K. Pachauri & A. Reisinger (Eds.), *Contribution of Working Groups I, II, and III to the Fourth Assessment Report of the Intergovernmental Panel on Climate Change*. IPCC.

IPCC. (2013). Climate change 2013. The physical science basis. In T. F. Stocker, D. Qin, G.-K. Plattner, M. M. B. Tignor, S. K. Allen, J. Boschung, Y. Alexander Nauels, V. B. Xia, & P. M. Midgley (Eds.), *Contribution of Working Group I to the Fifth Assessment Report of the Intergovernmental Panel on Climate Change*. Cambridge University Press.

IPCC. (2022). Climate change 2022. Impacts, adaptation, and vulnerability. In H.-O. Pörtner, D. C. Roberts, M. M. B. Tignor, E. Poloczanska, K. Mintenbeck, A. Alegría, M. Craig, S. Langsdorf, S. Löschke, V. Möller, A. Okem, & B. Rama (Eds.), *Contribution of Working Group II to the Sixth Assessment Report of the Intergovernmental Panel on Climate Change*. Cambridge University Press.

IPCC. (2023). Climate change 2023. Synthesis report. In The Core Writing Team, H. Lee, & J. Romero (Eds.), *Contribution of Working Groups I, II and III to the Sixth Assessment Report of the Intergovernmental Panel on Climate Change* (pp. 35–115). IPCC.

Jasanoff, S. (Ed.). (2004). *States of knowledge. The co-production of science and social order*. Taylor and Francis.

Jasanoff, S. (2015). Future imperfect: Science, technology, and the imaginations of modernity. In S. Jasanoff & S.-H. Kim (Eds.), *Dreamscapes of modernity. Sociotechnical imaginaries and the fabrication of power* (pp. 1–33). University of Chicago Press.

Jasanoff, S., & Kim, S.-H. (2009). Containing the Atom: Sociotechnical Imaginaries and Nuclear Power in the United States and South Korea. *Minerva, 47*, 119–146.

Jonas, H. (1979). *Das Prinzip Verantwortung*. Suhrkamp.

Keith, D. (2013). *A case for climate engineering*. MIT Press.

Keith, D. W. (2000). Geoengineering the climate: History and prospect. *Annual Review of Environment and Resources, 25*, 245–284.

Klein, N. (2015). *Die Entscheidung. Kapitalismus vs. Klima*. S. Fischer.

Kotir, J. H. (2011). Climate change and variability in Sub-Saharan Africa: A review of current and future trends and impacts on agriculture and food security. *Environment, Development and Sustainability, 13*, 587–605.

Latour, B. (2004). Why has critique run out of steam? From matters of fact to matters of concern. *Critical Inquiry, 30*(2), 225–248.

Latour, B., & Venn, C. (2002). Morality and technology. *Theory, Culture and Society, 19*(5–6), 247–260.

Law, J. (2016). STS as Method. In U. Felt, R. Miller, D. R. Moore, & L. Smith (Eds.), *The Handbook of Science and Technology Studies* (4th ed., p. 31-37). MIT Press.

Link, J. (2008). Sprache, Diskurs, Interdiskurs und Literatur: (mit einem Blick auf Kafkas Schloß). In H. Kämper & L. Eichinger (Eds.), *Sprache - Kognition - Kultur: Sprache zwischen mentaler Struktur und kultureller Prägung* (pp. 115–134). de Gruyter.

Linzenich, A., Arning, K., Offermann-van Heek, J., & Ziefle, M. (2019). Uncovering attitudes towards carbon capture storage and utilization technologies in Germany: Insights into affective-cognitive evaluations of benefits and risks. *Energy Research and Social Science, 48*, 205–218.

Lyons, K., & Westoby, P. (2014). Carbon colonialism and the new land grab: Plantation forestry in Uganda and its livelihood impacts. *Journal of Rural Studies, 36*, 13–21.

Neuber, F., & Ott, K. (2020). The buying time argument within the solar radiation management discourse. *Applied Sciences, 10*(13), 4637.

Niemeier, U. (2018). Climate-Engineering: Ein Wundermittel gegen den Klimawandel? In J. L. Lozán, S. W. Breckle, H. Graßl, & D. Kasang (Eds.), *Warnsignal Klima: Extremereignisse* (pp. 357–361). Verlag Wissenschaftliche Auswertungen.

Nordmann, A. (2014). Responsible innovation, the art and craft of anticipation. *Journal of Responsible Innovation, 1*(1), 87–98.

Oomen, J., & Meiske, M. (2021). Proactive and reactive geoengineering: Engineering the climate and the lithosphere. *Wiley Interdisciplinary Reviews: Climate Change, 12*(6), e732.

Orimoloye, I. R., Zhou, L., & Kalumba, A. M. (2021). Drought disaster risk adaptation through ecosystem services-based solutions: Way forward for South Africa. *Sustainability, 13*(8), 4132.

Osinbajo, Y., Duque Márquez, I., Nazareth, A., Thevasagayam, S., Caldwell, G., Kenewendo, B., Antonioli, D., Lopokoiyit, S., Perez, A., ElGizy, R., Sanjayan, M., Ogunbiyi, D., Nganga, J. (2022). *Africa CARBON Markets Initiative (ACMI): Roadmap report. Harnessing Carbon Markets for Africa.*

Pfaller, L., Hansen, S. L., Adloff, F., & Schicktanz, S. (2018). 'Saying no to organ donation': an empirical typology of reluctance and rejection. *Sociology of Health & Illness, 40*(8), 1327–1346.

Pinto, I., Jack, C., Lennard, C., Tilmes, S., & Odoulami, R. C. (2020). Africa's Climate Response to Solar Radiation Management with Stratospheric Aerosol. *Geophysical Research Letters, 47*(2), e2019GL086047.

Preston, C. J. (2013). Ethics and geoengineering: Reviewing the moral issues raised by solar radiation management and carbon dioxide removal. *Wiley Interdisciplinary Reviews: Climate Change, 4*(1), 23–37.

Rahman, A. A., Artaxo, P., Asrat, A., & Parker, A. (2018). Developing countries must lead on solar geoengineering research. *Nature, 556*, 22–24.

Ricke, K., Wan, J. S., Saenger, M., & Lutsko, N. J. (2023). Hydrological consequences of solar geoengineering. *Annual Review of Earth and Planetary Sciences, 51*, 447–470.

Rothe, D. (2020). Governing the end times? Planet politics and the secular eschatology of the anthropocene. *Millennium: Journal of International Studies, 48*(2), 143–164.

Sand, M., Hofbauer, B. P., & Alleblas, J. (2023). Techno-Fixing non-compliance-geoengineering, ideal theory and residual responsibility. *Technology in Society, 73*, 102236.

Santos, B. d. S. (2015). *Epistemologies of the South: Justice against Epistemicide.* Routledge.

Santos, B. d. S. (2016). Epistemologies of the South and the future. *From the European South: A Transdisciplinary Journal of Postcolonial Humanities, 1*, 17–29.

Schneider, L. (2020). Ein Technofix für das Klima? Die Interessen hinter dem Geoengineering im Meer. *Forum Umwelt und Entwicklung – Rundbrief, 1(2020)*, 23–25.

Schneider, L., & Ribeiro, S. (2021). Netto-null und geoengineering. *Heinrich Böll Stiftung*, letzter Zugriff. Retrieved July 17, 2024, from https://www.boell.de/de/2021/10/06/netto-null-und-geoengineering.

Shepherd, J. G. (2009). *Geoengineering the climate: Science, governance and uncertainty.* The Royal Society.

Smith, J. M., & Tidwell, A. S. (2016). The everyday lives of energy transitions: Contested sociotechnical imaginaries in the American West. *Social Studies of Science, 46*(3), 327–350.

Smith, S. M., Geden, O., Nemet, G. F., Gidden, M., Lamb, W. F., Powis, C., Bellamy, R., Callaghan, M., Cowie, A., Cox, E., Fuss, S., Gasser, T., Grassi, G., Greene, J., Lück, S., Mohan, A., Müller-Hansen, F., Peters, G., Pratama, Y., Repke, T., Riahi, K., Schenuit, F., Steinhauser, J., Strefler, J., Valenzuela, J. M., Minx, J. C. (2023). *The state of carbon dioxide removal -1st Edition.* University of Oxford.

Sovacool, B. K. (2023). Expanding carbon removal to the Global South: Thematic concerns on systems, justice, and climate governance. *Energy and Climate Change, 4*, 100103.

Stilgoe, J. (2016). Geoengineering as collective experimentation. *Science and Engineering Ethics, 22*, 851–869.

Suarez, P., Banerjee, B., & Mendler de Suarez, J. (2018). Geoengineering and the humanitarian challenge: What role for the most vulnerable? In J. J. Blackstock & S. Low (Eds.), *Geoengineering Our Climate? Ethics, Politics, and Governance* (pp. 193–197). Routledge.

Surprise, K. (2020). Stratospheric imperialism: Liberalism, (eco)modernization, and ideologies of solar geoengineering research. *Environment and Planning E: Nature and Space, 3*(1), 141–163.

Szerszynski, B. (2010). Reading and writing the weather. *Theory, Culture and Society, 27*(2–3), 9–30.

Szerszynski, B. (2017). Coloring climates: Imagining a geoengineered world. In U. Heise, J. Christensen, & M. Niemann (Eds.), *The Routledge companion to the environmental humanities* (pp. 82–90). Routledge.

Tagesschau. (2023). Grüner Kurswechsel bei der CO2-Speicherung. *Tagesschau*, letzter Zugriff. Retrieved July 17, 2024, from https://www.tagesschau.de/inland/innenpolitik/gruene-parteitag-co2-speicherung-100.html.

Tavoni, M., & Socolow, R. (2013). Modeling meets science and technology: An introduction to a special issue on negative emissions. *Climatic Change, 118*, 1–14.

Vogel, C., & Swilling, M. (2018). Climate change and vulnerability in South Africa: Sustainability transitions in a changing climate? In N. Mohamed (Ed.), *Sustainability transitions in South Africa* (pp. 40–57). Routledge.

Wagner, G. (2021). *Geoengineering. The gamble.* John Wiley & Sons.

Wieners, C. E., Hofbauer, B. P., De Vries, I. E., Honegger, M., Visioni, D., Russchenberg, H. W., & Felgenhauer, T. (2023). Solar radiation modification is risky, but so is rejecting it: A call for balanced research. *Oxford Open. Climate Change, 3*(1), kgad002.

CHAPTER 9

Greening Earth Through Outer Space: Promises and Contestations

Craig Henry Jones

1 Introduction

Outer Space has been a fertile area from which a multitude of variegated future imaginaries have been created and recreated, whether these be social, political, cultural, or technological in their focus. Indeed, the sociotechnical imaginaries of Outer Space are so pronounced that it is "already fully leaden with cosmic dreaming, theological wonderings, and science fiction fabulations" (Kearnes & van Dooren, 2017; p.179). Whilst these various Outer Space imaginaries have spanned centuries, they became particularly prevalent during the Cold War's *Space Race* and attendant *astroculture* (Diaz, 2018; Dick, 2018; Ellis, 2017; Eisfeld, 2018; Garrett, 2016; Geppert, 2018; Messeri, 2016; Scoles, 2016; Triscott, 2016). The sociotechnical imaginaries reproduced during this period broadly fell into science fiction pop culture or—perhaps more prominently—featured in the military and political discourses of the superpowers as an area of potential threat that required planning and prognostication to pre-empt potential threats (Carr, 2010; Holden, 1975; Poo, 2012). However, whilst

C. H. Jones (✉)
Lancaster University, Lancaster, UK
e-mail: c.jones45@lancaster.ac.uk

S. Becker, B. Fladvad (eds.), *Contested Imaginaries of Future Technologies*, https://doi.org/10.1007/978-3-032-11497-6_9

there remain plenty of military discussions regarding the potential (mis) uses of Outer Space (see Anantatmula, 2013; Bowen, 2020; Mistry & Gopalaswamy, 2012 for further discussion), the notion of governments as the principal driver(s) of Space policy and technologies has increasingly come to be regarded as *old space*, making way for an increasing level of involvement from private actors in the *new space* era (see Davidian, 2020 and Paikowsky, 2017 for further discussion on this distinction).

Recent years have seen a large increase in the number of private actors coming to be involved in Outer Space, a phenomenon and sector that has been dubbed the NewSpace Economy (NSE). Private actor involvement has rapidly increased over the course of the past decade and is now involved in all aspects of Outer Space operations—spanning launch capacities, satellite capabilities, crewed space launches, and hardware development (Grady, 2017; Luscombe & Sample, 2020). This growth in the number of actors involved in Outer Space operations and development has instigated a renewed discussion of—and interest in—Outer Space and the potential futures that may arise through working with(in) this domain. Indeed, these discussions and attendant sociotechnical imaginaries now span areas such as lunar bases (Dunbar, 2020; Klinger, 2017), Martian habitation to ensure human species survival (Zubrin, 2021), space-based solar power (Enel, 2024; ESA, 2022; GreenMatch, 2024; Space Solar, 2024), and asteroid mining (Rincon, 2013). Whilst each of these speculative technologies has received varying levels of attention in their respective rights—being linked through multiple, distinct discourses surrounding notions of *destiny*, speculative growth and new economies, and sustainable or green futures—this chapter takes asteroid mining as its main focus to explore these discourses and the way(s) the *green* futures of Outer Space are recreated by private actors operating within the NSE.

Amongst the speculative technologies noted above, plans for asteroid mining have had persistent traction within the NSE sector for over a decade, beginning in 2012 with the creation of Deep Space Industries (DSI) (now owned by Bradford Space) and Planetary Resources (now owned by ConcenSys), with the sector expanding over the past 10 years to include companies such as Asteroid Mining Company (AMC), AstroForge, Aten Engineering, Deltion Innovations Ltd., Kleos Space, Neora, Offworld, Planetoids Mine Company, Spacefab.us, Space Resources Australia, and TransAstra. Indeed, speculation regarding the potential for asteroid mining has resulted in the creation of a nascent industry sector that is presently estimated to be worth US$1.38 billion (The Business

Research Company, 2024) and increasing in value to approximately US$3.868 billion by 2028 (Statista, 2024). Whilst the value of an asteroid was first estimated by Cole (1963), the purported value of asteroids (also known as Near Earth Objects (NEOs)) has been a frequent staple of news headlines over the years (see Jamasmie, 2014, 2020 for some examples). This speculation has led to commentators dubbing current endeavours to mine extraterrestrial materials as a *new Space Race* or *modern Gold Rush* (see Cofield, 2016; Farrell, 2013; Grady, 2017; Pandya, 2019 for further discussion).

Plans for extraterrestrial extractivism have been posited as a means of opening new and emerging resource frontiers: a discourse that is reproduced by and through the efforts of both State and private actors, particularly through their positioning of green futures as contingent upon the mineral deposits targeted within their speculative efforts. Indeed, there are two core narratives espoused that are mutually reinforcing in the green discourses of Outer Space: the first posits that green futurity on Earth is contingent upon mining minerals in Outer Space, as this would ensure that mineral demands in the manufacturing of *green* technologies are met. The second holds that extraterrestrial futurity itself is contingent upon *green tech*, thereby reinforcing an increasingly normative discourse on asteroid mining's potential to realize a green future in different ways.

Taking asteroid mining as the Outer Space technology of focus throughout this chapter, the means by and through which the sociotechnical imaginaries of Outer Space are (ab)used to position it as a means of achieving *green* or sustainable futures are explored. The ensuing discussion draws upon fieldwork conducted as part of a doctoral study between 2016 and 2021. This research used a multiple method approach that generated data consisting of 20 in-depth interviews; 87 science fiction novels, short stories, films, and videogames; participant observation of three NSE conferences (generating fieldnotes, collecting advertising materials, taking 171 photographs, and attending over 50 talks); four national asteroid mining policy documents; grey literature on asteroid mining; website materials from asteroid mining companies being collected (specifically DSI and Planetary Resources at the time); and concept art. Interviews were conducted both in person during NSE conferences as these events provided access to key figures within the NSE community, and online when time would not allow for an in-person interview. This multiple method approach was adopted due to the recognition that the groups targeted for interview are small and difficult to access, and—due to their constituting *elites* in some regards—it has been noted in the literature that collecting multiple forms of data in such circumstances is prudent (see Moyser & Wagstaffe, 1987; Shore, 2002). Whilst this doctoral research produced a wealth of data, this chapter will draw primarily upon fieldnotes generated during NSE conference attendance, interview contents, and online materials. Through engaging with these data, this chapter explores the way(s) in which Outer Space and asteroid mining are repositioned by various actors as a route to achieving *green* futures whilst permitting the continued accumulation of capital demanded by a neoliberal private sector. The first part of the chapter explores the imaginaries and promises espoused by NSE advocates that are intended to create rapport and enhance legitimacy through purported egalitarian efforts. The latter part of the chapter briefly explores some of the issues that are frequently left out of these discussions, asking questions of land rights, ownership, extractive waste, and *whose* conception of the future is heard and, consequently, is deemed to *matter*. Following this, the chapter will conclude with a brief deliberation on how, as critical scholars, we can begin to interrogate some of these normative discourses of the sociotechnical imaginaries of Outer Space and where we may go from here.

Endeavours to engage in extraterrestrial extractivism have come to hold a special place within the geographical imaginary of Outer Space and its associated techno-utopianism (Deberdt & Le Billon, 2023). The sociotechnical imaginaries of Outer Space frequently feature the extraction and manipulation of all sorts of mineral deposits through what State and NSE actors refer to as In-Situ Resource Utilisation (ISRU) (ESA, 2021). Whilst ISRU is often framed through a practical lens, i.e. materials can be used where they are found rather than being launched into space, thereby reducing costs, various actors have posited that asteroid mining can enable unlimited growth as markets, human, and—with these—economic activity expand throughout the solar system (Lewicki et al., 2013). Indeed, arguments that asteroid mining poses unlimited potential regarding capital accumulation whilst simultaneously presenting an opportunity to *solve* issues of environmental degradation are not particularly new. Rather they are the latest manifestation of socio-ecological fixes being proposed in the face of capitalism in crisis and climate change (McCarthy, 2015) and as a means of using nature (however we may define it) as an accumulation strategy (Smith, 2007). Alongside arguments for supposedly unlimited growth and accumulation, other actors argue that mining in Outer Space is inevitable as going to other planets and travelling throughout the solar system are certain due to it being humanity's *destiny* (Sage, 2008), drawing upon colonial discourses of exploration and frontiers to an extent that has led Olson (2018) to refer to a colonial model of spacefaring that centres this as a mode of human destiny. A further argument utilized by NSE advocates for the development of an off-Earth economy and extractive industry is that of species survival (Taylor, 2022; Valentine, 2012). This line of argument posits that humanity must become a multiplanetary species to ensure continued survival at the species level, using other planets and celestial bodies to diversify the range of places inhabited should something happen to Earth. Rather than operating singularly, these discourses are often mobilized in concert to state the case for taking humanity and various activities off Earth and into Outer Space.

However, whilst these different discourses are often used to advocate for asteroid mining and subtend the sociotechnical imaginaries NSE actors seek to create and reinforce, perhaps the most frequent discourse is that of using space to create a green future for humanity and the Earth more generally. Due to the prominence of this discourse and the frequency with which it is used, I turn now to consider this strand of sociotechnical imaginary in its own right.

2 Asteroid Mining, Outer Space, and the *Green Imperative*

The creation of a green discourse for Outer Space sees multiple and variegated claims come together in an attempt to position Outer Space and asteroid mining as a *green* solution to contemporary issues of ecological destruction. Indeed, whilst terrestrial mining companies have sought to minimize resistance to their operations' social and environmental impacts through *greening* their image (Gamu & Dauvergne, 2018; Gilbert, 2020a, 2020b; Parsons et al., 2014), these impacts can be (in)directly observed and called out. However, asteroid mining—and extraterrestrial extraction more broadly—is unfolding in a realm of *invisibility*, an imagined space, the interactions with(in) which the characteristics and dynamics are narrated and reshaped by those in power (Steinberg, 2018; Gamu & Dauvergne, 2018; Gilbert, 2020b). This came through during interviews with NSE actors and can be found throughout grey literature associated with the asteroid mining sector.

A key argument used to prop up the *green* credentials of asteroid mining is the moral imperative, one that frames asteroid mining as fundamental to keeping the Earth habitable through the *off-worlding* of polluting industries. Matloff et al. dedicate an entire chapter of their book Harvesting Space for a Greener Earth to the moral argument for space-based industry and extraction. In it they write:

> …in order for humans to prosper and be good stewards of the planet and its myriad life forms, they must stop destroying the environment that gives it life. But how do we accomplish this goal and maintain all of the positive aspects that come from our twenty-first-century technological civilization? The answer is pretty simple. We must place heavy industry, with all of its inevitable pollution, in a place that is already hostile to life and in which life will almost certainly never arise – in space or on the Moon. A space-based infrastructure is not only possible but also essential if we are to restore our home planet and turn it into a safe place to live, pollution free. (Matloff et al., 2014, p.12)

This moral argument for the relocation of heavy industry into space is not confined to books and papers by space advocates and engineers only. This strand of thought is firmly embedded in discussions of Outer Space futurity and the role it will play in preserving Earth. Indeed, Jeff Bezos—one of the three billionaires looking to make space their personal domain—has made a similar point regarding the moving of heavy industry into Outer Space:

> Our descendants are going to move all heavy industry off of Earth — all the polluting industry will be done in space where we have infinite resources for all practical matters and Earth can be zoned, light industry and residential….Earth can be this amazing garden.[1]

This idea of Outer Space as a veritable cornucopia of infinite resources becomes enmeshed with the moral dimension of the *green imperative* in two distinct ways. Firstly, advocates link this through to the removal of polluting industries, to preserve Earth and "to provide a brighter future for all of mankind". Secondly, the moral case is linked through to raising living standards for everyone. Whilst Matloff et al. (2014) note at the start

[1]Speaking at Amazon India event, available at https://www.youtube.com/watch?v=jzfXlg-wyUU.

of their book that to provide everyone with the same standard of living would see a dramatic increase in greenhouse gas emissions, NSE advocates such as James—a NewSpace advocate, consultant, and co-founder of their own NSE company—argue that asteroid mining provides a neat solution to these problems:

> The fact of the matter is that if you look at the solar system, it's nonsense [that there aren't enough resources for a viable future], you know? It's...silliness to imply that...all humans, we have enough – in the solar system – resources to provide all humans with a standard of living equivalent to...Western democracies....We have huge numbers of people and we have resources that do far less environmental damage and we can get it at a far lower cost, so we can provide a much better standard of living for a much larger number of people, at much less damage than we've ever done in history.... (quote from interview)

Here, James' comments clearly outline an argument used by asteroid mining advocates to subtend the *green imperative* discourse: asteroid mining has to happen not only to save the Earth from ecological decline and climate catastrophe, but also to raise the living standards of everyone at the same time. With this in mind, we can see how the characteristics and dynamics of asteroid mining are being narrated and reshaped by those in power (Gamu & Dauvergne, 2018; Steinberg, 2018) to produce and perpetuate within this imagined space a utopic futurity, one in which scarcity ceases to be an issue without the attendant issues of pollution, whilst further entrenching and legitimizing a capitalist mode of production and exploitation.

Beyond the moral arguments advocates use to promote their industry, asteroid mining is advanced through a *green imperative* linking their activities to sustainability and market demands for certain choice elements that are required for renewable technologies. Thus, rather than simply framing the industry as a site of capital accumulation and immense profit potential, the industry has attempted to diversify its appeal, speaking to demands for renewable technologies. If we consider Fig. 9.1, Planetary Resource's infographic states the need for platinum group metals for advanced materials and catalytic converters, and it notes that one in four manufactured goods requires these metals. This is not simply designed to appeal to market demand (although this is a major aspect due to the private nature of these ventures) but to align asteroid mining narratives to ideas of a green

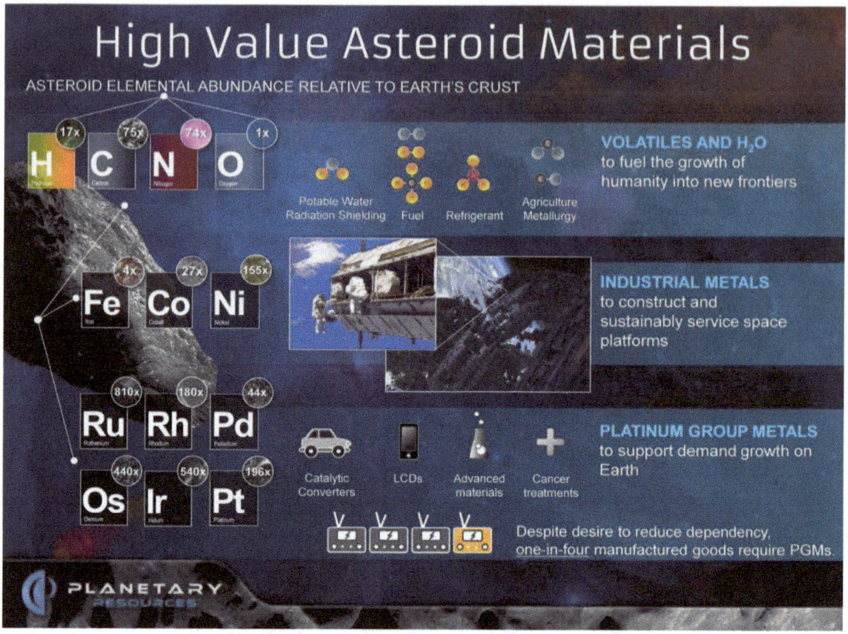

Fig. 9.1 Planetary Resources infographic. Source: Paul Cannon (2021)

futurity. Indeed, the narrative links being made between asteroid mining and sustainability are not limited to terrestrial sustainability but is a term also applied to the provision of materials to the cis-lunar economy. DSI's website makes this clear:

> This is the goal of Deep Space Industries: in-space delivery of the right materials, to the right place, for the right price, to support the sustainable expansion of Earth's economy into space.[2]

Not only does DSI position their activities as a means of "support[ing] the *sustainable* expansion of Earth's economy into space [emphasis added]" but they also link this back through to the utopic futurity outlined above: "We are journeying to unknown frontiers, and pushing the

[2] Information retrieved from analysed website material (DSI (2017), *Asteroid Mining: An Unlimited Future for All Mankind*. This webpage is no longer accessible).

limits of technology to provide a brighter future for all of mankind."[3] This final quote from DSI epitomizes the promises made by asteroid mining advocates to advance their interests. Using *all of mankind* as a hook that echoes the Outer Space Treaty's sentiment (see below), they promise a *brighter future*: an image that is deliberately ambiguous and allows people to project their own hopes and interpretations upon the statement but, when considered with the rest of the material, links back through to the *green imperative* used to justify asteroid mining. Indeed, this *green imperative* is not simply being applied to a terrestrial context but is being linked to extraplanetary futurity. Alongside DSI's above claim of expanding the Earth's economy into space, NSE actors are attaching their arguments for asteroid mining to *sustainable* multiplanetary exploration. For example, Steve —an NSE consultant involved in space advocacy campaigns—commented that "[t]here is no alternative. There's literally no alternative. We cannot sustainably go to Mars on a continuous basis and on a permanent basis unless we're using resources available in space".

Thus, asteroid mining is linked to a *green imperative* through a specific mode of corporate social responsibility, one that purports to be engaged in these activities to secure *a brighter future for all of mankind*. Asteroid mining companies and advocates thereby produce a new site by and through which demand can be manufactured and Outer Space is made into a site of capital accumulation. This perpetuates sociotechnical imaginaries that link the endeavours of NSE actors' and Outer Space activities to continued species and planetary survival through the *green* credentials of extraterrestrial extractivism, particularly asteroid mining.

3 Problems With(in) the Sociotechnical Utopia of Outer Space

Whilst the purported benefits of asteroid mining and Outer Space more broadly have been noted above—discourses ranging from its ability to provide unlimited growth through material abundance, inhabiting and working Outer Space being part of a collective *destiny*, protecting Earth through providing a *backup* for humanity and the Earth itself, through to the most sizeable argument of (re)producing a means by which a green future can be realized—the prospective futures of Outer Space remain

[3] Information retrieved from analysed website material (DSI (2017), *Who We Are*. This webpage is no longer accessible).

problematic. Indeed, issues pertaining to Outer Space and its supposed uses abound; however, drawing attention to such matters may be antithetical to the interests of involved private companies. Whilst there are attempts to sustain discourses of extraterrestrial futurity that recreate these spaces and activities therein as being almost inevitable and inherently beneficial, there remain several areas where problems arise within these oft-cited sociotechnical imaginaries. Broadly speaking, these can be summarized as issues regarding access to (terrestrial) land; questions of extraterrestrial property rights; mining waste and debris; and, generally, *whose* future is being spoken of and for. I will briefly consider each of these in turn.

Whilst discussions and the sociotechnological imaginaries of Outer Space frequently focus upon areas that are both spatially and temporally distant—focusing beyond the Earth—there are issues regarding these imaginaries that are distinctly terrestrial in nature. Indeed, the infrastructures required to realize speculative endeavours such as asteroid mining are contingent upon a host of terrestrial networks and assemblages which themselves can be deeply problematic. One such instance is the development of the Thirty Meter Telescope in Hawai'i, where developers wish to situate the telescope on the sacred mountain Mauna Kea. This has led to the well-noted instance of conflict between Western and indigenous onto-epistemological frameworks coming into contestation with one another surrounding space infrastructure (see BBC News, 2019; Matson & Nunn, 2017; Smiles, 2020; van Dyke, 2019 for further information and discussion). Indeed, this is perhaps the most notable instance at present of the colonial logics that are often woven into the imaginaries of Outer Space (Jones, 2021; Olson, 2018) becoming materially manifest within a terrestrial context. As activities pertaining to the NSE increase over the coming years, there will doubtlessly be further contestation between those seeking to build infrastructures to enable their speculative industries and those who are located within or in proximity to such developments. This may yield further issues regarding different onto-epistemological dispositions and claims to land/resources, intersecting with modes of neocolonial violence in some instances or other local tensions such as the NIMBYism (see Bagnall, 2017; Gov.uk, 2018; Griffin, 2020; Hebditch, 2021; Kelly, 2020).

Questions of tenure, rights, and ownership are not confined to the terrestrial when deliberating the multiple and variegated sociotechnical futures of Outer Space and its attendant extractive endeavours. We also find significant deliberations regarding access to and ownership of minerals in Outer Space itself: several nations are passing legislation regarding the prospective mining of asteroids but this remains an uncertain area. Indeed, the (in)ability to lay claim to any resource relies upon the physical and legislative enclosure of said resource (Bridge, 2004; Li, 2014; Steinberg, 2018; Tsing, 2003), and the fundamental questions regarding owning extraterrestrial resources have yet to be concluded, posing a significant hurdle to the sociotechnical imaginaries of extraterrestrial mining becoming a reality. Some have argued that a regulatory regime should already be introduced to prevent the oft-touted *gold rush* in Outer Space (e.g. Doshi, 2016), whilst others have posed salient questions regarding how such activities could be regulated and policed, and ownership claimed or enforced (Feinman, 2014; Fox, 2016, 2019). Importantly, among these deliberations, it has yet to be convincingly debated whether extraterrestrial territories and the resources therein are indeed still regarded as a *common* (Buck, 1999), or if they should be regarded as *terra communis* (communal land) or *terra nullius* (empty land), or should be managed as a type of cultural park system (see Cockell & Horneck, 2004; Collis, 2017 and Collis & Graham, 2009 for further discussion). At present, the principal mode through which Outer Space is addressed continues to adopt the language of the commons: Outer Space is still frequently referred to as *the common heritage of [hu]mankind* (using the phrasing of the Outer Space Treaty) and is a prominent example of a space that lies beyond national jurisdictions (Ranganathan, 2016). Although the notion of the commons is often invoked through the phrasing used when discussing Outer Space resources, this lies in contradistinction to the growing national and private interests in asteroids and their mineral deposits, with various actors seeking to claim, control, and commodify these materials. Without these areas being properly addressed, the sociotechnical pipedream of capital accumulation through extraterrestrial resource exploitation will continue to face a significant hurdle in reality.

Alongside these issues of land tenure/access and extraterrestrial resource rights is an area that has been given next to no attention in discussions regarding asteroid mining: mining waste and debris. Although matters concerning Outer Space debris are becoming increasingly prevalent, the ways this relates to potential asteroid mining are under-explored. Indeed, questions of Outer Space debris have found their focus through discussions on Kessler Syndrome (the cascading growth of space debris impacts described by Kessler & Cour-Palais, 1978; Kessler et al., 2010), and a similar issue regarded as Economic Kessler Syndrome (Adilov et al., 2018), and have sometimes come to the fore when something has gone awry (see Clark, 2012, 2019; Murray & Sample, 2021; Webster, 2025 for some notable examples). These matters have raised pertinent questions regarding the technical and legal regulation of space debris, though present endeavours focus on the prevention and mitigation of debris (Migaud, 2020), with much depending on the space agency or company in question (see ESA, 2025 for an example). Whilst the (in)ability to prevent space debris is placed upon the individual actor, removing present space debris is a contested area due to legal debates over where responsibility lies, how this should be addressed, and how the nature of space debris should be (re)defined within different legal contexts (see Muñoz-Patchen, 2018; Nelson, 2015–2016; Reibel, 1991). This contested matter will increase in complexity should extraterrestrial mining begin in earnest. To date, there has only been one paper that has thoroughly considered some of the issues posed by and through mining NEOs, with Fladeland et al. (2019) noting the potential for meteoroid stream formation resulting from the debris cast off from mining NEOs. This matter should, perhaps, be unsurprising due to issues of *waste* frequently being regarded as an externality within the terrestrial mining sector (Bridge, 2004; Steinberg, 2018). However, this should not be regarded as a trivial matter if asteroid mining and its green future(s) are to be taken seriously.

To illustrate the scale of this potential issue, we can estimate the quantity of sand-sized particles produced as asteroid mining waste. Taking the asteroids Bennu and Geographos as case studies[4] and using the volumes of these asteroids (see Williams, 2019 for data), we can begin to get a sense of this issue. The average size of a particle of sand is approximately 0.56mm^3. Using the volumes of Bennu and Geographos as examples, after a yield rate of 90% Geographos would produce $\sim 5.9 \times 10^{19}$ particles and Bennu would produce $\sim 2.7 \times 10^{17}$ particles in waste material. This would be an average of $\sim 3.01 \times 10^{19}$ particles produced as mining waste. The scale of waste here only represents two of some 16,000 NEOs and this waste poses potential material and spatio-temporal issues not only for the terrestrial context (as Fladeland et al., 2019 have demonstrated) but for the Outer Space environment more broadly. Consequently, the materialities of asteroid mining and their potential implications pose significant

[4] Respectively 0.90–1.36 and 1.66 Astronomical Units (AU) from the Sun.

questions to the *green* sociotechnical futures that are being recreated by NSE actors and asteroid mining advocates.

A final problem that confronts the seemingly normative sociotechnical imaginaries of a *green* Outer Space futurity is *whose* futures are being spoken of and for? This question is crucial as it cuts across all dimensions of Outer Space future discourses and provides an important challenge for interrogating sociotechnical imaginaries in general. It demands that we address who is reconstructing these discourses of futurity and what their purported interests are (and what they may otherwise be), and—perhaps most importantly—to ask who is being excluded from these discussions. Discussions regarding the future(s) of Outer Space and asteroid minerals are dominated by particular NSE companies and actors with vested interests in privatizing these resources. These actors have the capital and associated power to lobby governments and perpetuate particular socio-cultural imaginaries of Outer Space and its potentialities. This poses implications for the physical dimensions of mining in Outer Space: matters of resource access and ownership rely on regimes of inclusion and exclusion through physical and legislative means (Li, 2014; Tsing, 2003). However, of equal importance are the effects these NSE actors have on the wider discussions of asteroid mining. The discursive dimensions rely on excluding people and groups from the very act(s) of imagining and reimagining future spaces and the way(s) in which they and their attendant resources/materialities can be engaged with and distributed, and the purposes they can be directed towards. Indeed, popular discussions frequently talk about *the* future, presenting it as singular and often inevitable through framing conversation in the affirmative, eliding the fact that there are multiple futurisms that draw upon distinctly different social, cultural, and political influences that vie for different futures to be realized (Jones, 2021). Despite popular discussions framing the neoliberal enclosure of Outer Space and the resources therein as a done deal, this is far from final, and the contested nature of Outer Space's sociotechnical imaginaries is something that is worth far more deliberation.

4 Conclusion

Taking asteroid mining as a central speculative technology for utilizing Outer Space, this chapter has explored the recreation of sociotechnical imaginaries and the way(s) actors link justifications for such technologies to discourses of green futurity. This is done by state and private actors through mobilizing discourses of accessing unlimited resources, notions of human destiny using Outer Space to realize green futures on Earth, and developing Outer Space as a backup for the human species. However, whilst these topics are used in various combinations to justify and reinforce particular sociotechnical imaginaries—always discussed in the affirmative to ensure a seeming inevitability to their coming to fruition (Jones, 2021)—there are multiple problems that remain unresolved and, at times, unquestioned. As has been discussed in this chapter, there are numerous issues that are omitted from the NewSpace Economy's depictions of sociotechnical utopias of Outer Space, regarded as externalities or of little consequence by some of the actors involved. Such issues include questions of access to land—both in terms of the terrestrial infrastructure required to subtend such operations and questions of ownership of off-Earth resources— and questions of the scales and implications of mining externalities in the form of *waste*, and *whose* future is being spoken of and for. These deliberations have implications for the multiple and variegated spatialities that Outer Space and its attendant infrastructures intersect with. These spatial dimensions span questions of terrestrial land governance—where infrastructures are located, whose land they infringe upon or who is removed, and whose values or priorities are acted upon—and questions of extraterrestrial spatialities— how matters in orbit and beyond are governed, how resources are accessed and (mis)managed, and, through these frameworks, how the extraterrestrial domain is made sense of and related to. Importantly, these spatialities are not separate from one another; rather they are intertwined with the governance of one informing operations and understandings of the other.

Central to these issues and critical scholarship moving forward, there are multiple areas that need to be addressed and drawn to the fore rather than being left unquestioned, implicit, or for us to *wait and see* when it comes to the sociotechnical imaginaries of Outer Space generally, and asteroid mining specifically. As has been noted throughout this discussion, there are implicit normative assumptions bound up within the recreation of Outer Space futures, assumptions that usually present neoliberal and neocolonial discourses as the *de facto* norm, rendering sociotechnical imaginaries of Outer Space mining as inherently bound up in settler colonial and Western onto-epistemological relations that exclude alternative, i.e., indigenous or non-White, conceptions and cosmologies (see Noon et al., 2023; Olson, 2018; Smiles, 2020 for further discussion). Through engaging with the range of different futurisms that draw upon diverse social, cultural, and political backgrounds to reimagine the sociotechnical future(s) of Outer Space (Jones, 2021), it becomes possible to deconstruct the implicit assumptions bound up within *usual* discussions of Outer Space imaginaries. Importantly, throughout these deliberations, questions of governance—both *what* is governed and how—should be regarded anew through encountering, challenging, and reconsidering the normative assumptions that have taken root within the sociotechnical imaginaries of Outer Space. These deliberations need to address a foundational question to guide future debate within this area, namely: How do we turn sociotechnical futures into something just and equitable? By keeping this question at the centre of debates on Outer Space futures, perhaps we can move towards debate that encourages the implicit assumptions of different futures to be drawn to the fore and fundamental principles of social justice and equity to be applied to the multiplicity of futures that exist.

Acknowledgements I would like to extend my thanks to the ESRC for funding the research that has informed the work for this chapter (funding codes ES/J500094/1 and ES/X00645X/1). As this research was conducted during the course of my PhD studies and subsequent postdoctoral position, I would like to express my gratitude to my supervisor, Professor Nigel Clark, and mentor, Dr Saskia Vermeylen, for all of their support and encouragement. Beyond the remit of academia, I would also like to note the contribution of my partner, Dr Ellie Fielding-Redpath, for her continuous support throughout all of my endeavours.

References

Adilov, N., Alexander, P. J., & Cunningham, B. M. (2018). An economic "Kessler Syndrome": A dynamic model of earth orbit debris. *Economics Letters, 166*, 79–82.

Anantatmula, V. (2013). U.S. initiative to place weapons in space: The catalyst for a space-based arms race with China and Russia. *Astropolitics, 11*(3), 132–155.

Bagnall, S. (2017). Snowdonia satellite launch pad bid underway. *Daily Post.* Retrieved August 07, 2017, from https://www.dailypost.co.uk/business/snowdonia-satellite-launch-pad-bid-13443140

BBC News. (2019). Mauna Kea: Hawaii protesters delay giant telescope construction. *BBC News.* https://www.bbc.co.uk/news/world-us-canada-49035815

Bowen, B. (2020). *War in space: Strategy, spacepower, geopolitics.* Edinburgh University Press.

Bridge, G. (2004). Mapping the Bonanza: Geographies of mining investment in an era of neoliberal reform. *The Professional Geographer, 56*(3), 406–421.
Buck, S. J. (1999). *The global commons: An introduction*. Earthscan Publications Ltd.
Cannon, K. (2021, August 7). Mining Near-Earth asteroids makes little sense: So why does the idea persist? https://planetaryintel.substack.com/p/mining-near-earth-asteroids-makes
Carr, M. (2010). Slouching towards dystopia: The new military futurism. *Race & Class, 53*(1), 13–32.
Clark, S. (2012, October 4). How dangerous is space debris? *The Guardian*. https://www.theguardian.com/science/across-the-universe/2012/oct/04/astronomy-space
Clark, S. (2019, August 31). The greatest threat to life on Earth may come from space. *The Guardian*. https://www.theguardian.com/science/2019/aug/31/greatest-threat-to-life-on-earth-may-come-from-space-asteroids-satellite-debris
Cockell, C., & Horneck, G. (2004). A planetary park system for mars. *Space Policy, 20*(4), 291–295.
Cofield, C. (2016, November 21). Extraterrestrial gold rush: What's next for the space mining industry?. *space.com*. https://www.space.com/34774-whats--next-for-space-mining.html
Cole, D. M. (1963). $50,000,000,000,000 from the Asteroids. *Space World, 4*(2), 1–8.
Collis, C. (2017). Territories beyond possession? Antarctica and outer space. *The Polar Journal., 7*(2), 287–302.
Collis, C., & Graham, P. (2009). Political geographies of Mars: A history of Martian management. *Management & Organizational History, 4*(3), 247–261.
Davidian, K. (2020). Definition of NewSpace. *New Space, 8*(2), 53–55.
Deberdt, R., & Le Billon, P. (2023). Outer space mining: Exploring techno--utopianism in a time of climate crisis. *Annals of the American Association of Geographers, 113*(8), 1878–1899.
Diaz, E. (2018). Art and the new space age. *New Left Review, 112*, 144–160.
Dick, S. J. (2018). Space, time and aliens: The role of imagination in outer space. In A. C. T. Geppert (Ed.), *Imagining outer space: European astroculture in the twentieth century*. Palgrave Macmillan.
Doshi, P. D. (2016). Regulating The final frontier: Asteroid mining and the need for a new regulatory regime. *Notre Dame Journal of International & Comparative Law, 6*(1), Article 15.
Dunbar, B. (2020, October 28). Lunar living: NASA's Artemis Base Camp Concept. *NASA*. https://blogs.nasa.gov/artemis/2020/10/28/lunar-living-nasas-artemis-base-camp-concept/

Eisfeld, R. (2018). Projecting landscapes of the human mind onto another world: Changing faces of an imaginary world. In A. C. T. Geppert (Ed.), *Imagining outer space: European astroculture in the twentieth century.* Palgrave Macmillan.

Ellis, E. G. (2017). How NASA visualizes stunning worlds without really seeing them. *Wired.* Retrieved October 16, 2020, from https://www.wired.com/2017/04/nasa-visualizes-stunning-worlds-without-really-seeing/

Enel. (2024, May 03). Photovoltaic panels in space: A possible revolution in solar energy. *enel.* https://www.enel.com/company/stories/articles/2024/05/solar-panels-in-space

ESA. (2021, n.d.). Asteroid/Moon mining in-situ resource utilisation. *The European Space Agency.* https://www.esa.int/About_Us/Business_with_ESA/Global_Space_Economic_Forum/Asteroid_Moon_mining_in-situ_resource_utilisation

ESA. (2022, August 08). Space-Based Solar Power overview. *ESA.* https://www.esa.int/Enabling_Support/Space_Engineering_Technology/SOLARIS/Space-Based_Solar_Power_overview

ESA. (2025). New Space Debris mitigation policy and requirements in Effect. *ESA.* https://esoc.esa.int/new-space-debris-mitigation-policy-and-requirements-effect

Farrell, P. B. (2013, January 08). Asteroid mining 2022 a $1 trillion bet for Earth. *MarketWatch.* https://www.marketwatch.com/story/asteroid-mining-2022-a-1-trillion-bet-for-earth-2013-01-08

Feinman, M. (2014). Mining the final frontier: Keeping earth's asteroid mining ventures from becoming the next gold rush. *Journal of Technology, Law & Policy, XIV*(Spring), 202–235.

Fladeland, L., Boley, A. C., & Byers, M. (2019). Meteoroid stream formation due to the extraction of space resources from asteroids. In *Conference paper for the 1st International Orbital Debris Conference,* December 9-12. https://arxiv.org/ftp/arxiv/papers/1911/1911.12840.pdf

Fox, S. J. (2016). SPACE: The race for mineral rights *The sky is no longer the limit* Lessons from earth! *Resources Policy, 49,* 165–178.

Fox, S. J. (2019). Policing mining: In outer-space greed and domination vs. peace and equity a governance for humanity! *Resources Policy, 64,* 101517.

Gamu, J. K., & Dauvergne, P. (2018). The slow violence of corporate social responsibility: The case of mining in Peru. *Third World Quarterly, 39*(5), 959–975.

Garrett, D. (2016). The improbable, bold history of space concept art. *Next.* Retrieved October 16, 2020, from https://howwegettonext.com/the-improbable-bold-history-of-space-concept-art42c1fb1b6035

Geppert, A. C. T. (2018). European astrofuturism, cosmic provincialism: Historicizing the space Age. In A. C. T. Geppert (Ed.), *Imagining outer space: European astroculture in the twentieth century.* Palgrave Macmillan.

Gilbert, P. R. (2020a). Speculating on sovereignty: *Money mining* and corporate foreign policy at the extractive industry frontier. *Economy and Society, 49*(1), 16–44.

Gilbert, P. R. (2020b). Making critical materials valuable: Decarbonization, investment, and "political risk". In A. Bleicher & A. Pehlken (Eds.), *The material basis of energy transitions* (1st ed., pp. 91–108). Elsevier Science & Technology.

Gov.uk. (2018). One giant leap: Vertical launch spaceport to bring UK into new space age. *gov.uk*. Retrieved July 15, 2018, from https://www.gov.uk/government/news/one-giant-leap-vertical-launch-spaceport-to-bringuk-into-new-space-age

Grady, M. (2017). Private companies are launching a new space race – here's what to expect. *The Conversation*. https://theconversation.com/private-companies-are-launching-a-new-spacerace-heres-what-to--expect-80697

GreenMatch. (2024, October 31). What is space-based solar power? *GreenMatch*. https://www.greenmatch.co.uk/blog/2020/02/space-based-solar-power

Griffin, A. (2020). Satellites to be launched into space from Scotland after approval of new plan. *The Independent*. Retrieved August 20, 2020, from https://www.independent.co.uk/life-style/gadgets-and-tech/news/spacesatellites--scotland-launch-uk-hie-orbit-a9678501.html

Hebditch, J. (2021). *Scotland's first space launch as billion-dollar US company choose Shetland site for blast-off*. Retrieved February 10, 2021, from https://www.dailyrecord.co.uk/news/scottish-news/scotlands-first-spacelaunch-billion-23474515

Holden, C. (1975). Futurism: Gaining a toehold in public policy. *Science, 189*, 120–123.

Jamasmie, C. (2014, June 11). Asteroids mined for fuel to generate trillion dollar market, says firm. *mining.com*. https://www.mining.com/asteroids-mined-for-fuel-to-generate-trillion-dollar-market-says-firm-63951/

Jamasmie, C. (2020, October 29). NASA finds rare metal asteroid worth more than global economy. *mining.com*. https://www.mining.com/nasa-finds-rare-metal-asteroid-worth-more-than-global-economy/

Jones, C. H. (2021, May 24). Enclosing the Cosmos: Privatising Outer Space and Voices of Resistance. *Society + Space*. https://www.societyandspace.org/articles/enclosing-the-cosmos-privatising-outer-space-and-voices-of-resistance

Kearnes, M., & van Dooren, T. (2017). Rethinking the final frontier: Cosmo--logics and an ethic of interstellar flourishing. *GeoHumanities, 3*(2), 1–20.

Kelly, M. (2020). Scottish rocket launchpad gains planning approval, *Construction News*. Retrieved August 20, 2020, from https://www.constructionnews.co.uk/civils/scottish-rocket-launchpad-gains-planningapproval-20-08-2020/

Kessler, D. J., & Cour-Palais, B. G. (1978). Collision frequency of artificial satellites: The creation of a debris belt. *Journal of Geophysical Research: Space Physics, 83(A6)*, 2637–2646.

Kessler, D. J., Johnson, N. L., Liou, J. C., & Matney, M. (2010). The Kessler syndrome: Implications to future space operations. *AAS, 10–106*. https://www.threecountrytrustedbroker.com/media/kesseler_syndrome.pdf

Klinger, J. (2017). *Rare earth frontiers: From terrestrial subsoils to lunar landscapes*. Cornell University Press.

Lewicki, C., Diamandis, P., Anderson, E., Voorhees, C., & Mycroft, F. (2013). Planetary resources – The asteroid mining company. *New Space, 1*(2), 105–108.

Li, T. M. (2014). What is land? Assembling a resource for global investment. *Transactions of the Institute of British Geographers, 39*(4), 589–602.

Luscombe, R., & Sample, I. (2020). SpaceX successfully launches NASA astronauts into orbit. *The Guardian*. Retrieved May 30, 2020, from https://www.theguardian.com/science/2020/may/30/spacex-nasa-crewedspaceflight-launch-dragon-capsule-elon-musk-trump

Matloff, G., Johnson, L., & Bangs, C. (2014). *Harvesting space for a greener earth*. Springer.

Matson, Z. M., & Nunn, N. (2017). Space infrastructure, empire, and the final fronties: What the mauna kea land defenders teach us about colonial totality. *Society & Space Magazine*. Retrieved February 19, 2021, from https://www.societyandspace.org/forums/investigating-infrastructures

McCarthy, J. (2015). A socioecological fix to capitalist crisis and climate change? The possibilities and limits of renewable energy. *Environment and Planning A, 47*(12), 2485–2502.

Messeri, L. (2016). *Placing outer space: An earthly ethnography of other worlds*. Duke University Press.

Migaud, M. R. (2020). Protecting earth's orbital environment: Policy tools for combatting space debris. *Space Policy, 52*, 101361.

Mistry, D., & Gopalaswamy, B. (2012). Ballistic missiles and space launch vehicles in regional powers. *Astropolitics, 10*(2), 126–151.

Moyser, G., & Wagstaffe, M. (1987). Studying elites: Theoretical and methodological issues. In G. Moyser & M. Wagstaffe (Eds.), *Research methods for elite studies*. Allen & Unwin.

Muñoz-Patchen, C. (2018). Regulating the space commons: Treating space debris as abandoned property in violation of the outer space treaty. *Chicago Journal of International Law, 19*(*1*), 233–259.

Murray, W., & Sample, I. (2021). Debris from Chinese rocket could hit Earth at weekend, says expert. *The Guardian*. https://www.theguardian.com/science/2021/may/06/chinese-rocket-falling-crash-to-earth-saturday-china-space-station-long-march-5b-us-space-command

Nelson, T. G. (2015–2016). Regulating the void: In-orbit collisions and space debris. *Journal of Space Law, 40*(*1–2*), 105–130.

Noon, K. A., De Napoli, K., Swanton, P., Guedes, C., & Hamacher, D. (2023). Safeguarding indigenous sky rights from colonial exploitation. In J. F. Salazar & A. Gorman (Eds.), *The Routledge handbook of social studies of outer space*. Routledge.

Olson, V. (2018). *Into the extreme: U.S. environmental systems and politics beyond earth*. University of Minnesota Press.

Paikowsky, D. (2017). What is new space? The changing ecosystem of global space activity. *New Space, 5*(*2*), 84–88.

Pandya, J. (2019, May 13). The race to mine space. *Forbes*. https://www.forbes.com/sites/cognitiveworld/2019/05/13/the-race-to-mine-space/

Parsons, R., Lacey, J., & Moffat, K. (2014). Maintaining legitimacy of a contested practice: How the minerals industry understands its 'social licence to operate'. *Resources Policy, 41*, 83–90.

Poo, A. (2012). Movement futurism. *The American Prospect, 23*(8), 25.

Ranganathan, S. (2016). Global commons. *European Journal of International Law, 27*(*3*), 693–717.

Reibel, D. E. (1991). Environmental regulation of space activity: The case of orbital debris. *Stanford Environmental Law Journal, 10*(*97*), 97–136.

Rincon, P. (2013, January 22). New venture 'to mine asteroids. *BBC News*. https://www.bbc.co.uk/news/science-environment-21144769

Sage, D. (2008). Framing space: A popular geopolitics of American manifest destiny in outer space. *Geopolitics, 13*(*1*), 27–53.

Scoles, S. (2016). How space scientists turn exoplanets into places we can 'See'. *Wired*. Retrieved October 16, 2020, from https://www.wired.com/2016/09/space-scientists-turn-exoplanets-places-can-see/

Shore, C. (2002). Introduction: Towards an anthropology of elites. In C. Shore & S. Nugent (Eds.), *Elite Cultures: Anthropological perspectives*. Routledge.

Smiles, D. (2020). The settler logics of (outer) space, *Society & Space Magazine*. Retrieved October 31, 2020, from https://www.societyandspace.org/articles/the-settler-logics-of-outer-space

Smith, N. (2007). Nature as accumulation strategy. *Socialist Reister, 43*, 16–36.

Space Solar. (2024, n.d.). Space solar. *Space Solar*. https://www.spacesolar.co.uk/

Statista. (2024, July 22). Market Value of Asteroid Mining 2017–2025. *Statista*. https://www.statista.com/statistics/1023115/market-value-asteroid-mining/

Steinberg, P. E. (2018). Editorial: The ocean as frontier. *International Social Science Journal, 68*(299–230), 237–240.

Taylor, S. M. (2022). F*ck earth: Unmasking mars colonization marketing, from planetary perceived obsolescence to apocalyptic "new earth" rhetoric. *Journal of Religion, Media and Digital Culture, 11*(*1*), 54–84.

The Business Research Company. (2024, October 30). Asteroid mining global market report 2024. *The Business Research Company*. https://www.thebusinessresearchcompany.com/report/asteroid-mining-global-market--report#:~:text=The%20global%20asteroid%20mining%20market,(CAGR)%20of%2023.9%25.

Triscott, N. (2016). Transmissions from the noosphere: Contemporary art and outer space. In J. S. Ormrod & P. Dickens (Eds.), *The Palgrave handbook of society, culture and outer space*. Palgrave Macmillan.

Tsing, A. L. (2003). Natural resources and capitalist frontiers. *Economic and Political Weekly, 38*(48), 5100–5106.

Valentine, D. (2012). Exit strategy: Profit, cosmology, and the future of humans in space. *Anthropological Quarterly, 85*(4), 1045–1067.

van Dyke, M. B. (2019). Dozens arrested as Hawaiians protest $1.4 billion telescope on sacred mountain. *The Guardian. https://www.theguardian.com/us--news/2019/jul/18/hawaii-mauna-key-protest-arrests-observatory*

Webster, E. (2025, February 19). SpaceX rocket debris crashes into Poland. *BBC News*. https://www.bbc.co.uk/news/articles/c62z3vxjplpo

Williams, D. R, (2019, September 27). Asteroid fact sheet. *NASA*. https://nssdc.gsfc.nasa.gov/planetary/factsheet/asteroidfact.html

Zubrin, R. (2021). *The case for mars: The plan to settle the red planet and why we must*. Free Press.

Index[1]

[1] Note: Page numbers followed by 'n' refer to notes.

S. Becker, B. Fladvad (eds.), *Contested Imaginaries of Future Technologies*, https://doi.org/10.1007/978-3-032-11497-6

FSC
www.fsc.org
MIX
Papier | Fördert
gute Waldnutzung
FSC® C083411

Kolibri 360 GmbH
Ferdinand-Jühlke-Straße 7
99095 Erfurt, Deutschland
produktsicherheit@kolibri360.de